W9-BIU-735

GLOBALIZATION AND ECONOMIC ETHICS

Also by Albino Barrera

Economic Compulsion and Christian Ethics
(Cambridge University Press, 2005)

God and the Evil of Scarcity: Moral Foundations
of Economic Agency
(University of Notre Dame Press, 2005)

Modern Catholic Social Documents and Political Economy
(Georgetown University Press, 2001)

Globalization and Economic Ethics

Distributive Justice in the Knowledge Economy

Albino Barrera

palgrave
macmillan

GLOBALIZATION AND ECONOMIC ETHICS

First published in 2007 by
PALGRAVE MACMILLAN™
175 Fifth Avenue, New York, N.Y. 10010 and
Houndmills, Basingstoke, Hampshire, England RG21 6XS
Companies and representatives throughout the world.

PALGRAVE MACMILLAN is the global academic imprint of the Palgrave Macmillan division of St. Martin's Press, LLC and of Palgrave Macmillan Ltd. Macmillan® is a registered trademark in the United States, United Kingdom and other countries. Palgrave is a registered trademark in the European Union and other countries.

ISBN-13: 978-0-230-60089-8
ISBN-10: 0-230-60089-1

Library of Congress Cataloging-in-Publication Data

Barrera, Albino.
    Globalization and economic ethics : distributive justice in the knowledge economy / Albino Barrera.
        p. cm.
    Includes bibliographical references and index.
    ISBN 0-230-60089-1 (alk. paper)
        1. Distributive justice. 2. Information society—Economic aspects.
    3. Economic development—Social aspects. 4. International economic integration—Social aspects. 5. Economics—Philosophy. I. Title.

HB523.B365 2007
174'.4—dc22   2007007681

A catalogue record for this book is available from the British Library.

Design by Newgen Imaging Systems (P) Ltd., Chennai, India.

First edition: December 2007

10 9 8 7 6 5 4 3 2 1

Transferred to digital printing in 2008.

In thanksgiving for Claire,
my kind and caring sister

Contents

Preface

How should we divide societal resources and output among ourselves? According to need, contribution, equality, economic efficiency, or deserts? Why? How should we rank these criteria of distributive justice in order of their importance? These are among the biggest unresolved questions of political economy, and they have become even more divisive in the face of globalization.

Global economic integration adds urgency to addressing disagreements over distributive criteria because: there is now a much larger economic pie at stake, economic activity has accelerated and excluded many who have been unable to keep up with the pace, market participation has become more exacting in its requirements, there are enormous rents to be reaped, and there is stiffer competition for global commodities and energy supplies in the wake of emerging economic powerhouses like China and India. Globalization has improved the lives of hundreds of millions who have wallowed in poverty until recently, just as it has impoverished nations and individuals unable to fend for themselves in the face of the market's unintended consequences. Indeed, debate over what distributive justice requires has become increasingly strident and contentious even as the issues themselves have become even more complex and intractable. There is need for a clear-eyed method in giving people and nations their economic due. Equally important, however, is the task of articulating the conceptual and practical justification for the principle used for such a distribution. The bitter discord over globalization largely reflects philosophical disagreements over the proper criteria to use for distributive justice.

Efficiency and need have by far been the most widely preferred criteria. On the one hand, advocates of unfettered markets tout the pivotal role of economic efficiency in providing the great wealth we have enjoyed in the modern industrial era. On the other hand, critics of laissez-faire capitalism argue for need satisfaction as a way of ameliorating the market's perennial failure to provide for the more vulnerable segments of the population. Though nothing in their philosophical justification makes efficiency and need mutually exclusive, these two norms often require diametrically opposed economic policies when it comes to actual implementation. For example, while efficiency generally calls for minimal government intervention in market operations, need satisfaction frequently requires intrusive extra-market initiatives, such as legislation on minimum wage, affirmative action, and consumer protection. Thus, in his classic work *Equality and Efficiency: The Big Tradeoff*, Arthur Okun (1975) notes that beyond a certain point, equity-oriented policies become a drag on economic efficiency. Simon Kuznets (1955, 1963) posits his famous inverted U-shaped relationship between equity and growth; inequality worsens in the earlier stages of economic growth and gradually improves over time. Despite the absence of conclusive empirical evidence confirming the Kuznets phenomenon, efficiency and need have nevertheless been viewed by and large as competing criteria of distributive justice.

Need as a benchmark of distributive justice can be justified on the basis of the inherent dignity of the human person. However, we can make an additional case for need as a distributive rule by appealing to its instrumental utility in bringing about market efficiency. The thesis of this study is that far from being rival principles of distributive justice, efficiency and need are, in fact, complementary norms given the special requirements of the emerging knowledge economy. They have become necessary conditions to each other because of the central role of human capital in generating and sustaining long-term efficiency in the digital age. Information and communication technologies (ICTs) have transformed the economic terrain. The principal sources of wealth creation in the past two centuries were natural resources and industrial capital. Today, it is knowledge. Not surprising, the highly skilled and digital-savvy *homo oeconomicus* has taken center stage in contemporary economic life. Future growth and development are dependent on the widespread satisfaction of human needs in the earlier rounds of economic activity. However, a community can maintain need satisfaction as an economic policy only to the degree that it is efficient in the use of its scarce resources in producing its necessities. Indeed, far from being at odds with each other, efficiency and need satisfaction mutually reinforce one another in the information economy.

I use both the properties of the market and the features of the knowledge economy as analytical tools with which to demonstrate this linkage between efficiency and need satisfaction. Any substantive assessment of economic distribution must take into account its attendant circumstances. At present, this all-important context has at least two major components to it. First, globalization is breathtaking, not so much for the extent to which it is integrating the world economy into a single entity, but for the information age it has intensified. Thus, it is the knowledge economy and its attributes that provide the immediate context to any meaningful discussion of distributive justice in globalization. Second, we must delve deeper beneath the knowledge economy and examine the bedrock on which it stands—the marketplace. The market has intrinsic characteristics that define the limits of what economic exchange (whether in the industrial age or the digital era) can or cannot achieve. The market has particular qualities that shape the terrain within which economic life unfolds. Thus, in this study, I assess what ought to be our yardstick of distributive justice within the twofold context of the properties of the market and the attributes of the knowledge economy.

Chapter 1 examines the substantial overlap between two of the most contentious problems in economic ethics today: (1) the clashing claims of the different norms of economic justice and (2) the opposing schools of thought on whether globalization has been a "common climb to the top" or a "race to the bottom." At the root of disagreements over the ills or benefits of global economic integration are differences in the philosophical commitments on what ought to be the appropriate criterion of distributive justice. This is reflected in the choice of statistics employed by pro- and antiglobalizers to make their case.

Before assessing the competing rules of distributive justice, I examine the nature of the knowledge economy in the two chapters of part I. The information and communication revolution is different from the industrial revolution because it is the market itself that has been radically transformed and not merely transportation (e.g., steam engine) or production (e.g., electricity, steel, oil), as in the nineteenth century. Thus, chapter 2 explains that microelectronics has made the market more efficient at being efficient. This foreshadows major changes in our economic life, precisely at a time when we are increasingly heavily reliant on the market as it seeps into every facet of society. It is important to anticipate the problems accompanying such "marketization" including the superfluity of data that have to be processed, the disruption of livelihoods and lifestyles, and the ceaseless substantive readjustments on the part of economic agents. Chapter 3 outlines the need for ever-more advanced human capital in view of the exacting features of the knowledge economy, namely: the faster pace of economic life, the much fiercer competition for innovations and networking, and the increasing value of time.

Part II reviews the case for economic efficiency as the appropriate criterion of distributive justice. Chapter 4 contends that efficiency matters, and more so in the information age. ICTs have made the market even better at creating value. Thus, impeding the marketplace from what it does best (allocating scarce resources to their most valued uses) leads to ever larger opportunity losses over time, especially in a highly dynamic setting. Besides, no community can flourish in the long term unless it is judicious in the use of its endowments. Efficiency is essential for a self-sustaining, growing economy; it is an unavoidable constraint that distributive justice must satisfy. Nonetheless, chapter 5 cautions that as important as efficiency is, it is not sufficient because of the distributive dimension of the price mechanism. Efficiency does not arise in a vacuum; it requires wide-ranging socioeconomic preconditions if the market is to work properly and produce its much-acclaimed economic benefits. These foundational institutions often lead to a self-reinforcing dynamic that permanently marginalizes those at the fringes of the economy. The resulting price adjustments from economic exchange can inflict adverse unintended consequences on certain segments of the population, often the very people who are least able to bear these burdens. To make matters worse, the market will not self-correct its harmful outcomes but may, in fact, even aggravate them over time. There is need for extra-market remedial action in order to rectify the limitations of efficiency as the proximate goal of economic operations.

Part III weighs need as a fitting norm of distributive justice. Chapter 6 suggests that it is in the self-interest of communities to ensure that people have access to their essential needs for personal growth and development. Human capital has to be continuously upgraded in an extremely fluid environment such as the information age in which tacit knowledge holds the key to creating value. In other words, need satisfaction is a precondition of long-term efficiency in the knowledge economy. Furthermore, chapter 7 delineates how such a strategy of need satisfaction broadens the base for economic initiative and technological creativity, thereby adding further to the stability and quality of the pool of human capital available to the community.

Part IV considers entitlement as a suitable canon of distributive justice. Chapter 8 describes a feature of the marketplace in which many factor inputs are left unpaid for their real social contribution. These ownership externalities arise because of the public-good nature of the marketplace in which no one with the requisite purchasing power may be excluded from the services it provides. Moreover, just as technologies, currencies, and languages become even more valuable to early adopters as more people use them, the market also exhibits network externalities as it confers ever-greater benefits on its participants as it expands its geographic reach and scale. Unfortunately, the resulting gains are difficult, if not impossible, to assign to their rightful owners, thereby exacerbating the gap between private and social costs or benefits. By its nature, the market rarely pays factor inputs according to their true social contribution because of its manifold unintended consequences (externalities). Sociohistorical location, chance, and contingencies are often decisive determinants of what people receive from the marketplace. Consequently, employing entitlement as a norm of distributive justice requires extensive corrective work if we are to satisfy its twin conditions of justice in acquisition and justice in transfer.

Chapter 9 concludes this study by claiming that far from clashing with each other, need, equality, efficiency, and entitlement are all interdependent criteria. Need satisfaction has become inseparable from economic efficiency in the knowledge economy. Moreover, there is an intrinsic egalitarianism embedded within a strategy of need satisfaction. By rewarding people according to what they bring to the marketplace, the entitlement principle maintains the incentives essential to the market's smooth operations; it enhances efficiency as a viable benchmark of justice. Thus, efficiency, need, equality, and entitlement supplement each other in the information age. In assessing the benefits and ills of globalization, we avoid two common errors in economic reasoning (the fallacies of composition and division) through the integrated use of these different standards of distributive justice.

The empirical studies on many of the issues we examine can literally fill volumes. Thus, my use of empirical evidence is necessarily selective and is merely illustrative rather than definitive as I examine the preceding questions. Besides, statistics can often be presented in support of both sides of most economic disagreements. Moreover, one must remember that empirical studies are contingent by nature because their results are dependent on heuristic models, simplifying assumptions, and econometric techniques, not to mention data selection, quality, and measurement.

This study offers a fourfold contribution to the literature besides adding to what we already know about the knowledge economy and globalization. First, it calls for a change in our thinking regarding the practical implementation of distributive justice. While need, equality, efficiency, and entitlement may arguably be described as competing norms during the industrial age, these have become symbiotic components of a necessary comprehensive approach to distributive justice in the era of microelectronics. This highlights not only the complexity but also the richness of contemporary political economy.

Second, this book is different from many that have been written on globalization because it employs the nature of the market as a starting point of analysis. This makes for a more balanced approach because we are forced to acknowledge both the gains and losses from cross-border exchange. In paying heed to the inherent limitations of the market, we avoid exaggerating the much-heralded advantages of international trade. In the same manner, by duly acknowledging the exceptional institutional capabilities of the marketplace, we cannot readily dismiss global economic integration as irredeemably harmful. Any objective look at economic globalization must take into account the intrinsic properties of the market. At the same time, this research project has provided an occasion to use empirical evidence from recent economic history in advancing our understanding of both the market and the knowledge economy.

Third, ownership externalities are rarely discussed in economic ethics. Moreover, the case for treating the market as a network externality has yet to be made in the literature. This study has been a good opportunity to examine the economics and ethics of globalization partly through the prism of these two largely unexplored externalities.

Finally, the convergence of efficiency and need satisfaction into inseparable norms in the knowledge economy narrows the gap between free market proponents, who have advocated all along for allocative efficiency, and critics of globalization, who have under-scored the plight of those who have been adversely affected by trade. In proposing that sustainable efficiency and human capital develop-ment are two sides of the same coin, this study claims that pro- and anti-globalizers are not really too far apart from each other. They are merely stressing different dimensions of the same phenomenon. In appreciating how economic efficiency and need satisfaction are neces-sary conditions for each other, both sides of the debate have reason to be open and attentive to each other's arguments.

Why is it urgent to ascertain which criterion of distributive justice has precedence and who is right about globalization? Why is it impor-tant to determine which claims of proponents and critics are valid and which are not? Even as globalization is still merely in its nascent stages and much of it has yet to unfold, we have already witnessed both the considerable good and the wide-ranging injuries it can inflict. Understanding the nature and dynamics of global economic integra-tion allows us to take an active role in shaping its processes and out-comes. There is much at stake in being ahead of the curve and in laying the ground rules that will determine the direction and the tenor of how we are going to evolve and function together as a truly single global economic community. In grappling with difficult questions, such as distributive justice in the knowledge economy, I hope this book has made a modest contribution toward the formation of a postindustrial economic ethos that takes greater personal and collective responsibility for market outcomes and, more importantly, for each other's well-being.

Many have been kind and generous in the course of this project. Ernest Bartell, Wilfred Dolfsma, Dan Finn, Ted Tsukahara, and Pat Welch provided valuable advice, guidance, encouragement, and suggestions for improvement that I have tried to incorporate while keeping this work to a reasonable length. Any remaining errors are solely my responsibility. I am deeply grateful for their example, beneficence, and friendship. Maran Elancheran and the staff of Newgen Imaging Systems and Elaine McLean helped with copyediting and proofreading. Rebecca Francescatti did the index. It has been such a pleasure to work with Aaron Javsicas, Kate Ankofski, Elizabeth Sabo, and the staff of Palgrave MacMillan, and I truly appreciate their assistance throughout the publication process. My students make the long hours of hard work truly worth it. Indeed, I consider myself to be greatly blessed with such good mentors, peers, friends, and family.

February 11, 2007
Providence, Rhode Island

Chapter 1

Overlapping Questions: Globalization and Distributive Justice

Proponents and critics of globalization find little common ground for discourse. Even looking for an analytical framework with which to assess the claims and counterclaims of both sides of the debate is a highly contentious task. The two dominant questions of contemporary economic ethics are: (1) should globalization be reined in or even halted and then reversed altogether, and (2) what criterion ought we use for distributive justice? This chapter argues that these two seemingly separate issues overlap. On the one hand, most of the criticisms directed against global economic integration have been about the inequitable distribution of its burdens and benefits. On the other hand, advocates of unfettered market operations laud the enormous gains reaped from allocative efficiency. Thus, the debate on globalization can be framed in terms of the long-standing debate on the right principle to use for distributive justice. In what follows, I briefly sketch the arguments for and against globalization, summarize the contrasting canons of distributive justice, and then present a framework for analyzing these two overlapping issues.

Globalization: A Blessing or a Burden?

For many, globalization has been an economic godsend; for others, it has been an unmitigated bane. The divergent positions on global economic integration can be divided into five schools of thought.[1] In the first school are those who believe that "it is much ado about nothing."[2] By traditional measures of trade openness or of financial flows, the quarter century preceding World War I was as integrated as the global economy today.[3] Thus, globalization is nothing new; we have already seen it in economic history. Other scholars have criticized this view by pointing to the significant qualitative differences between nineteenth- and twentieth-century globalization, such as contemporary international vertical specialization; the emergence of transnational firms; intense intra-industry trade; the greater number of countries, especially emerging nations, actively participating in the global marketplace; the rise of super-exporters (e.g., East Asia); the sheer volume of trade; the boom in trade in services; and the increasing proportion of trade in ideas rather than in tangible goods.[4]

The second school hails globalization as "a common climb to the top." This is the proverbial case of the "rising tide raising all boats." By its nature, international trade unleashes expansive benefits because of gains from specialization and a division of labor according to nations' respective comparative advantages. Advocates of globalization point to the disparity in the economic performance of countries that have embraced cross-border exchange in a full-throated manner compared to those that have isolated themselves from the global marketplace. Hundreds of millions have seen their incomes rise and their lives improved. The economic miracles in East Asia are eloquent testimony to the empowering effect of the marketplace. A sample of the exponents of this view include Bhagwati (2004), Irwin (2002), Dollar and Kraay (2001a and b), Friedman (1999), Wolf (2004), and many mainstream (neoclassical) economists.

Scholars from the third school believe that globalization leads to neoclassical convergence. Left on their own, market economies will converge to a common steady state. In other words, as poorer nations tend to grow faster than richer countries, these emerging economies will eventually catch up with their wealthier counterparts. International inequalities will decline on their own. For example, there was an unconditional convergence in the income levels of the major Atlantic economies during nineteenth-century globalization.[5] The same unconditional convergence is unfolding today between the leading developed nations and newly industrializing countries (NICs).[6]

The fourth school of thought views globalization as a leading cause of unequal development and increasing international inequality. Nations reap benefits from global exchange only in proportion to their bargaining power, their level of development, and the depth and quality of their institutions and social capital. Moreover, the rules of international trade are said to be skewed against poor nations, as in the case of OECD agricultural subsidies and discriminatory trade barriers on manufactures, such as apparel and footwear in which poor countries enjoy a comparative advantage.[7] Furthermore, contrary to traditional economics, technological change and innovation may in fact be endogenous, rather than exogenous. If this endogenous growth theory[8] truly works in practice, then we would expect the knowledge economy—a central feature of contemporary globalization—to exhibit increasing, rather than decreasing, returns to scale. This bodes ill for poor nations because they will be left much farther behind by the developed economies that will grow even faster and much wealthier. And indeed, there is abundant empirical evidence indicating an increasing income gap between nations. In fact, the above-mentioned claim of an unconditional convergence applies only to industrialized nations, but not to less developed countries (LDCs).[9] In contrast to the nineteenth-century experience, there is an unconditional divergence between industrialized and emerging nations. Many studies and anecdotal accounts describe the poor's worsening plight. It is often claimed that wealthier economies gain more from international trade than poor nations. Thus, critics from this fourth school of thought equate twentieth-century globalization with neocolonialism. Neoliberalism and the Washington Consensus[10] are viewed with great suspicion and skepticism.[11]

Finally, there are those who view globalization as a "race to the bottom." Nations strip themselves of environmental and labor standards in an effort to be competitive in the global marketplace. Thus, many point to the deplorable working conditions in emerging nations eager to attract foreign direct investments (FDIs) and expand their international market share. The power of the marketplace is illustrated well in the steep and continuing decline of American labor unions, especially in manufacturing, and in the increasing loss of national sovereignty, as in the case of the European Union's (EU) need to reform its social economy to compete better in global trade.[12] Key member states, such as France and Germany, have grappled with the question of whether or not to scale back their generous social welfare and be more market-oriented. There is concern that globalization has shifted the cost of social protection from employers to workers.[13] Even Paul Samuelson, the "father of modern economics," has expressed reservations about the bedrock neoclassical claim on the beneficial impact of free trade. Such gains from cross-border exchange are not guaranteed; unfettered trade may at times and under certain conditions be more hurtful than beneficial.[14]

There are other descriptions of the divisions in the literature besides these five schools of thought. For example, some propose four distinct approaches to globalization, namely: neoliberal, developmental, neocolonial, and earthist.[15] Neoliberalism is exemplified by mainstream, neoclassical economics and proponents of the Washington Consensus. The social development approach is comprised of the multilateral development agencies, such as the World Bank, United Nations Development Programme (UNDP), United States Agency for International Development (USAID), and other similar organizations. Just like neoliberalism, these institutions affirm the value of international trade as a means toward poverty alleviation, but differ from neoliberalism in their broader concerns that include providing health care, education, and other basic needs for the poor. The neocolonial school sees the expansion of markets as a new form of colonial exploitation. The earthist approach calls for protecting the environment and a closer scrutiny of the impact of markets on local communities in the face of rampant globalization.

The antiglobalization movement could also be divided into two groups, namely: the fair trade or back-to-Bretton-Woods school and the localization school.[16] The fair trade approach believes that the market is not intrinsically harmful; it only needs reform. It holds that the rules of international trade are skewed in favor of industrialized countries. As a consequence, emerging nations do not reap much benefit and have in many instances even been harmed by cross-border exchanges. The position of Oxfam International on trade is representative of this outlook. On the other hand, the localization school stresses the importance of local communities and the environmental impact of trade. It is the more radical kind of opposition as it calls for the abolition of the World Trade Organization (WTO), the World Bank, and the International Monetary Fund (IMF)—organizations that it considers to be at the root of the many ills of globalization. However, these radical critics do not offer any alternatives to replace the essential services provided by these multilateral institutions.

This is not the place to resolve the question of who is right or wrong. Neither am I going to rehash and evaluate the arguments for and against global economic integration. But, we can have a better understanding of this debate by using the various criteria of economic justice as a template with which to evaluate the claims being made for or against globalization. In other words, a large part of the debates over international trade is a carryover from disagreements on the appropriate norms to use for distributive justice in the marketplace. Narrowing the gaps between the contending philosophies on economic justice goes a long way toward bridging the divide between pro- and antiglobalizers. It is to this that we now turn our attention.

Distributive Justice

Economic ethics can be divided into three major areas of concern, namely: the division of output, the question of commodification, and the ethical basis of economic thought and analysis.[17] The first deals with questions of distributive justice and constitutes the bulk of the literature on economic ethics. The second pertains to the propriety of using market rules in noneconomic matters. For example, should we permit a market for kidneys? Should we allow commercial transactions on human ova or frozen embryos? Are there certain goods or services that should never be bought or sold (blocked exchanges)? The third set of issues grapples with the anthropological premises of economic modeling and their impact in changing actual economic behavior.[18] This book will focus exclusively on the first topic: What precisely are the appropriate criteria to use in dividing societal resources?

The term "distributive justice" comes from Aristotle who defines it in the fifth book of his *Nicomachean Ethics* as the geometric, proportionate allocation of wealth, honors, or whatever else is divided within the community according to merit. Like cases are treated in like fashion, while unequal cases deserve unequal treatment.[19] Marx proposes the communist distributive principle: "[F]rom each according to his ability, to each according to his needs!"[20] Ryan (1942) lists six canons of distribution: arithmetical equality, proportional needs, effort and sacrifice, comparative productivity, relative scarcity, and human welfare.[21] Rescher (1966) adopts and expands Ryan's norms and calls them distribution according to equality, need, ability-achievement, effort, productivity, social utility, and supply and demand.[22] Rawls (1971) presents his difference principle, while Nozick (1974) responds with an altogether different approach through entitlements. Miller (1976) believes that the claims of social justice are founded on rights, needs, and deserts. Frolich and Oppenheimer (1992, 1994) and Konow (2003) see needs, efficiency, and deserts as the key principles of justice. Scott et al. (2001) subscribe to equality, equity/merit, efficiency, and need. In his recent history of distributive justice, Fleischaker (2004) reduces the concept to two variants: Aristotle's distributive justice and Rawls's justice as fairness.[23] In what follows I will limit myself to a quick review of the main criteria that repeatedly arise in various studies and surveys. This is necessarily a selective reading of an overwhelmingly vast literature on the nature of distributive justice.[24]

Justice as Fairness

John Rawls's groundbreaking *Theory of Justice* addresses the problem of how to arrive at a common vision of justice in a pluralistic world where people subscribe to different notions of the good.[25] He argues that people who are uncertain as to what their position will be in society and what resources will be available to them will be amenable to the following simple rules. First, every person will be accorded the maximum liberties possible that are consistent with everyone else enjoying the same right. Second, inequalities will be permitted only to the extent that they benefit the least advantaged, and only if these inequalities are attached to societal roles that are open to all. Rawls argues that people will readily agree to these terms because they would certainly want those at the bottom of society to be treated fairly and properly, in case they ended up in such a position. The attractive feature of Rawls's method is that there is no need to appeal to any substantive moral theory, only to people's self-interest.

Entitlement

Robert Nozick disputes Rawls's theory of "justice as fairness" and argues against redistribution and the undue interference of government in what is properly private economic terrain.[26] For example, take the case of a basketball player who is greatly enriched by people coming in droves to pay to watch him play. Nozick observes that the government's act of taking away a portion of such earnings (as taxes) and then redistributing the proceeds to other members of the community (presumably the poor) is nothing less than forced labor. Nozick calls for minimal government intervention and asserts that people ought to be able to keep for themselves earnings from their labor and their properties. What is important is that people had legitimately acquired such properties either through a just initial acquisition or through a just transfer from someone who had lawful ownership of the said holdings. As the market operates strictly by the right to private property ownership, it merely divides outcomes according to what people have brought to the marketplace and what they have contributed to the common productive effort. Hence, in judging the fairness of the market's disposition of societal output, inequality is not a relevant consideration—only the proper enforcement of property rights. In short, people are entitled to keep what they have earned, regardless of how unequal such an outcome might be.

Utilitarianism

Utilitarianism is concerned with consequences rather than with the processes by which justice is attained (consequentialism). Moreover, human welfare is measured by the utility levels of individuals, that is, the degree to which their preferences are satisfied (welfarism). In addition, the good of the entire community is conveniently measured by simply getting the sum of individual utility levels (sum-ranking).[27] There are numerous appealing reasons to employing utilitarianism as the preferred criterion of distributive justice. In the first place, people are assumed to know what is in their best interest, and they are given the liberty to pursue whatever ends they may choose for themselves. There is a liberal openness in the way market participants are left free to set and pursue their own goals. Second, utilitarianism dovetails market operations well. In fact, in the textbook model of perfect competition, the unfettered market's resulting allocative efficiency is the "greatest good for the greatest majority."[28] This greatly simplifies our task because the market automatically brings about distributive justice. If efficiency were the basis for distributive justice, there would have been no need for any other additional procedures or redistributions.

Need-Based Distribution

Distribution according to need is a rule that most people would accept as valid and urgent, particularly when we are confronting life-and-death emergencies. Because of the corporeal nature of human beings, people need material goods, such as food, clothing, shelter, and medicine, in order to stay alive, enjoy basic health, grow, develop, and function. Thus, in extreme cases of starvation, most people would say that goods should be allocated according to need. In fact, there is an implicit "right of necessity" in Aquinas's position that it is no theft at all in using somebody else's property in dire cases of imminent death or severe destitution.[29] Properties may be owned in private, but under exigent circumstances they become common in use.

The difficulty with need as a norm of distribution is the slew of unanswered questions it leaves in its wake: What constitutes a dire emergency? What ought to be included in the basket of legitimate needs that will be supplied? To what extent are these needs to be satisfied? Who has responsibility for meeting such needs? There are many competing accounts of the content and scope of what constitutes minimum needs, and I will limit myself only to two of the most widely known theories.[30] Rawls suggests a set of primary social goods that are essential for any reasonable conception of a good life. These primary social goods are rights and liberties, opportunities and powers, income and wealth, and the bases of self-respect.[31] These are universal necessities that allow people to pursue whatever goals they may have set for themselves in whatever place or time. Alternatively, we also have Sen's (1993) and Nussbaum's (1992) "functionings and capabilities." Both are highly critical of the use of utility as a measure of human welfare (welfarism). The ability to function in life is a far better measure of human well-being than preference satisfaction.

Egalitarianism

Finally, we have egalitarianism as a possible yardstick of distributive justice. In some sense, there is a foundational egalitarianism undergirding the various approaches to distributive justice. For example, utilitarianism presupposes equality because every person's preferences count. Rawls sees a fundamental equality in people's right to possess and enjoy his aforesaid list of four primary social goods. Nozick's entitlement criterion is about equal rights to self-ownership and to enjoying the fruits of one's legitimate private properties. Sen's and Nussbaum's "capabilities and functionings" approach is ultimately about empowering every person to work toward his or her life goals. Religious traditions' plea for the satisfaction of basic needs is founded on an equal dignity accorded to every human being.[32] In other words, the divergent measures of distributive justice can arguably be viewed as subsets of egalitarianism because they all aim to equalize something. Their claims are ultimately founded on the equality of a common right or entitlement that every person should have. Hence, far from being a separate school of thought itself, egalitarianism can be viewed as an overarching framework.

Alternatively, egalitarianism can also be regarded merely as a special case of the all-encompassing standards of justice. In his positive multicriterion theory of distributive justice, Konow (2003) considers whether or not egalitarianism should be included as a separate principle of justice at the same level as efficiency, need, and entitlement. He decides not to classify egalitarianism as a separate principle because he views it merely as "a special case of general principles."[33] In various empirical studies and in his own experimental work, Konow finds that most people favor egalitarianism only in exceptional circumstances, such as whenever supplies are low and there is not enough to go around. Equal distribution is also viewed to be the fairest or the least controversial alternative in cases in which there is insufficient information on ethically relevant characteristics, such as effort, costs, contribution, or choices. It is also the preferred rule of distributive justice in cases of uncertainty that lead to costly disputes or extensive information searches regarding contributions, rewards, or other relevant variables on which to base compensation. Finally, at a deeper level, most calls for equality are actually appeals for fairness based on an equality of opportunity. But equality of opportunity can be easily subsumed under need satisfaction; both compensate people for factors beyond their control that impede their ability to function effectively just like other members of the community. Given these widespread views on egalitarianism, Konow concludes that equality is not a general principle of justice but is merely a special case of the principal criteria of justice. Thus, he limits his study only to efficiency, need, and entitlement.

Whether viewed as a separate norm of distributive justice or as an overarching framework, or whether treated as a special case or as a general principle of justice, egalitarianism ultimately has to address the question of "equality of what?" There is no consensus on this issue. Various proposals have been advanced, ranging from minimal claims to the broadest and most intrusive requirements, to wit: an equality of basic civil and political rights and liberties (simple egalitarianism), equality of opportunity (welfare egalitarianism), equality of resources to act and pursue ends, equality in material outcomes (socialist egalitarianism), and equality of welfare.[34] These diverse approaches are not mutually exclusive. For example, an equality of welfare can encompass equality in civil and political liberties, opportunity, or material outcomes.

Overlapping Questions

Many of the disagreements over globalization are often a continuation of the long-standing fight over the proper criterion to use for distributive justice. Global economic integration merely provides the immediate occasion and terrain for the latest, most intense round of the debate.

The schools of thought that laud globalization as "a common climb to the top" or as "a neoclassical convergence" base their claims on the market's much-vaunted ability to allocate scarce resources to their most valued uses. Obviously, for proponents of globalization, efficiency is the primary, if not exclusive, principle of distributive justice. In contrast, the schools of thought that severely criticize globalization as "a race to the bottom," as an uneven development, or as neocolonialism are deeply concerned about people who have either been left out of the entire process or who have been adversely affected by an expanding marketplace. For these critics, the principle of need is the key norm of distributive justice. Thus, the literature on the value or disvalue of globalization can be assessed along the lines of the tension between the two main rival measures of distributive justice: need versus efficiency. *At a deeper level, many of the disagreements over the benefits or ills of globalization are about the appropriate yardstick to use for distributive justice.*[35]

Measures of inequality inevitably have underlying value judgments.[36] The use of statistics to support arguments on the gains or losses from globalization is not value-free but reflects philosophical beliefs. For example, proponents of globalization focus on inequality between individuals and use aggregate measurements of poverty and inequality. Moreover, they prefer relative, rather than absolute, measures of inequality. Using the entire world population as a single unit of analysis, they show a closing gap between the rich and the poor. Indeed, statistics show an unmistakable improvement in both economic and social indicators across entire nations and regions of the world, evidence of the value of globalization as a vehicle of poverty alleviation according to its proponents. The economic gains of the NICs, such as China, Taiwan, South Korea, Singapore, Malaysia, Brazil, and Thailand, are simply too impressive to ignore. In the case of China, the gains are nothing short of breathtaking. The improvement in the lives of hundreds of millions of people is clearly evident not only in the economic sphere, but more importantly, in life expectancy, education, and mass ownership of some of the basic comforts of life (TV, telephones, computers, and consumer electronics). Thus, the "common climb to the top" and the "neoclassical convergence" schools of thought conclude that global economic integration has reduced inequality.

In contrast, those who view globalization as a "race to the bottom" or as an uneven development measure inequality across countries (rather than across people) and are able to show the opposite effect of a steadily worsening gap between rich and poor nations in the post–World War II era.[37] Antiglobalizers are concerned with inequality across nations and use disaggregated data on selected vulnerable segments of society that are at greatest risk, disregarding the total gains accumulated by the whole. They use absolute, rather than relative, measures of inequality. Moreover, many market skeptics are more attentive to personal narratives rather than cold, impersonal statistics. They detail heartrending stories of severe destitution, exploitative sweatshops, ruined ecologies, and ever more powerful monopolies that destroy small- and medium-scale firms and farms.[38] And indeed, based on the living conditions of at-risk populations, critics can easily show that market exchange has harmed the marginalized—people who are unable to participate in a meaningful manner in the economy. For example, they are keen to call attention to the plight of sub-Saharan Africa and impoverished parts of Latin America. They point to Chinese farmers driven off their land and entire villages displaced by an unrelenting industrialization. Far from reaping benefits from global economic integration, many have, in fact, been affected negatively by trade and capital liberalization.

Pro-globalizers defend the use of aggregate measures because these data provide critical information on the direction of the entire economy and its overall ability to reduce poverty via the trickle-down effect. Antiglobalizers, for their part, are skeptical of aggregate measures because these do not show the differential impact of market shocks on various reference groups, shocks that may cancel each other out in the calculation of averages. Aggregation and the use of group averages tend to hide poorly performing outliers.

Both sides cite and use extensive empirical evidence to support their respective positions. The bibliography, analytical studies, and anecdotal accounts backing both sides of the debate are vast. It seems that we have the proverbial case of whether the glass is half empty or half full.

For example, from 1982 to 2001, the proportion of LDCs' population subsisting on less than a $1 a day dropped from 40 percent to 21 percent. Furthermore, in absolute terms, there were 1.5 billion people in 1981 living on less than $1 a day compared to 1.1 billion in 2001. These measures indicate a narrowing gap between the rich and the poor and affirm the position of pro-globalizers.[39] However, antiglobalizers are quick to point out that at the end of the nineteenth century, the gap between the richest and the poorest countries was tenfold. Today, this gap has widened to sixty-fold.[40]

Both sides are looking at the same phenomenon but are stressing completely different dimensions of the issue. The key difference in the choice of these statistics is the weight accorded to China and India, two nations that have seen major improvements in their citizens' economic well-being. If we use national entities as the basic unit of analysis, these two countries, accounting for a third of the entire world population, only count as 2 out of 174 countries. Under this method of accounting, a small country such as Haiti with a population of 8.1 million, for example, carries as much weight as China, with a population that is nearly 160 times bigger (1.275 billion), or India, with a population that is over 120 times larger (1 billion).[41] Not surprisingly, the equal weights assigned to each country, regardless of the size of their population, grossly downplays the immense strides achieved in these two countries, especially China.[42] Thus, proponents of globalization argue that the proper unit of analysis is not individual countries against each other, but people relative to one another.

Take a second illustration of this phenomenon of a "half-full or half-empty glass." The absolute increase in the number of people living below $2 a day supports the conclusion that globalization has impoverished many. There were 2.45 billion people living under $2 a day in 1981; by 2001, this had risen to 2.736 billion.[43] On the other hand, instead of focusing on the absolute number of disadvantaged people, proponents of globalization point to a decline in the relative proportion of the world population living under $2 a day: It was 66.7 percent in 1981 versus 52.9 percent in 2001.[44] The number of people living under $2 a day did increase in absolute terms from 1981 to 2001, but not as fast relative to the growth in global population. Thus, market advocates assert that globalization has indeed been a boon to poverty alleviation. This is a case in which both sides employ the same statistics but use them differently to arrive at diametrically opposed conclusions.

In sum, disagreements on the selection of measures of inequality reflect even deeper and more substantive differences in their value judgments regarding distributive justice. Advocates of globalization prefer aggregate measures because they believe in the trickle-down effect of allocative efficiency and the substantial value it creates. Thus, for these proponents, the principle of efficiency not only subsumes the principle of entitlement-desert, but it also takes precedence over the principle of equality-need. In contrast, critics of globalization are acutely sensitive to the unmet needs of vulnerable groups. Consequently, from their point of view, the principle of equality-need is more important. Both sides of the debate have their philosophical differences on what constitutes genuine economic welfare and progress.

Which claims are correct? Should we evaluate contemporary globalization according to the principles of efficiency and entitlement or according to the principle of need, or both? Why? These are the questions I aim to examine in this book.

Framework of Analysis

For this study, I employ Konow's (2003) threefold theory of distributive justice based on efficiency, need, and entitlement-desert.[45] Egalitarianism is not explicitly included as a separate principle because, as we will see in chapter 6, it is already part of need as a criterion of distributive justice, as are Rawls's primary goods and the difference principle in his conception of justice as fairness. Thus, of the five schools of distributive justice sketched in the preceding section we will evaluate efficiency (utilitarianism), need (Sen, Nussbaum, and Rawls), and entitlement (Nozick). Two issues will be addressed. Are they mutually exclusive? If so, how does one rank them in order of priority?

Meta-approaches

There are three meta-approaches in thinking about social justice, to wit: hegemonic, skeptical, and pluralist.[46] The hegemonic school of thought maintains that "it is in fact possible to ascertain a single substantive standard of social justice that is rationally persuasive."[47] Those who subscribe to this position believe that their proposed norm for distributive justice is clearly superior to alternatives by any reasonable measure. There is a very specific and objective standard of what constitutes social justice, one that is universally applicable across national borders and across generations. Examples include Marx's distribution according to need, Rawls's justice as fairness, and Nozick's entitlement theory.

The skeptical view is the antithesis of the hegemonic approach. Skeptics do not believe in an objective "social justice" because people protect their self-interest. Those with the stronger bargaining position or whose power prevails in the end get to impose their vision of distributive justice. There is no single "principle" of social justice, only interests to be preserved and promoted. Examples of such a perspective include libertarians like Hayek and utilitarians, who believe that people should be left free to pursue their own ends and exercise sovereignty over their own properties. There is a vast multiplicity of interests and, as a result, a correspondingly wide variety of possible "social justice" outcomes.

The pluralistic position falls between the hegemonic and skeptical schools of thought. Unlike the single, all-embracing rule espoused by hegemonic adherents, the pluralist approach sees social justice as comprising a much broader set of principles in order to deal adequately with the complexities of the economic terrain. There is no single panacea or "silver bullet" that resolves all social justice conflicts.

However, unlike the infinite expansibility and amorphous "social justice" preferred by the skeptics, a pluralist conception limits itself to only a handful of valid principles. For the pluralist, social justice is more than just about tastes and preferences; it is imbued with a truly objective basis. Thus, it is possible to weigh skeptics' innumerable conceptions of "social justice" relative to each other and whittle them down to a much smaller set of clearly exceptional criteria. Which norm applies depends on the context, such as the end that is pursued. For example, for Aristotle, social justice is founded on what constitutes excellence in the good society. For Miller (1976), rights, need, and deserts take precedence. Other pluralist views of social justice include Walzer's (1983) "spheres of justice" and Sen's (1993) and Nussbaum's (1992) "capabilities and functionings."[48] Walzer argues for a complex equality in which different realms of social life are governed by their respective rules on what justice requires. For example, while purchasing power is an effective method for allocating scarce goods and services in the economic arena, it would be wrong to employ purchasing power as the yardstick in politics. Money should never be used to buy votes or secure public office. Neither should it determine outcomes in the judicial court system or in education. In other words, equality is complex because various realms of society are shaped by rules of justice that are specific to their particular spheres. Sen's and Nussbaum's standard of "capabilities and functionings" is pluralist because it acknowledges that there is no single formula to endowing people with the capacity to act in pursuit of their goals. The requirements for acting effectively are conditioned by culture and time. For example, we would expect a completely different assortment of requisite "capabilities and functionings" between the nineteenth-century's industrial economy and our own information age. To these pluralist approaches, we can also add Konow's (2003), Frolich and Oppenheimer's (1992, 1994), and Scott et al.'s (2001) wide, but clearly limited, set of criteria for social justice, namely: efficiency, need, equality, and deserts.

Context

Context occupies a central role in the study of justice, which is about giving people their due. After all, justice's requisite measurements and its need for precision cannot be satisfied in abstraction but must be set within the particulars of time, place, and history. There has to be a reference group, a clear articulation of the clashing claims, and an understanding of the circumstances of the competing claimants. It is context that provides these. Context also paves the way for a richer and a more nuanced application of the principles of justice. It is also a necessary condition for the above-mentioned pluralist meta-approach to distributive justice. For example, in his surveys on what people thought about justice, Konow (2003, 1199) finds evidence of a trade-off between needs and efficiency as competing criteria of distributive justice. As the urgency to satisfy basic needs subsides and as economic performance and incentives begin to falter, people switch over to using efficiency as the preferred or the primary basis for allocation. Context is the medium that permits a multi-criterion theory of justice such as Konow's.

I use context in two important and distinct ways in this study. First, I believe that a significant shortcoming of many commentators on the values or disvalues of globalization is their failure to take the nature of the market into account. The ills or benefits spawned by global economic integration in its wake are largely reflective of the market's inherent properties. To gain a better appreciation for why globalization has been such a blessing for some and an onerous burden for others, it is important to understand the mechanics and dynamics of the market-place. Thus, chapters 4 and 5 briefly outline both the allocative and distributive nature of the market's core mechanism—its array of prices.

Second, I employ a globalizing knowledge economy as the context for evaluating the three primary principles of distributive justice we have identified in this chapter. We will assess the impact of the knowledge economy and market expansion on the relative claims of these three criteria. As a collateral benefit of such an exercise, we also get a glimpse into both the strengths and the limitations of the arguments made for or against globalization.

Using the nature of the market and the globalizing knowledge economy as the context of this study, I will address the question of whether the principles of efficiency, need, and entitlement are mutually exclusive. And if they are, which criterion should apply in contemporary globalization? How do we rank these norms in order of importance?

Part I

The Knowledge Economy

A distinctive feature of contemporary globalization is the shift in the source of wealth and value creation from natural resources and industrial capital to knowledge. ICTs have been instrumental in causing this transformation. Chapter 2 maintains that the current technological revolution is atypical because it is the market itself and its core process that have been radically transformed. Good information is the lifeblood of the marketplace, and microelectronics provides this information faster and in great abundance. As a consequence, the market has become even better at allocating scarce resources to their most valued uses. In other words, the market has become more efficient at being efficient. Chapter 3 describes how the knowledge economy is exacting in its demands on human capital. Economic life has become even more competitive and dynamic, its pace has accelerated, and it requires even greater acuity on the part of market participants.

Chapter 2

Microelectronics and Market Efficiency

The Difference Technology Makes

Twentieth-century globalization has been described as "much ado about nothing" because by traditional measures of trade and financial openness, the quarter century preceding World War I was just about as, if not more, integrated as our contemporary era.[1] Scholars have disputed this claim, noting that similarities between these two periods of globalization are more apparent than real because of fundamental differences in their trade and production structures.[2] In particular, contemporary production has been subdivided along key components that are then farmed out to specialized export-manufacturing sites around the world especially in the NICs of Asia and Latin America.[3] Moreover, trade in the past two decades has been increasingly a global exchange in ideas (such as financial instruments) rather than in traditional goods and commodities.[4] Closer inspection of these recent shifts in business organization and in the composition of international trade reveals an even more significant contrast—the emergence and impact of ICTs.

The main drivers of twentieth-century economic integration have been capital mobility, technological change, and the shift in government attitudes toward liberalizing their domestic markets.[5] These three factors were similarly responsible for nineteenth-century globalization. However, the key difference lies in the radically transformative impact of technology in contemporary globalization.

A common pattern in economic history is the pivotal role of technological discoveries in precipitating major economic changes. Thus, for example, recall the role of the wheeled plow, the horse collar, and the three-field system of crop rotation in greatly increasing the productivity of medieval agriculture. Remember the carvel construction technique in shipbuilding that saved wood and led to the development of lighter and larger ships. These technological advances in ship construction were essential for the age of discovery.[6]

The modern economy is no exception to this pattern in economic history as many scholars believe that the first and second Industrial Revolutions were possible only because of path-breaking technological inventions and innovations, such as the steam engine, steel, and electricity. Technological changes come in varying degrees. Four types have been proposed, to wit: incremental innovations, radical innovations, changes in technology systems, and technological revolutions.[7] Incremental innovations are the everyday, run-of-the-mill refinements in the normal course of business operations as workers get better at what they do through "learning by doing." Radical innovations, on the other hand, are improvements that are deliberately pursued and developed through a specific program of research and development (R&D). These are the more substantive advances that spawn new products, markets, and investments. Nylon, aluminum, plastic, home video cameras, and other consumer electronics are examples that come to mind. Changes in technology systems are a step up from radical innovations in that they are not "localized" but have a system-wide impact affecting several sectors, as in the case of the petrochemical industries. Of interest and relevance to us for this study, however, is the last and the most sweeping of these categories: the techno-economic paradigm shifts that induce permanent and wide-ranging socioeconomic changes.

Freeman and Perez (1988) describe these technological revolutions as "techno-economic" phenomena because of their dual character. In the first place, they are technological in nature because they revolve around significant improvements in how we engineer manufacturing processes and products. These technical achievements are so sweeping as to reduce drastically the cost of production; they precipitate extensive market changes in their wake. Thus, these events are also properly described as economic in nature. It is from these two features that Freeman and Perez coin their term "techno-economic."

These technological revolutions are occasioned by the availability of a new set of core inputs (for the economy) characterized by three important qualities: a deep and continuing drop in their relative prices, nearly inexhaustible supplies for the foreseeable future, and ubiquity in use and application.[8] And because these newfound inexpensive inputs seep into every facet of society and radically transform the way people live, eat, work, and relate to each other, they have also been described as "all-purpose technologies."[9] They give rise to clusters of innovations along a wide front: technical, organizational, and managerial. Moreover, these diverse changes mutually reinforce each other to produce even further innovations in a self-sustaining beneficial cycle. Thus, there is a cascading stream of ever-new products, services, and processes. These general-purpose technologies could indeed be aptly described as "inducing a pattern of discontinuity in the material basis of economy, society, and culture."[10]

These techno-economic paradigm shifts have been used as the basis for a theory of business cycles. Periodic fluctuations in prices and employment in the modern economy can be explained through these bursts of revolutionary and disruptive technical changes.[11] These epochal shifts are believed to come in recurring periods of fifty years in what has come to be known as Kondratieff or long-wave cycles.

There have been five of these modern economic epochs, and we are currently in the fifth. Freeman and Perez (1988, Figure 3.1, 50–57) outline an excellent schematic summary of these long-wave cycles.[12] The first was the "early mechanization Kondratieff" dating from 1770–80 to 1830–40 with the development of a mechanized textile industry built on the ready availability of cheap cotton and pig iron. This was followed by the "steam power and railway Kondratieff" (1830–40 to 1880–90), characterized by the widespread use of steam engines and the emergence of a rail transport system that greatly reduced the inland cost of moving materials, goods, and people. Cheap coal and transportation became the core set of inexpensive inputs that transformed society.

The third long-wave cycle was the "electrical and heavy engineering Kondratieff" from 1880–90 to 1930–40. Steel and electricity formed the core set of cheap and widely available inputs that spawned the heavy industries of the modern economy (e.g., machine tools, heavy chemicals, and electrical machinery). The fourth was the "Fordist mass production Kondratieff" (1930–40 to 1980–90) made possible by cheap energy, oil in particular. This was the epoch of mass transportation and petrochemicals. The current cycle is the "information and communication Kondratieff" (1980–90 onward), distinctive for the wonders of microelectronics.

Each of these long-wave cycles precipitated a "golden age."[13] Abundant cotton, labor, and coal of the first two Kondratieff cycles gave rise to the "Industrial Revolution." Low-cost steel (third Kondratieff) inaugurated the "Victorian boom." Plentiful petroleum (fourth Kondratieff) ushered in "la belle époque." Inexpensive microelectronics (fifth Kondratieff) heralded the "Keynesian boom."

Information and Communication Kondratieff

Freeman and Perez (1988) use the long-wave cycles only to account for why the business cycle can be viewed as a process of adjustment to the structural crisis precipitated by technological change. This is unfortunate because they fail to bring out the full significance of the last Kondratieff cycle. I propose that our current information and communication long-wave cycle is qualitatively different from the earlier Kondratieff cycles and deserves to be treated as a separate class by itself. The contemporary economic impact of microelectronics exceeds those of earlier "carrier inputs" in the first four Kondratieff cycles for at least two reasons. First, they fulfill the three features of all-purpose technologies to a supereminent degree, and secondly, they alter the very heart of the market process itself.

Microelectronics as an All-Purpose Technology

All-purpose technologies are characterized by rapidly falling relative costs, unlimited supplies, and ubiquity in use and application.[14] Steam power and electricity, in particular, were the key innovations that animated the first and second Industrial Revolutions respectively. The generation and distribution of energy at will, in desired quantities and wherever needed, radically improved both the manufacturing and transportation sectors with ripple effects throughout the social fabric.[15] Nonetheless, despite the spectacular gains they engendered as the quintessential technological revolutions of their era, they still pale in comparison with ICTs. Microelectronics exceeds all previous carrier inputs in all three areas of price, supplies, and ubiquity.

Compare the rate of decline in the prices of the past and present carrier inputs. Between 1790 and 1850, the cost of steam power fell by a total of only 50 percent over sixty years. The cost of rail transport in the United States declined by 40 percent between 1870 and 1913, a drop in prices of 3 percent per year. The cost of electricity showed an annual decline of 6 percent between 1890 and 1920. In contrast, the real price of computer processing power has dropped by an average of 35 percent per annum in the past thirty years.[16] The average cost of processing information was $75 per million operations in 1960. This dropped to less than $.0001 by 1990 and is expected to decline even further.[17] The fall in the price of ICTs as carrier inputs has been so precipitous and dramatic that it has even been claimed that if the automotive industry's costs dropped to the same extent over the past twenty years, cars would now cost $5 and give us 250,000 miles per gallon.[18]

It took seventy years (1780–1850) for the price of cotton cloth to fall by 85 percent in Britain. In contrast, the price of semiconductors declined by 85 percent in only three years (1959–62).[19] The real price of electricity decreased by 7 percent per year between 1890 and 1920 while the real, quality-adjusted, price of computers dropped by 20 percent per year from 1990 to 2000.[20]

This wide disparity is also seen in communications. The cost of a phone call decreased by 10 percent per year between 1930 and 2000. The telegraph remained relatively expensive throughout the past 150 years. On the basis of prices from the year 2000, it cost $70 a word in the 1860s and declined to $10 per word in the 1870s. In contrast, within seven years of making the Internet available for commercial use, it cost less than a cent to e-mail a twenty-page document. A transatlantic phone call today costs a few pennies.[21]

These differential rates are also reflected in the market penetration of these all-purpose technologies. It took more than a century before steam became the dominant source of power in Britain. Electricity supplied 50 percent of the power requirements of U.S. manufacturing only by 1919, ninety years after the discovery of electromagnetic induction.[22] In contrast, 50 percent of U.S. residents were using computers just thirty years after the invention of microprocessors and only fifty years after the invention of computers. The market penetration of the Internet is nothing short of breathtaking. It was already in use by 50 percent of the U.S. population only seven years after its commercialization.[23] Measured from the time of their invention to adoption by U.S. households, the Internet (1975), the personal computer (1975), and the cell phone (1983) have taken only a tiny fraction of the time that previous technologies—electricity (1873), the telephone (1876), the automobile (1886), the radio (1905), the television (1926), the VCR (1952), and the microwave (1953)—took to gain widespread use.[24]

The speed of adoption can also be gauged by examining the experience of LDCs. For example, by the outbreak of World War I, only 30 percent of the total rail lines in the world were in emerging nations. In contrast, within seven years of the Internet's commercial launch, users in LDCs already constituted 10 percent of total Internet subscribers (2000). Moreover, many of these emerging nations showed double-digit growth rates in ICT adoption.[25]

The cost of previous carrier inputs declined at a much slower rate and over a longer period of time. It is believed, for example, that growth in the use of electricity was stunted on account of the protectionism during the interwar years. In contrast, prices of microelectronics and their derivative products and services have declined much faster, and as a result, they have had a much deeper impact and market penetration than previous carrier inputs. In addition, ICTs came at a time when governments had been actively opening up their markets to each other.[26]

Microelectronics is altogether unique as an all-purpose technology because it is reducing cost simultaneously across the entire spectrum of the production infrastructure, from numerically controlled manufacturing, to new forms of faster and cheaper methods of communication[27] that require less upfront capital investment and maintenance, and to even more inexpensive and efficient transportation systems that facilitate international subcontracting and just-in-time inventory management. Moreover, this radical improvement in processes has transpired across all segments of the economy. In addition, the use of microelectronics has been so pervasive as to give rise to an entirely new array of products, services, and industries. This is especially true for consumer electronics. All these elements of the revolution point to far-reaching changes in socioeconomic life requiring even quicker responses from economic agents both to take advantage of profit opportunities and to avoid losses from a rapidly evolving marketplace. These new demands will be ever more taxing on human capital.

Core Efficiency

Twentieth-century globalization is not merely "much ado about nothing" even in the face of trade and financial statistics that show the nineteenth-century global economy to be far more integrated. Krugman (1995) notes that our contemporary experience is qualitatively different in the manner in which the whole world has become a single integrated workshop with final products being assembled from parts manufactured in different continents. Dicken (2003, 11–12) differentiates the "shallow integration" of nineteenth-century cross-border trade in goods versus the "deep integration" of contemporary globalization in which intermediate goods are heavily traded through networks of transnational firms. Baldwin and Martin (1999) argue that ours is more of a trade in ideas than in traditional goods. These authors are merely describing the symptoms of an even deeper qualitative transformation. It is the improvement in the market's core process itself that spells the difference between these two economic epochs, and the consequences of such an advance are as wide-ranging as they are profound.

Even more important than the rapid diffusion of ICTs is the manner in which microelectronics has transformed the economic terrain itself. The real core set of inexpensive inputs for the fifth Kondratieff cycle may not be microelectronics but information. The pivotal role of technologies in improving the flow of information in the economy is not a recent, postindustrial phenomenon. There has been a constant stream of information-related technological innovations that have led to better managerial control of mass production processes and flows, distribution, and consumption since the 1830s.[28] These "control innovations" have included both organizational changes and new equipment.[29] However, these technological changes were mostly a mix of incremental and radical innovations.[30] At best, they were changes in technology systems, but not the kind of revolution that radically shifts the technological foundations of society. It was not until the advent of microelectronics in the 1980s that we truly see a "control innovation" that is extremely cheap, abundant, pervasive, and truly transformative in its impact. In fact, our contemporary information and communication long-wave cycle is at its heart the paradigmatic "control innovation."

The ready availability of low-cost information alters the market process itself. Recall the centrality of information in the marketplace. Economic agents exchange goods and services in an effort to improve their pretrade welfare. This requires knowledge of what other economic agents have to offer, what goods they want in return, at what terms, and where and when to consummate such exchanges. In other words, a good part of the transaction costs (search, bargaining, and enforcement) of economic exchanges is about securing reliable information.

Rents also illustrate the importance of information in the economy. Market participants with superior or advance information are able to position themselves for profit-making opportunities. Arbitrage is largely about having information at the right place, in a timely manner, and in an exclusive fashion. Arbitrage works only because the information is privileged (asymmetric) and is not widely available to others.

Neoclassical microeconomics is about consumers and businesses allocating their resources to maximize their welfare. It is a dynamic optimizing exercise because these market participants have to adjust their decisions constantly in response to new market opportunities and to how other economic actors behave. Thus, procuring, analyzing, and using information to good effect is the core process of microeconomics. Recall that the other name for microeconomics is price theory. No other social mechanism is as effective as the market price in conveying a continuous stream of information on an incredibly large volume of goods and services in a timely and cost-effective manner across widely dispersed economic agents. Price is merely the means to an even larger end: getting information across cheaply, quickly, effectively, and continuously. The market is such an important societal institution because there is nothing to date that can replace its singular ability to collate, process, convey, and orchestrate a proper response to economic information as it becomes available.[31] It is only in understanding the role of information in economic life that one can appreciate the profound implications of the fifth Kondratieff cycle, why it is truly a paradigm shift from the four earlier long-wave cycles, and why it deserves to be treated as a class by itself.

In drastically cutting the cost of collecting, storing, and analyzing data, microelectronics is pushing the market and its participants to become even more effective and efficient in the way they use and share information. Thus, it has even been said that "IT [information technology] and the Internet amplify brain power in the same way that the technologies of the industrial revolution amplified muscle power."[32] If the marketplace is about allocating scarce resources to their most valued uses, then microelectronics is about making the market even more efficient. Perfect information is a necessary condition for perfectly competitive markets to achieve allocative efficiency. We are closer to approximating such Pareto efficiency to the extent that microelectronics provides us with better and more complete information, ceteris paribus.[33] The carrier inputs of earlier Kondratieff cycles, such as cotton, steam power, steel, and electricity, revolutionized locomotion and production. In contrast, the impact of microelectronics is altogether different because its effects reach into the economy's core process itself. It is the market itself that is subject to radical change. Its decision-making process reaps the most benefits from the inexpensive carrier input of the fifth long-wave cycle: information. *The market economy has become more efficient at being efficient!*

The market's enhanced efficiency is evident in some of the characteristic features of contemporary globalization: more intense competition, an accelerated economic pace, self-sustaining technological and organizational innovations, lower production costs to the point of taming worldwide inflation, and, most of all, a market-driven global economic integration that is wider and deeper than at any time in history. The following sections and the next chapter examine some of the specific causes and consequences of the market's improved efficiency.

Features of the Knowledge Economy

Superfluity of Data

Mayer-Schönberger et al. (2000) dissect the information and communications revolution into four interlocking technological breakthroughs.[34] The first significant development was the ability to digitize information, that is, to reduce data to a binary code, thereby leading to the following results:

1. Greater access to nontraditional forms of data besides text and numbers, such as drawings, pictures, audio, and video. Data in various formats can now be easily processed or shared. Not only does this expand data sources, but it also makes available different media for disseminating information or for communication.
2. Enormous savings in data storage and duplication.
3. The ability to share and transmit data over long distances via satellite, cable, or wire with the click of a mouse. Distance becomes increasingly irrelevant to data sharing.
4. Substantial cost savings from standardization and economies of scale. Prior to digitization, different means of transmission (such as radio, telephone, telegraph, and television) required their own dedicated systems that were not interchangeable. With the binary code, a single universal transmission network can serve different media, thus, avoiding a costly duplication of equipment. Moreover, this means that data can be switched easily from one medium to another because of the convenience afforded by standardization.

The second technological breakthrough was the discovery and development of silicon chips, that is, integrated circuits to process data. The pace of innovation for these chips has been remarkable with their processing capacity doubling every eighteen months (Moore's law). This is the immediate cause for the continued precipitous drop in the cost of data processing and storage mentioned earlier.

The third major technological development was the relentless expansion in network bandwidth, that is, the amount of data that can be transmitted over the network. The advance in these capabilities is even more impressive—a tripling of capacity every year (Gilder's law). This means that every three years, while processing speed increases fourfold, transmission capacity increases by an astounding twenty-sevenfold, nearly seven times that of processing speed.

The fourth technological building block was the simultaneous standardization and decentralization of the information highway. The

Internet is radically decentralized as it is not controlled by any single entity. At the same time, it is also standardized in its electronic infrastructure (TCP/IP).[35] Consequently, it reaps the best of both worlds. On the one hand, its decentralization opens the door to a much broader user base, which in turn offers a much wider pool of innovators who improve the Internet's architecture and explore its other potential uses. And on the other hand, standardization provides economies of scale for all facets of the information highway, from the hardware and software to the engineering and design of their supporting infrastructure. Decentralization and standardization feed off each other. Cost savings from standardization make the Internet that much more accessible, while the resulting increased usage leads to even greater economies of scale in the next rounds of economic activity.[36]

Together, these four technological breakthroughs (digitization, Moore's law in data processing speed, Gilder's law in data transmission capacities, and an information highway that is both decentralized and standardized) have been responsible for the spectacular fall in the cost of information processing—a rate of decline in prices never before seen in any of the carrier inputs of the earlier four Kondratieff cycles. Microelectronics outclasses these earlier carrier inputs by any measure used to define all-purpose technologies in terms of cost, unlimited supplies, or ubiquity. As a consequence, we are now literally flooded with data. As empirical proof of this claim, consider the indispensability of using the Internet in the normal course of the day, our complete dependence on search engines to find our way through the Web, and the emergence and overnight success of MySpace, YouTube, Google, eBay, Yahoo, and other similar dotcoms characterized by a common feature—their ability to manage data and information in a cost-effective, orderly, and useful manner. This is not even to mention the blogosphere.

Market Widening

I use the term "market widening" to refer to the extension of the market's reach both across and within nations. Late-twentieth-century globalization is considerably different from the two earlier periods of global economic integration in terms of the number of countries involved. Nineteenth-century globalization was principally centered on Europe, the New World, and Australia. The three decades after World War II saw an expansion in the scope of global markets, thanks to the different rounds of General Agreement on Trade and Tariffs (GATT) negotiations. In contrast, contemporary globalization is characterized by (1) a much larger number of countries engaged in international exchange, (2) the expansion in the volume of global trade, (3) the increasing share of emerging countries in international exchange, and (4) the growing openness of economies to trade (measured in terms of exports plus imports as a percentage of gross domestic product [GDP]).[37]

International trade has been growing much faster than GDP. For the period from 1980 to 1989, global GDP rose at an annual rate of 3.2 percent while merchandise exports grew at 6 percent per year. While global GDP decelerated to an annual growth rate of 2.8 percent for the period from 1990 to 2004, merchandise exports even accelerated slightly to an annual growth rate of 6.36 percent. Combining these two time periods (1980–2004), world output grew at an annual rate of 2.6 percent while merchandise exports rose by 6.89 percent per year.[38] The growth of merchandise exports at nearly three times the rate of GDP only goes to underscore the vibrancy of cross-border exchange. Growth in trade is expected to exceed growth in output by a factor of two or more for the next two decades.[39]

Market widening is also evident in the continued rise in the number of countries that have liberalized their merchandise trade in the last quarter of the twentieth century. More countries have voluntarily integrated themselves into the global marketplace.[40] Between 1985 and 1995 alone, 33 developing countries switched from a statist, inward-looking trade posture to more open, outward-oriented policies.[41] The share of exports from developing countries has been steadily growing over time from 25 percent in 1960 to 29 percent in 1980 to 33 percent in 2004.[42] In 1973, only 12 to 13 percent of developed countries' imports of manufactures came from emerging nations; by 2003, this had risen threefold to around 40 percent.[43] Trade barriers and tariffs have dropped as part of the Uruguay round of trade negotiations. Moreover, even emerging nations themselves have begun the process of liberalizing their capital markets.[44] Indeed, emerging nations have become increasingly active participants in the global marketplace.

This phenomenon of market widening is also evident in the increasing penetration of trade in local economies.[45] Compare, for example, the traditional measure of trade openness across time (ratio of exports and imports to GDP). For the global economy as a whole, it was 38 percent in 1980 and increased to nearly 50 percent by 2003. For developing nations, it was 47 percent for 1980 and increased to 70 percent in 2003. Emerging nations in Asia began with a ratio of 50 percent in 1980 and rose to a remarkable 77 percent by 2003.[46] The world's export-to-GDP elasticity rose by nearly a third from around 1.6 in 1970 to 2.3 by 2004.[47] Not only have more countries been opening themselves to trade, they have also been increasing the volume of their trade with the rest of the world.[48]

Many scholars believe that the global economic integration of the past three decades has also been as a result of the shift in government policies toward greater liberalization. Market widening is reflected in the internal reforms pursued by countries in their respective domestic economies. Isolated communities and heavily subsidized sectors of the local economy have been gradually incorporated into the marketplace. For example, many governments have begun to privatize state-owned enterprises.[49] Protective policies from an earlier, failed era of import substitution have been gradually rescinded. Members of the EU have been grappling and debating among themselves, with much acrimony, on whether or not they should give up their social economy, become more market-oriented, and be more flexible in their labor markets in line with the requirements of global competition.[50] All these reflect the continued move among nations to subscribe further to market rules. It is a development that has been unfolding for quite some time and is described in Yergin and Stanislaw's (1998) book, *Commanding Heights*.

Market widening has been a notable cause of contemporary global economic integration. However, there is also a feedback effect in which globalization causes even further market widening. Countries, such as Russia, China, and Vietnam, which have been outside the scope of traditional Western capitalism, have been willing to embrace painful domestic economic reforms and even grant concessions in an effort to gain membership in the WTO. Note, too, the proliferation and acceleration of regional economic integration efforts.[51] After witnessing the tremendous strides achieved by neighboring China, and perhaps fearful of being left too far behind, India followed suit in embracing a more open economy beginning in the early 1990s. This is no small feat as India has long been steeped in a tradition of central planning, economic nationalism, and protectionism. While governments should rightly be given credit for opening their markets, it is very likely that they did not have much choice on the matter. The opportunity cost of not being part of the global marketplace would have simply been too great for these governments to bear. It would have been self-defeating to shut themselves out of international commerce. Thus, government liberalization can be said to be both a cause and effect of contemporary globalization.

This feedback effect (of globalization pushing market widening further) is seen not only at a macroeconomic or governmental level but even more so at the microeconomic level of the firm. For example, recall the well-documented deindustrialization of developed nations.[52] Survival for many manufacturing operations in the OECD has required their relocation in less expensive overseas sites.

An even better example of a microeconomic-driven market widening is the recent surge in international vertical specialization, a phenomenon in which firms procure their supplies from different parts of the world, even for their core products and activities. To stay competitive, firms have had to slice up their products into ever-finer value-added components for subcontracting to countries that are able to offer these parts at the lowest price. This is particularly true for the automotive, airplane, and electronics manufacturers who have turned the entire world into a single workshop supplying parts for their final products.

This is in sharp contrast to the heyday of vertical integration in the industrialized nations in which firms manufactured their own parts. Ronald Coase's (1937) "Nature of the Firm" provides a theoretical explanation for why this erstwhile practice once made economic sense. The transaction costs of subcontracting these parts to other firms were so high that it was cheaper for manufacturers to simply supply their own requirements. Thus, until recently, the "Big Three" U.S. automotive firms produced their own engine blocks, transmission boxes, electrical systems, and stamped metal sidings. Today, there is no such thing as an American-made car because components have come from all over the world.[53] The same phenomenon is true for both Airbus and Boeing[54] and for electronic goods such as computers and mobile phones.[55] The range of products subject to international vertical specialization is clear testimony to the pressure that globalization has exerted on economies to open their markets. It is not surprising that the surge in international vertical specialization coincided with the breakthroughs achieved in data digitization, processing, storage, and transmission, thereby reducing the cost of communications, supervision, coordination, and data sharing. The drop in these transaction costs has greatly facilitated overseas subcontracting and has intensified or expanded the scope of market-based activity (e.g., eBay, B2B). Microelectronics is a significant cause of international vertical specialization and market widening.

Market Deepening

I use the term "market deepening" to refer to the expansion of economic exchange to include services that were not traded across borders until the advent of ICTs.[56] The most well-known example, of course, has been business process outsourcing (BPO) that covers routine back-office operations: data entry, paper processing, transcription, digitization, telemarketing, tech support, and call centers. However, outsourcing has moved up the skills ladder to include software programming, 3-D animation, desktop publishing, accounting and bookkeeping, tax preparation, financial analysis, engineering and architectural design work, and even medical consultation.[57] In addition to these, banking, insurance, investment, and other financial services are now traded heavily across national boundaries. Even the legal profession outsources its more routine work, such as legal research, patent applications, and divorce papers. It is estimated that as many as 12,000 legal jobs have been outsourced, and these are expected to more than double to 29,000 by 2008.[58]

Data on the full extent of such outsourcing has been extremely hard to come by. However, initial estimates point to a robust growth of offshore employment from 2003 to 2008: IT services (89 percent), retail banking (226 percent), packaged software (176 percent), retail (50 percent), and insurance (90 percent).[59] In 2000, global spending on business-processing outsourcing was nearly $100 billion and is projected to rise to as much as $175 billion by 2008.[60] This trend is also reflected in other aggregated statistics. Exports of services as a proportion of world output has been increasing over time. In 1984 it was 3 percent and had risen to 4.9 percent by 2004. The ratio for emerging nations more than doubled, from 2 percent in 1984 to 4.7 percent in 2004.[61]

For the period 1980–2002, the annual growth rate in the global export of services (8.1 percent) has outpaced that of merchandise exports (6.8 percent).[62] The cumulative growth rates in the export of services between 1994 to 2003 for some emerging nations have been impressive: nearly 700 percent for India and more than 200 percent for China, Brazil, and Argentina. Global outsourcing of services is projected to grow at 30 percent per year between 2003 and 2008.[63]

International outsourcing of services has been made possible by the technological innovations of the knowledge economy. Any economic operation that can be conducted through a telephone line or be reduced to a binary code can now be easily traded.[64] And as in the case of market widening, global economic integration also feeds back into pushing market deepening even further. For example, the need to reduce costs in order to keep up with the competition has driven firms to follow suit and outsource services and functions that used to be nontradables and previously supplied from within the companies themselves.

Numerous anecdotes reflect both the power and the promise of globalization in pushing market widening and market deepening even further. International outsourcing is no longer only for the large companies. Even small-scale, first-time entrepreneurs subcontract their manufacturing overseas. Richtel (2005) describes the experience of start-ups in children's pajamas and in software development. Without low-cost overseas subcontractors, these small U.S.-based businesses could not have gotten off the ground as domestic costs would have been four to ten times more in the case of the children's pajamas, and three to fifteen times more in the case of software programming. These foreign subcontractors were not difficult to find and contact through the Internet, trade shows, and local firms specializing in searching for overseas expertise.

Note some striking observations from these anecdotes. First, international outsourcing is not merely an option but a necessity for many firms' viability. Second, international outsourcing is getting to be relatively easier to arrange and even small-scale start-ups, which Richtel calls "micro-outsourcers," are able to follow this business model. There are thousands of Web sites providing information on various manufacturers and service providers overseas, not to mention trade shows both in the United States and abroad. E-mail, instant messaging, and excellent phone links have allowed local business owners and foreign manufacturers to stay in constant communications throughout the production process.[65]

Third, even micro-outsourcers are able to slice up their products into ever-finer value-added segments. Take the case of the children's pajama start-up. As soon as they get the manufacturing squared away, the entrepreneurs intend to "hire a freight management [firm] . . . to receive the shipments, check the merchandise's quality, [and] then send it along to customers" (Richtel 2005). This kind of business is aptly called a "virtual" business because the owners have no manufacturing facility, no storefront, and no warehouse. Everything is conducted via electronic communications. Such companies illustrate the new business horizons made possible by both ICTs and global market widening and deepening. International vertical specialization has seeped down all the way to the smallest operations.

Fourth, outsourcing used to be limited to the noncore activities of firms. However, the dividing line between what is core and noncore for businesses is shifting. In the case of the children's pajama start-up, product design and marketing have become the core. In an earlier age, it would have most likely been the design, manufacturing, warehousing, and marketing of the pajamas. In other words, ICTs and globalization have made it increasingly possible to whittle down the firm's core activities to a bare minimum. Even the U.S. automakers are seriously considering entrusting some of their manufacturing and assembly operations to smaller, specialized subcontractors.[66]

The personal accomplishments of these micro-outsourcers typify the extent to which market widening and deepening have changed socioeconomic life. More important, however, these anecdotes illustrate how globalization is generating change down to the level of the individual economic agent. As a researcher on outsourcing trends notes, outsourcing is occurring at every level from the manufacture of steel, cars, software, and computer chips, to the "little lady who make[s] scarves."[67]

In sum, both market widening and deepening are about the increasing "marketization" of society in which more interpersonal, intra-national, and international relations transpire through the marketplace.[68] Market rules govern ever-larger realms of socioeconomic life. Work that used to be performed internally within the household, firm, or government is taken over by the marketplace. Examples include growth in the provision of paid child care outside the family, the outsourcing of many noncore activities (such as accounting and payroll), and the privatization of many functions traditionally reserved for government, such as collecting back taxes and running prisons and schools. Of special interest to us in this study are the international exchanges. These have grown over the past twenty-five odd years as a result of a self-feeding process of global economic integration.

Self-reinforcing Market Expansion

There is a self-reinforcing dynamic to market expansion. First, the market has created a need for itself; people are ever more reliant on it in the knowledge economy. Even as the digital age produces a deluge of new information at an accelerating pace, it turns out that it is also the market that is capable of processing such immense amounts of information. Google and other similar multibillion dollar search-engine portals are excellent examples of how the market itself provides a solution for dealing with the superfluity of data it has spawned. Or, note the credit-reporting agencies that collate data on people's creditworthiness. It is much cheaper for banks, financial institutions, and many other businesses to simply rely on these specialist firms than to have to gather, store, and update such data themselves.[69] This is not to mention society's savings through economies of scale and avoiding a costly duplication of effort. In both of these examples, we, in effect, are dealing with a market for information. Observe the paradox in this. We are driven to even greater "marketization" as a way of coping with the increased demand for sifting, processing, and using a profusion of information that the market itself had generated in the first place. In other words, there will be an increased reliance on the market for data-information management in the knowledge economy. Thus, recall the earlier point that twentieth-century globalization is different from its earlier variants because it is increasingly about an exchange of ideas than of commodities.[70]

Second, the augmented demand owing to market widening and deepening brings about economies of scale that translate into a decline in the cost of goods and services. This leads to a further rise in quantity demanded. More important, this drop in prices intensifies competition and the push for ever more advanced technological change and innovation. Moreover, there is also an operative bandwagon effect in that competitors are forced to adopt the latest innovations lest they lose their market share.

Third, market widening and deepening also mean larger potential short-term rents, thereby escalating the search for the next generation of new technologies. The availability of ever-larger profits to be made reveals needs in the economy that remain to be filled and provides entrepreneurs with the necessary incentives. (Take the case of the wildly successful iPods as an example.) Moreover, intense competition, risk, and uncertainty drive private initiative to network with each other. These collaborative exchanges widen and deepen the marketplace even further, turning it into a catalyst and medium for ever more profound change and technological advances. This is discussed further when we get to competitive networking in the next chapter.

Finally, the balanced growth theory of development economics is helpful in illuminating the nature of a self-reinforcing market expansion in contemporary globalization. Mid-twentieth century development economists believed that poor nations could not industrialize because they had small markets for industrial goods.[71] Industry had difficulty taking root in these countries because of insufficient demand. Thus, some proposed a "big push" development strategy in which investments were to be made across a wide range of industries. Such a broad development effort was expected to result in different sectors of the economy providing markets for each other. This phenomenon is currently unfolding both in China's domestic economy and in East Asia. A wide variety of industries in these emerging nations are thriving simultaneously; their success is convincing proof of the value of mutually reinforcing demand. Take the Chinese apparel industry, for example. It is said that there is no country that can beat

China when it comes to its vertical supply chain in this industry because it has a large pool of independent button, fabric, thread, and zipper makers bound together in an interlocking web of superefficient exporters.[72] These manufacturers are, in effect, collectively supporting each other by providing complementary demand for their respective outputs. They reap incalculable economies of scale in the process and become even more competitive abroad.

Another example of the mutually reinforcing momentum of market deepening and widening can be seen in the linkage between the real and the financial sectors. A deep and well-developed financial market has been found to be instrumental in the establishment of an ICT sector in the local economy.[73] Because of their risk profile, ICT industries are better suited for equity financing rather than bank or debt financing and, consequently, a functioning capital market is essential for their development. The causation is not merely one-way. In their own turn, the peculiar requirements of ICT firms push capital markets into ever-new frontiers and products (e.g., venture capital).[74] Observe how the marketplace serves as the critical link between the financial sector and ICT industries.

To sum up, there is a self-reinforcing dynamic to market expansion. Market widening and deepening can take a life of their own. The knowledge economy will be ever more reliant on the market.

Knowledge as the New Source of Value Creation

There has been a noticeable shift in the source of wealth and value creation. In the industrial epoch, natural resources and investment capital were the primary generators of economic value and wealth. The manufacturing sector was the main seller and buyer in the product and factor markets and pulled along the rest of the economy. Value creation was largely dependent on the transformation of natural resources into finished goods. In contrast, knowledge is the main driver in the information economy. Economic value is predominantly generated through a more intelligent disposition of resources, through new and cost-effective ways of doing things, and through the creation of intellectual property, such as software, pharmaceuticals, and entertainment. In what could be described as the learning or reflexive economy, production is now centered on "knowledge-intensive design process" rather than the more traditional "material production process" of the industrial era.[75] Thus, many describe ours as the "weightless economy" in which the value of goods comes more from their intangible inputs (such as design and engineering) rather than the cost of their raw materials. These changes have been driven largely from the supply-side given the ready availability of ICT tools and the improvement in human capital.

There are also demand-side factors behind the shift in the source of value creation. A rise in people's wealth and in the value of their time leads to an increase in the demand for services, such as entertainment, finance, and investments.[76] Furthermore, an aging population with purchasing power will surely push the demand curve outward for new drugs, medical procedures, and technologies that improve or prolong the quality of life. Nonetheless, whether from the demand- or supply-side, or both, microelectronics has been a catalyst in putting knowledge at the heart of value and wealth creation in the postindustrial economy.

Empirical evidence confirms this shift in the source of value and wealth creation. As of the mid-1990s, more than 50 percent of GDP in the leading OECD nations is knowledge-based. Moreover, the share of high-technology goods in OECD manufacturing and exports has more than doubled to 20–25 percent between 1970 and 1993.[77] The physical weight of U.S. output is approximately the same as a hundred years ago, even as its value has increased twenty-fold. In addition, the value of the stock of U.S. intangible capital, such as R&D and education, exceeded that of physical capital stock as of the 1980s.[78] The ten most valued firms in the world in the late 1990s held intellectual properties whose value surpassed that of their capital stock.[79] This trend toward a weightless economy will strengthen even further as more people avail of e-commerce and telecommuting.[80] The composition of global manufactured exports is another indicator of the central role of knowledge in today's economy. The 30 most valuable manufactured goods exports comprise 44 percent of total global merchandise exports. Of these 85 percent are complex technologies with the remaining 15 percent taken by simple commodities.[81]

Computer and data processing is expected to be the fastest growing source of employment between 1998 and 2008, more than doubling during the period. For the period between 1983 and 2003, mathematical and computer scientists increased fourfold, the fastest growing type of occupation.[82] There has been a continuous decline in the number of production laborers in favor of creative workers.[83] Between 1980 and 1996, there has been a steady increase in the ranks of managers and professionals as a proportion of the labor force for most of the major developed countries. Moreover, as of 1996, the proportion of these workers was anywhere from 10.6 percent (Italy) to as high as 32.78 percent (Canada).[84] The well-documented increasing disparity in the earnings of skilled versus unskilled workers can be attributed to technological bias rather than trade; the more sophisticated the technologies employed, the greater is the demand for technical competence.[85] Moreover, the high returns to education are also indicative of an increasingly knowledge-based economy.[86]

In his book *The End of Work*, Jeremy Rifkin claims that most of the new jobs created are temporary and low-paying, heralding the disappearance of the mid-level jobs. Such "de-skilling" is not borne out by empirical evidence. In fact, for the United States, these mid-level jobs held steady as a proportion of employment (1980 = 34.4 percent; 1998 = 34.6 percent). More than that, contrary to Rifkin's prediction, high-wage work increased from 28.2 percent in 1980 to 33 percent in 1998. It was low-wage work that saw a decline from 37.4 percent in 1980 to 32.4 percent in 1998. This empirical evidence is confirmed by numerous other studies that indicate an even greater demand for skilled workers in the face of even more "information-rich activities" in the new economy.[87]

Even as it is still in its nascent stage, the knowledge economy's impact has already been impressive. For example, it cost $60,000 in 1985 to conduct a Ford crash test. In contrast, the same results could be achieved in 2000 through computer simulation at a cost of $100. In 1991, Amoco's cost for prospecting for oil was $10 per barrel. By 2000, three-dimensional seismic exploration technology reduced such costs to $1 per barrel. In 1970, the cost of transmitting the *Encyclopedia Britannica* from coast to coast in the United States was $187. By 2000, the entire content of the Library of Congress could be transmitted from coast to coast for $40.[88]

The repercussions of the knowledge economy are also evident in productivity growth. Between 1945 and 1973, American labor productivity grew at 2.5 percent per year.[89] This dropped to an annual rate of 1.4 percent between 1973 and 1995 but jumped to nearly 3 percent per year from 1996 to 2000. The high correlation between industry productivity and ICT investments strongly suggests that the effects of microelectronics have begun to be felt across the real economy. The Internet alone is estimated to have been responsible for an annual productivity gain of 0.25 to 0.5 percent. This accounts for 8.3 to 16.6 percent of the productivity gains from 1995 to 2000.[90]

Ceaseless, Substantive, and Sharper Readjustments

By its nature, the market is in a constant state of adjustment. It never stands still because of pecuniary externalities. As we will see in chapters 4 and 5, a key feature of the market is its price mechanism, which serves as a cost-effective vehicle for gathering, processing, and disseminating information in a timely fashion across a wide geographic area. Price adjustments induce changes in people's decisions, which collectively move the entire economy toward the most efficient use of its scarce resources. This is the allocative dimension of price. Unfortunately, these price movements have collateral effects that reshuffle economic burdens and benefits across market participants. This de facto income redistribution is the unavoidable distributive dimension of price and is the proximate reason for why not everyone necessarily benefits from market exchange. Schumpeter's (1942, 81–86) famous term "creative destruction" already connotes the mixed blessing that capitalism is to different people. It is a boon to those who benefit from the new value created, but is an encumbrance for those for whom value is destroyed. Even as they are empowered by markets, economic actors must be prepared to deal with its ripple effects, both pleasant and unpleasant. The combined impact of these two dimensions of the price mechanism is succinctly summarized in the following assessment:

> Market economies are dynamic systems engaged in a continuous process of structural change. Economic progress is in large part a result of successful adaptation and adjustment to such change.[91]

Held et al. (1999, 187) describe it as "continuous structural adaptation." We can also call it a process of "formative disequilibria"[92] because the much-sought allocative efficiency is attained only through the bothersome process of having to adjust constantly to change.

Contemporary globalization has intensified the perpetual motion that seems to be a feature of the marketplace. Freeman and Perez (1988, 38) note that instability is an expected rite of passage in moving from one Kondratieff cycle to the next. After all, techno-economic paradigms arise in response to the bottlenecks and inadequacies of the preceding carrier inputs. New "all-purpose technologies" precipitate structural crises of adjustment as socioeconomic institutions adapt to the requirements of a fresh set of carrier inputs. Recall, for example, the tectonic changes in industrial organization and social living after the introduction of the steam engine, the electric motor, and, of course, the automobile. Moreover, the resulting capital-deepening phase of such long-wave cycles generally leads to overinvestment, as in the case of the railroad mania that led to a boom and then a bust in Great Britain in the nineteenth century. There were once 5,000 railway companies and 2,000 car manufacturers in the United States in the early days of these industries.[93] We have witnessed the same "over-shooting" phenomenon in the ICT boom and bust in the United States at the turn of the millennium.[94] The bursting of "irrational exuberance"[95] and its dotcom bubble in 2001 is part of the painful but necessary structural adjustment toward better allocative efficiency, just like all the other Kondratieff cycles. The OECD's deindustrialization, cross-border turbulence, rapid capital flow, and ICT volatility have been among the factors driving our current period of "formative disequilibria" requiring constant and substantive readjustments. Each of these is briefly examined in what follows.

Deindustrialization

The modern economy's center of gravity shifts from agriculture to industry to services as a regular part of economic growth.[96] Advanced developed countries are currently undergoing a process of "deindustrialization" as industrial resources (labor, capital, etc.) are increasingly switched toward the further development of services as a sector. Contemporary globalization has exacerbated the ill effects of deindustrialization by speeding up the rate of change. In the normal course of economic growth, the higher productivity in manufacturing relative to services causes an orderly transfer of labor from the former to the latter. Workers can be trimmed back in the industrial sector because of the increase in its productivity; surplus labor is then transferred to services. This is reminiscent of nineteenth-century growth in which gains in agricultural productivity released farm labor and other resources for use in industry. The best-case scenario, of course, is a seamless transition across sectors. Unfortunately, this is highly unlikely even in the best of times. The rate of job destruction in manufacturing is not synchronous with job creation in services, and many are left unemployed or underemployed. Thus, despite its acknowledged long-term gains, Schumpeter's "creative destruction" is not always a welcome phenomenon even in the most capitalist economies.[97]

Globalization accelerates deindustrialization and, in the process, aggravates the latter's attendant problems. ICTs have precipitated a much faster pace for economic life, a shorter product life cycle, more intense competition, and, most of all, international vertical specialization.[98] An immediate consequence of these developments is a much faster transfer of manufacturing from developed to emerging economies than would otherwise have been the case. Furthermore, there is the additional problem of an outmigration in the services sector as well because ICTs have made cross-border trade in services possible for the first time (e.g., call centers, engineering design, and accounting). This spells double trouble for developed countries because the services sector is supposed to create new employment for displaced industrial workers. And yet, it is itself under the same competitive pressure from the global marketplace. Erstwhile nontradables such as services have lost their ability to provide a safe haven by absorbing labor from manufacturing. Not only is the services sector unable to create remunerative jobs fast enough, but it is itself losing jobs to offshore competition. This is a serious dilemma because both economic theory and evidence point to the services sector as the predominant generator of employment and wealth in the advanced stages of economic development. Given the "new" competition in this sector, one that used to be sheltered from cross-border trade, developed nations find themselves having to speed up innovation in services.

Picture a ladder whose lower rungs correspond to natural comparative advantage based on a country's natural resources. The upper rungs pertain to created comparative advantage in which nations use their social and human capital to fashion ever-new products and services.[99] As countries develop, they move higher and higher up the ladder. And as they do, they leave to the next country behind them the economic activities and goods in which they no longer enjoy comparative advantage. This is the flying-geese pattern of development. Advanced nations graduate onto ever more sophisticated products and, in the process, hand down less complex industries to emerging economies. Thus, the more developed countries are in effect able to "pull up" trailing countries behind them. It is a win-win situation, with the leading nations able to push the technological frontier further and create higher value-added jobs.[100] What is even more important to note, however, is that until recently, developed countries were able to climb up the ladder of created comparative advantage at their own pace. But, not anymore.

In the knowledge economy, there is stiff competition across the entire length of the ladder, in areas of both natural and created comparative advantage at the same time. Countries down at the bottom of the ladder are able to compete even for the upper rungs. Take the case of software programming. These are sophisticated, high-tech services that would have been the next step up to replace manufacturing industries that had been handed down to emerging nations. However, with the advent of ICTs, Bangalore now competes with Silicon Valley for many of these high-tech service jobs. In other words, there are more and more cases in which it is the trailing countries lower on the ladder that are forcing the more developed countries up the ladder. Instead of the leading countries "pulling" along the emerging nations, we have a "push" phenomenon in which emerging nations are driving the industrialized nations to climb up the ladder much faster.

The principal implication of this change is that developed countries are now no longer able to climb up the ladder of comparative advantage at their own pace. This means that they have less time to shift labor and other resources in an orderly fashion to the new emerging high-tech sectors. In the "pull" phenomenon, they had the leisure of time and forewarning to get themselves ready for the upper rungs of the ladder and to minimize disruption as they hand down industries to the next countries in line. Moreover, tariff barriers had afforded developed countries' manufacturing industries some protection and time for a well-conducted changeover. In contrast, the services sector of leading nations in contemporary globalization can be put at risk overnight by technical advances in microelectronics.[101] Service jobs can be lost as quickly as they are created. Thus, in the knowledge economy, developed countries have had to move much faster up that ladder whether or not they are in a position to create new areas of comparative advantage for themselves that can generate export revenues and alternative employment. This accelerating flux in the labor market is also reflected in measures of job stability. For example, for the years between 1983 and 1998, there was a drop across all age groups in the median length of time U.S. males worked for the same employer.[102] There was a much quicker labor turnover.

The massive U.S. trade deficits partly stem from the problems spawned by the "push" phenomenon. Techno-economic paradigm shifts take time and substantial investments (e.g., education and skills training) before taking root. The necessary lead time for the technological breakthroughs or substantive innovations that create jobs in the upper rungs of the ladder will only get much longer given the ever-increasing complexity of products and services. To make matters worse, even the jobs that flow from such discoveries will not be secure for long because of an ever-shorter product life cycle that compels developed countries to move higher up the ladder faster. In other words, there has been an accelerated pace in climbing up the ladder of comparative advantage. The process of deindustrialization, as we know it from traditional economic theory and history, is changing. It has picked up speed and is ever more difficult to control, thereby leaving the more developed countries open to even more disruptive shocks in their domestic economies. With greater interdependence from global economic integration, the speed of adjustment is forced upon nations; they no longer set the pace of their own economies.

This is true even for the largest and the most dominant economies, such as the United States, EU, and Japan.

Cross-border Turbulence

The infrastructure of the knowledge economy is conducive to transmitting cross-border disturbances. As already mentioned, a distinctive feature of the fifth long-wave cycle is the pervasive impact of ICTs. ICTs have seeped into every facet of society and have radically altered the way people live and relate to each other. The health of different economic sectors has become so intertwined. Take the case of commodities as an illustration. At the height of recent Chinese economic growth, dry-bulk shipping freight rates increased 600 percent in just 18 months, between mid-2002 to its peak in December 2004. This was followed by a weaker Chinese demand for steel, which led to a steep decline in steel prices. From a price of $650–$700 per ton, hot-rolled coil (the industry benchmark) dropped to $480 per ton in two months, a reduction of 26 to 31 percent. With the resulting fall in the demand for iron ore and coking coal, key ingredients in the manufacture of steel, bulk-shipping rates sank 55 percent in less than six months from its peak in December 2004 to June 2005.[103] Observe the magnitude of the swings in prices within short periods of time without any forewarning. Furthermore, note the speed with which economic changes are transmitted across industries—from a weakened demand from end users of steel to an immediate fall in shipping rates.

Coffee was a lucrative crop to the point of being called "black gold." However, with the entry of Brazil and Vietnam as big coffee producers and with the shift in Western consumer preferences from coffee to pop soda, coffee prices have been extremely volatile and have also hit all-time lows, inflicting great hardship on small coffee farmers. The livelihood of small-scale coffee growers in Africa and Central America has been heavily dependent on the vagaries of the weather in Brazil.[104]

ICTs have strengthened and generated new forward and backward linkages in the global economy, in addition to widening and deepening the market. These intensified ties within the real economy make for a much broader and much faster transmission of cross-border turbulence than would have otherwise been the case in the absence of an ICT-led globalization. More countries are vulnerable to such shocks. Equally important, there will be more such unexpected ripple effects coming from many more parts of the world. Note, for example, how the ten-year per capita income growth rates of emerging nations have become much more volatile since the 1980s.[105]

Let us examine one other example of market integration and its concomitant risk of cross-border turbulence. Indonesia was severely hit by the 1997–98 Asian financial contagion that started in neighboring Thailand. Its GDP contracted by 13 percent in 1998 alone. It was still suffering from the lingering effects of the crisis well into 2002 as seen in its lower consumption (25 percent smaller than the pre-1998 crisis level) and the twofold increase in the number of people below the poverty line than would have otherwise been the case. Various regions of the country have been recovering since then, albeit at different rates. What is surprising to note is that in a study of the lasting impact of this economy-wide crisis at the local level, scholars found a seemingly counterintuitive result. It is commonly believed that the poor are more vulnerable to such macroeconomic shocks. Not in this case. Poorer regions fared much better in the face of the crisis and its aftermath. Because of uneven government policies and Indonesia's geography, some districts were isolated from the national economy. These were the poorer districts. They were insulated from the cross-border turbulence of 1998 and were not as adversely affected as a result.[106] This differential impact across the diverse regions of Indonesia serves to remind us that while market integration brings extensive benefits, it also comes with potential dangers.

Rapid Capital Flow

Capital market liberalization is another significant venue for the rapid transmission of cross-border disequilibria. Even more important, however, is the manner by which these financial linkages magnify such disruptions. In fact, compared to the real economy, the global financial market is an even better illustration of volatility as a constitutive feature of the knowledge economy. For example, goods and commodities have to be transported in the real economy, and there is consequently a physical limit to how much of them can be traded in a single transaction. Even trade in services is circumscribed by the human limitations of service workers. In contrast, there is a near-perfect transportability of financial instruments across borders, courtesy of ICTs, and, as a consequence, there are practically no limits to how much economic value can be traded across borders.

Moreover, financial trading is instantaneous, at the click of a mouse. This makes for a swift transmission of economic ripple effects across the globe. In contrast, there are physical constraints in the real economy. Manufacturing, transporting, warehousing, and selling goods and commodities take time. For example, excess inventories have to accumulate, be detected, and then corrected through the economy's regular business cycles. There are no such time lags for financial trading. Furthermore, a disproportionate segment of portfolio and foreign exchange trading is speculative in nature and, consequently, volatile and damaging to the economy. In addition, there is a "herd" or a "cascading" effect that magnifies the initial disturbance. Besides, rumors that underlie some of these shocks can be self-fulfilling as in the case of foreign currency trading.

The 1997–98 Asian financial crisis demonstrates the speed and magnitude of the shocks that ICT-driven capital markets can generate. Moreover, it reminds us of how turmoil in the financial sector spills over into the real economy. The freer trading of capital across borders is universally acknowledged to be a constitutive feature of contemporary globalization. Consequently, we should brace ourselves for disruptive and damaging disequilibria as ICTs push the world into a truly single, integrated capital market. This is an important and unavoidable hallmark of the knowledge economy.

ICT volatility

Unlike previous all-purpose technologies, ICTs are more vulnerable to turbulence because of the heavily speculative nature of their financing, their widely dispersed production sites spread across different countries, and the more rapid and steeper drop in their prices. Information technology has been widely considered to be the leading and the most vibrant sector in the global marketplace. There is both an upside and a downside to this. The upside is that ICTs can pull along many other sectors of the global economy. The downside is that these technologies are much more susceptible to market disturbances than ordinary goods and can readily transmit and magnify such shocks to the rest of the international community. The use of ICTs is so pervasive that the sale of semiconductors is extremely sensitive to changes in the state of the world economy. For example, using the standard deviation of monthly growth sales as a measure of volatility, industrial production fluctuates anywhere from 0.5 (for the G-7) to a maximum of 7.0 (Hong Kong SAR [Special Administrative Region], Taiwan, South Korea, and Singapore). In contrast, the volatility for the world sales of semiconductors is 14.0, or twice that of the maximum recorded in industrial production. World semiconductor sales and electronic exports growth are many times more variable compared to GDP growth.[107]

Or, take the case of ICTs' production through international vertical specialization. Most of the world's consumer electronics and personal computers are manufactured and assembled in Asia. Electronic exports constitute nearly 10 percent of the GDP of the region, even going as high as 25 percent for the smaller economies. These products have been subdivided in their value chain in manufacturing and farmed out to different countries in the region.[108] An economic downturn in the West leads to a drop in demand for consumer electronics and computers. This in turn prompts nations assembling these products (primarily China and Taiwan) to curtail their imports of microelectronic parts from their Southeast Asian neighbors. This domino effect is not surprising considering that as much as 50 to 75 percent of the value of these electronic exports are imported intermediate inputs (coming from within the region). Thus, these countries face the risk of serious supply logjams owing to political instability or natural disasters along the entire manufacturing chain. This is particularly true for nations that have failed to diversify and are heavily dependent on such exports. ICT exports as a percentage of GDP range anywhere from 1 percent (Hong Kong SAR) to as much as 20 to 25 percent (Singapore and Malaysia, respectively) of local economies. Given such enormous dependence on ICT production and exports, these countries are heavily exposed to downswings in ICT demand. For example, a 10 percent drop in ICT exports can cause as much as a 1.75 to 2.25 percent decline in GDP growth in Singapore and Malaysia, respectively.[109]

The same volatility applies in the case of ICT financing. As we will see in a later discussion of the role of ICT financing in the development of domestic capital markets, ICT firms are heavily reliant (1) on external, rather than internal, financing, (2) on equity, rather than debt, financing, and (3) on short-term, rather than long-term, debt for whatever loans they may incur. Such a capital structure means that the ICT sector is wide open to macroeconomic disruptions and swings in consumer confidence.[110] It also means that it can easily transmit turbulence to other parts of the economy. Recall the roller coaster ride of the dotcom bubble and crash in the years just prior to and immediately after the turn of the millennium. The great uncertainties and consequent risks surrounding ICTs make the sector particularly dependent on venture capital. Firms that succeed reap unimaginable gains, while the many others that fail lose their investments. The leading edges of the industry literally have a "feast or famine" dynamic, thus making investments in this field truly speculative. All these contribute toward wilder fluctuations in the stock prices of ICT firms. Furthermore, such swings in ICT stock prices are instantly transmitted across borders; ICT stock prices are highly correlated across countries.[111] To make matters worse, as we have seen in the aftermath of the dotcom bubble, tumult in ICT stocks spills over into the rest of the equity markets and into the real economy.

Finally, the knowledge economy is intrinsically more volatile because of its increasing returns to scale (IRS).[112] This makes for sharper swings in the marketplace. Economic activities characterized by IRS are likely to grow faster than the rest of the economy in an upswing and contract much more severely in a downturn.[113] On the basis of U.S. industry output data from 1977 to 2001, there is empirical evidence that IRS industries[114] have indeed been more volatile compared to rest of the economy.[115]

Summary

ICTs have radically transformed the cost and the manner by which data is produced, processed, and used. By greatly improving the speed, volume, and quality with which information is provided to economic agents, microelectronics has made the market even more efficient at allocating scarce resources to their most valued uses. Moreover, they have also been instrumental in expanding the geographic reach of the market and the size and intensity of international trade. These technologies have also occasioned the shift in the source of value and wealth creation from natural resources and industrial capital to knowledge. Indeed, contemporary globalization is distinctive because it is both a cause and effect of the information age. This knowledge economy has been characterized by a superfluity of data and ceaseless substantive adjustments, thereby placing greater demands on market participants. It is to these new demands that we now turn our attention.

Chapter 3

Requisite Agility

W e continue to examine various features of the knowledge economy in this chapter. In what follows, we will look at the need for ever more advanced human capital in response to the faster pace of economic exchange, the more severe competition, and the higher value of time in the information age.

Accelerated Pace of Economic Life

The pace of economic life is not merely faster, it is, in fact, accelerating. The rate of innovation itself is speeding up. This is a result of a number of mutually reinforcing causes, namely:

- better information and communications links,
- improved transactions infrastructure,
- shorter-lived rents, and
- shortened product life cycles.

Better Information and Communications Links

Timely and correct decisions on the part of market participants are vital to allocative efficiency. This requisite accurate and alert response is largely dependent on access to quality and time-sensitive information. As we have seen earlier, the distinctive input of our unfolding Kondratieff cycle is information. The cost of gathering, storing, processing, analyzing, and disseminating data has dropped steeply, exceeding the decline in the cost of earlier carrier inputs. This speeds up economic life for at least two reasons. First, more and better data are readily available. We are by no means anywhere close to the condition of complete information in the textbook's perfectly competitive market, but contemporary market participants are at least far better informed than at any time in the past. Ceteris paribus, more complete and more precise data make for more informed and faster decisions. Second, besides better and more comprehensive data, market participants also have more powerful computers with which to process, analyze, and turn data into actionable information. Without such distillation and synthesis, data are useless and will be nothing more than incoherent numbers and letters. The widespread availability of inexpensive, yet powerful, tools reduces the turnaround time in transforming data into useful information and then acting on it. Not only can more data be processed, but they can be analyzed from many different angles and scenarios, and at a fraction of the time it would have taken without ICTs.[1] The personal computer and the Internet have enabled economic agents to manage and utilize complex and immense amounts of data within a much shorter period of time, truly an information revolution.

The acceleration of economic life is also due to better communications. The breakneck expansion in bandwidth and the simultaneous standardization and decentralization of the electronic superhighway have connected people to each other like never before. This "death of distance"[2] means easier communications and, therefore, easier coordination and collaboration among economic agents. This greatly reduces both the effort and the time needed to get widely dispersed people to make collective decisions and to follow through on them. Equally important, ICTs facilitate joint efforts in analyzing and integrating data into useful information. This ease in communications has been partly responsible for spawning another distinctive characteristic of our current global economic integration: the slicing up of the value chain in manufacturing (a.k.a. international vertical specialization), a phenomenon we will examine at length in chapter 4. The Internet alone has led to expansive streamlining and efficiency gains for business management, such as simplified paperwork and better supply chain administration.[3] In fact, the digital age has inaugurated a new era of "real-time management" in which information is immediately internalized in corporate decision making. The availability and use of the most up-to-the-minute data reduce lags and lead to an agile responsiveness that includes faster reengineering. Firms become more cohesive, more flexible, and therefore, more competitive.[4]

The acceleration of economic life is evident in the faster response of firms to excessive inventory. ICTs improve inventory management by providing better and timelier information. Firms monitor their widely dispersed supply chains round-the-clock and rapidly adjust their production in response to shifting market demand. This avoids the buildup of unsold stocks, thereby shortening the resulting corrective downswing (to reduce inventory). This had been called the "bullwhip effect" in which changes in consumer demand snowball into bigger problems up the supply chain because poor information delays critical decisions from being taken.[5] The quicker response facilitated by ICTs leads to a sharper downturn in economic activity and a faster transmission of shocks; however, it also reduces the amplitude and duration of the ensuing business cycle.[6] Empirical evidence shows that better inventory management has led to a reduction in stock levels over time, accompanied by a corresponding drop in output volatility for the major developed nations.[7] Indeed, ICTs have led to less damaging business cycles by facilitating prompt corrective action.

In sum, ICTs have engendered twin, mutually reinforcing, information and communications revolutions; it is a wired global marketplace. This has led to an accelerated economic life because market participants make faster and more informed decisions given their access to better and more complete data. Moreover, they are equipped with ever more powerful tools with which to process information. The resulting quicker turnaround time is also true at a collective level. People are able to decide and act jointly at a more rapid pace because of the ease with which they can communicate with each other. Furthermore, such an ability to exchange data and ideas expeditiously has the collateral effect of speeding up further the analysis and transformation of data into useful, actionable information.

Improved Transactions Infrastructure

The quickening momentum of the marketplace is also due to the improvement in the transactions infrastructure afforded by ICTs. Most of the costs incurred in completing economic exchanges are the frictional costs, namely: the time, effort, and money expended in searching for the appropriate trade, bargaining over the best possible terms, and then executing and enforcing the contract. Microelectronics has been instrumental in lowering the costs of consummating transactions, especially for the most expensive and time-consuming phase for most market participants: searching for the right good or service provided by the right trading partner at the right terms, at the right time, and at the right place. Recall the preceding chapter's anecdote on how even small-scale, "garage-based" businesses procure their supplies from overseas, courtesy of ICTs. These micro-outsourcers have had little trouble transacting with suppliers halfway across the globe.[8] An even better example is eBay and its hugely successful concept of bringing buyers and sellers together. Web-based marketing has made it possible for buyers to track down goods they could not get elsewhere or that would have taken much effort to find. And yet, with the click of a mouse, these buyers are able to locate these goods and even do comparison shopping. And, of course, the reverse is also true with respect to the ease and convenience of identifying potential buyers for just about any good.[9] Indeed, the spectacular growth and success of eBay and the auxiliary industries it has spawned reflect the extent to which the knowledge economy has transformed the transactions infrastructure of the marketplace.

The savings on transaction costs are substantial. For example, a Brookings Institute study on the impact of the Internet enumerates a wide variety of data-intensive industries that have reaped sizable savings on paperwork, time, and effort by shifting to Web-based operations.[10] The processing of healthcare payments costs \$10–\$15 for a paper-based claim versus \$2–\$4 for a mix of paper and electronic data filing. It would have cost less than a \$1 per claim if everything were done on the Web. For the year 2000 alone, this would have generated a savings of \$27 billion just by switching to the Internet. Many other cost reductions can be squeezed out of the healthcare industry, such as the use of electronic medical records. This saves on storage and minimizes errors. Furthermore, Web-based medical records permit speedy access to personal health information from anywhere in the event of an emergency.

The ease and swiftness with which transactions can be consummated via ICTs are illustrated best in financial services. Paying via the traditional check (which has to be physically transported, sorted, and then cleared) is estimated to be at least ten times more expensive than paying via the Web. Personnel and brick-and-mortar costs are minimized with the use of automatic teller machines. This is not to mention the convenience of having round-the-clock access to a "virtual" teller. Investors could avoid brokers and buy an increasing number of financial instruments directly from their providers. Comparison shopping has become much easier for the mortgage lending industry.[11]

The Web has streamlined governmental transactions including the dissemination of information via the Web instead of the phone, the collection of taxes via the Internet, and the electronic filing of many requisite forms and data required by local, state, and federal agencies. The savings and the possibilities of e-government are only beginning to be explored.[12]

Besides the drop in search costs afforded by e-commerce, there are also savings with respect to bargaining. Because of the transparency afforded by the published terms and conditions in Web-buying or selling, and because of the ease with which comparison shopping can be done, market participants need not expend time or effort in haggling. The prevailing price and the terms and conditions are readily available for all to see. Again, the best example of this is the auction-style marketing of eBay.

Besides lowering search and bargaining costs, ICTs have also improved the execution of exchanges. The infrastructure that enables economic agents to access more complete data lends itself to facilitating communication and the completion of exchanges. Note, for example, that the biggest segment of business-to-consumer e-commerce is online consumer travel spending (a third of the total). The bulk of personal travel purchases is expected to move online within a decade.[13] Consumers are increasingly forgoing traditional brick-and-mortar travel agents and completing transactions online with service providers (airlines, hotels, and resorts). This is also true even for the more complex products like financial instruments.[14] Today, even initial public offerings (IPOs) can bypass traditional brokers and go directly to buyers, as in the case of Google.[15] ICTs have cut the middlemen, saving both time and expense.

Short-Lived Rents

As already noted, information is the lifeblood of the market. Asymmetries and imperfections in the distribution of information give rise to economic rents. Arbitrageurs reap large gains for themselves because they are privy to data not available to others. ICTs level the playing field while at the same time raising the bar for all market participants by providing public access both to a superfluity of data and the necessary tools to sift through, analyze, and then profit from such information. The market is an extremely fluid environment because people continually adjust their economic decisions based on new information constantly provided by its price mechanism. Economic rents are instantaneously dissipated in the idealized model of perfectly competitive markets with perfect information and perfect mobility (ease of entry and exit).[16] However, in the real world of imperfect and rigid markets, considerable rents can be made, but only if one can beat the competition to it, or only if one can keep the information from becoming public or widely known. ICTs raise the bar for everyone because they reduce, if not eliminate, many of the bottlenecks and asymmetries in the distribution of information. Such greater transparency leads to a "compression of [firms'] profit margins" and these gains are ultimately passed on to consumers.[17]

ICTs have improved even the lives of farmers.[18] ITC, one of the largest Indian corporations, launched and funded the e-Choupal initiative that brought the Internet to the South Asian countryside. Rural farms have been among the biggest beneficiaries of this newfound source of information. Prior to e-Choupal, farmers had to transport their produce to markets without knowing ahead of time what price they would get for them. Middlemen took advantage of this information asymmetry by underpricing these crops. After all, it would have cost more for farmers to transport their harvest back to their village than to simply accept the offer of these unscrupulous buyers. However, with access to the Internet, farmers come to the marketplace better prepared and aware of the prevailing prices. They even check the futures market of the Chicago Board of Trade to get an idea of when they should sell their crops. The Internet has made it much more difficult for middlemen to prey on the farmers.

Microelectronics has leveled the playing field by providing greater transparency. But in so doing, it has also narrowed the window for profit-making opportunities. Time is now of the essence for competitors; the prize goes to the quick and the nimble. There is no substitute to a prompt response to changing market conditions. This need to react swiftly and effectively to new information, the ready availability of e-tools with which to process data, and the narrowing window of opportunity to reap rents all contribute toward an accelerating pace in the knowledge economy.

Shortened Product Life Cycle

The product life cycle is a useful model for understanding nations' changing patterns of comparative advantage over time. A good or service typically goes through three major phases: a new product phase, growth in its production and usage, and a mature phase. In the nascent stage, firms cultivate a market for their innovations or inventions. As demand increases, economies of scale lead to lower prices and the development of export markets. Other countries improve the product, manufacture it themselves with the use of foreign or local investments, and eventually end up dominating the export markets. This is the mature stage. Now, the original producing nation has to move to the next generation of technological innovations as it relinquishes its previous comparative advantage to the next tier of countries behind it.[19]

The knowledge economy leads to ever shorter product life cycles for a number of reasons. First, the length of the cycle is primarily dependent on how long it takes competitors to imitate and catch up with the first mover. Today, there is less breathing room and less of a lead time for first movers because one of international trade's unintended consequences is its transfer of technologies across borders.[20] Moreover, ICTs facilitate a much faster dissemination of engineering specifications and manufacturing processes. Better information and communications infrastructure makes for greater openness, a more expeditious exchange of ideas and information, and easier access to industry practice. Furthermore, more powerful e-tools allow for a quicker dissection of technologies. In addition, better human capital means that competitors can easily whittle away the lead time of first movers. In addition, firms have banded together in R&D networks in response to globalization. Such collaboration translates into even more brainpower, and this, in turn, means a much faster response to first movers. A more organized R&D makes for quicker imitation, or even improvement, of first movers' products and processes. This contributes to competitive leapfrogging, that is, the phenomenon of having a profusion of new generations of the same product, as in the case of cell phones and personal computers.[21] Indeed, there has been an acceleration in both knowledge creation and knowledge destruction.[22]

Second, the liberalization of capital markets has contributed to a faster diffusion of technological change. Foreign direct investments have long been known to be invaluable vehicles for transferring technologies because the latter are embedded in the capital, plant, personnel, and equipment that usually come as a package with such cross-border capital movements.[23]

Third, in anticipation of the brevity of the product life cycle, firms (and their competitors) are already busy working on the next generation of products. Such multiple, parallel efforts enhance the likelihood of a cluster of technological breakthroughs, some of which may be so superior as to render recent innovations suddenly outdated.

Fourth, given the rapid obsolescence of technologies, especially in microelectronics, firms already plan for a quick depreciation and replacement of such assets, especially ICT hardware.[24] This is another effective channel for diffusing technological change because cutting-edge engineering developments are immediately embodied in the latest capital equipment. The more rapid retirement of equipment eventually becomes standard industry practice as firms seek to maintain their competitive edge relative to each other. As a result, product life cycles are shortened even further.

This shorter product life cycle, especially for ICTs, is evident in the short-lived nature of rents. For example, in the mid-1990s, 70 percent of the computer industry's revenues came from products less than two years old.[25] Exceptional profits and wages are rare for ICT producers.[26] Lagging or imitator firms have easily caught up with the industry leaders, thereby precipitating a steep decline in the price of microelectronics. ICT producers have been hurt by this sharp deterioration in their terms of trade. In fact, the principal beneficiaries of ICTs have not been their manufacturers but their users on account of the consumer surplus reaped from the unrestrained fall in the price of microelectronics.

Empirical Evidence and Consequences

Empirical evidence confirms an acceleration in the pace of economic life.[27] There has been an unmistakable rise in long-run growth rates. Consider the United States. Its growth rate in GDP per capita was 0.6 percent per year from 1800 to 1840. In contrast, this growth rate had increased to 2.3 percent per year between 1960 and 1999; it is expected to rise even further to 2.5 percent per year in the coming decades.[28] This speedup in the long-run growth rate is believed to be due to the increasing returns to knowledge.[29]

A quickening economic momentum can also be inferred from the geographic concentration of certain industries. Inexpensive ICTs and transportation have dispersed many manufacturing activities worldwide through international vertical specialization. However, some industries, such as textiles and cars, have moved in the opposite direction of greater geographic concentration. This phenomenon is due to the "new" competition in which great premium is attached to rapid product development and short changeover times.[30] Suppliers locate themselves near their major final markets. Thus, many automotive-parts manufacturers serving the United States are found in Canada and Mexico. For textiles, we find concentrations of subcontractors for the U.S. market in Mexico and the Caribbean. The value attached to proximity to final markets is indirect evidence of the increasing pace of economic life.

We can draw a similar inference from the growing volume and value of air freight. Take the case of the United States. Measured in terms of freight-tons miles, cargo transport by air grew at 231 percent between 1980 and 2000, a growth rate that was more than twice as fast as intercity trucks and four times faster than the railways.[31] Or note the growth of expedited mail service. From 1974 to 2004, the average daily volume of express packages handled by FedEx grew at a cumulative growth rate of 753 percent.[32] Even the U.S. Postal Service had to offer an express mail service to remain competitive.

The NICs have achieved within a generation what took developed nations nearly a century to accomplish. This telescoping development process is additional evidence of a much faster economic life. Moreover, even as our contemporary ICT-led globalization is merely 25 years old and still has a long way to go, the gains from ICTs are already comparable to those attained from earlier Kondratieff carrier inputs. For example, the benefits for railways in the nineteenth century were around 5–10 percent of U.S. GDP and 10 percent of GDP for England-Wales. Today, the gains from ICTs are believed to be already around 4.1 to 5.6 percent for the United States and 4 to 5.4 percent for Singapore, two of the biggest beneficiaries of ICTs.[33] The acceleration in the pace of economic life is also reflected in both the astonishing drop in ICT prices (compared to earlier carrier inputs) and the consequent speed and scale of market penetration by the Internet, the personal computer, and the cell phone. As we have seen in chapter 2, these signature technologies of the information age have recorded a much faster rate of adoption than the icons of earlier epochs, such as electricity, the telephone, the automobile, the radio, and the television.[34]

Besides being notoriously difficult to measure, productivity gains from all-purpose technologies take time before becoming fully evident. For example, it took 40 years for the electric dynamo's impact on productivity to be fully felt.[35] The case of microelectronics has been radically different. The Internet became available for universal use only in 1993. Within seven years, however, the Internet had already significantly transformed manufacturing, financial services, health care, higher education, retail services, and the trucking and automotive industries. Its cumulative savings across these sectors alone (70 percent of GDP) already amounted to 1.2 to 2.5 percent of GDP, or an equivalent productivity gain of anywhere from 0.25 to 0.50 percent.[36]

The frenetic pace of economic life has reached such a point that some people have started to question whether or not it has become detrimental.

"Hyper-acceleration" refers to a situation where all parties would gain from slowing down the rate of learning but where the rules of the game are such that they give incentives to continuously accelerate the rate.[37]

Extra-market mechanisms are needed to slow down technical change. There are anecdotes of deliberate attempts to slow down change from the most unlikely sources.[38] Major Japanese automotive firms found that it was self-defeating to compete with each other in such a manner as to reduce the product life cycle of their car models. Huge expenditures were required to develop new models and to iron out kinks in the entire supply and manufacturing chain for every new generation of cars. These firms eventually slowed down change so as not to shorten any further the product life cycle of automobiles. A similar phenomenon, but with a different outcome, applies to computers and other ICT-products. The rate of obsolescence has been so fast that end users delay making their purchases in anticipation of the next generation of microelectronics. This is not merely to save on the cost of new equipment but also to defer the substantial investment of time and effort needed to learn how to use the upgraded hardware and software. Consumers switch only at the last moment in order to avoid having to keep up with every new edition of the software or hardware. Unlike the Japanese auto industry, however, the ICT sector is more competitive and thrives on creative destruction. It would have been unthinkable and uncharacteristic of it to slow down change deliberately. Developments in microelectronics, such as Moore's law and Gilder's law described earlier, highlight the impressive speed of contemporary economic life.

It is very likely that the next Kondratieff cycles will be much shorter and their accompanying structural adjustment periods much faster. After all, recall that our current (fifth) long-wave cycle's extraordinary contribution is the improvement in the core economic process itself in which the market has become even more efficient at being efficient. Furthermore, technological breakthroughs can be expected to be more frequent and more consequential from now on because of the even closer linkage between science and technology, better information and communications infrastructure, collaborative networking in R&D, and the competitive innovation that has characterized the ICT sector.

Finally, the increasing intensity of competition in the marketplace is also indirect evidence of an accelerating pace in economic life. As profit opportunities become short-lived, firms fiercely compete with each other in going after these rents within the brief period of time they are available. Such rivalry and quickening pace have spilled over into the workplace. There is a widespread perception of an increasing intensification and speed of work in contemporary globalization.[39]

Stiffer Competition and Competitive Innovation

As a result of the faster rounds of economic activity and the enormous potential rents that can be reaped within a narrowing time-frame, firms are forced to be even more forward-leaning than ever before. As early as the late nineteenth century, technological change was systematized and no longer left to ad hoc discoveries from chance and contingency. R&D became a formal, and increasingly larger, part of business operations in the twentieth century. Today, the tempo and appetite for discovery and innovation have increased even further with the advent of ICTs. We are in an era of accelerating and fiercer competitive innovation, for a number of reasons, namely: more capable market participants, shorter payback period, greater stress on responsiveness, more frequent requisite adjustments, larger potential short-term profits, outsized returns, government intervention, and mutually reinforcing features of the knowledge economy. Each of these is examined in what follows.

More Capable Economic Actors

The enhanced capacity to acquire, process, and use information due to ICTs has made competitors all the more agile and capable and, consequently, all the more threatening to each other. By its nature, competition is ultimately concerned with positional goods[40] because it is about jockeying for relative standing within a group. For example, even as the proverbial pie may be getting bigger with everybody enjoying a bigger slice in absolute terms, there will most likely still be strife over the size of such slices relative to each other.

As already noted, economic actors make faster and better informed decisions because of more complete data, better analytical tools, and easier communication with their colleagues. In other words, ICTs have enabled people to read the signals more accurately, make decisions swiftly, and then act on such findings—a much quicker turnaround time. Market participants bent on staying ahead of, or at least keeping up with, their peers can do no less than this. There is an operative, intense, demonstration effect at work in which keeping up with the competition is paramount.

Economic actors also make much better decisions over time because they learn from their own and others' mistakes and successes. Tacit knowledge is pivotal in getting a head start on the competition.[41] This is a kind of knowledge that is not transferable and is embodied in the subject. Moreover, tacit knowledge builds on itself; it can improve over time depending on how open the subject is to learning. Thus, in an extremely competitive environment, one would expect economic actors to be assiduous in constantly upgrading their tacit knowledge. Technological and organizational changes and continuous rounds of economic transactions provide a steady stream of opportunities for improving the quality and the scope of personal or collective tacit knowledge. Not only do market participants have more powerful tools in sifting through relevant data, but they get even better at interpreting and using such information over time. All these make for even tougher competition down the road.

Furthermore, there is urgency in responding swiftly because of the risk of getting too far behind. Gaps that are not immediately addressed may subsequently require more effort to close, if they can be closed at all, because of a rapidly accelerating pace of innovation and change, an autocorrelated[42] tacit knowledge, and path dependence[43] in the economy. There is need for a prompt response to new information or disequilibria just to keep up with peers in the industry. Thus, it is not surprising that "nonallocative efficiency" is said to be often more critical for economic growth compared to traditional allocative efficiency.[44] A large part of this "nonallocative efficiency" (also known as X-efficiency) stems from the competitive pressure bearing down on firms. For example, the sustained increase in productivity despite the dotcom bust at the turn of the millennium is due not merely to ICTs but also to the stiff competition that has driven firms to eke out every possible cost savings.[45]

Fierce competition is one of the more significant consequences of the Internet Revolution.[46] There is greater ease of entry for new economic actors because a truly successful start-up, no matter how small, has a better chance of getting its product or service known in the broader national, and even global, marketplace through the Web. There is a better dissemination of market opportunities because of the cheaper and freer flow of electronic information. As a consequence, the playing field among competitors is a little more level because the Internet provides a relatively inexpensive medium compared to traditional print and media advertising outlets.[47] For example, note the countless thriving small e-businesses that the Internet has spawned in its wake. Better yet, take a look at the small businesses that have flourished on account of eBay.

Shorter Payback Period

A second reason for more intense competition is the abbreviated payback period as a result of an ever shorter product life cycle. This compels innovators, patent holders, and first movers to reap as much rent as they can, as quickly as possible, and to prolong their lead or exclusive control by forestalling the competition from catching up. On the other hand, for industries that require huge upfront investments, rents must be sizable enough to compensate for a much shortened payback period. However, such large rents will invite unwanted attention and further entry into the industry. And because the payback period is all too brief, new entrants will be as assiduous in their own efforts to reap as much of the rents as they can before these are whittled away as the product matures. This dynamic is self-reinforcing because as the competition for the ever diminishing rents heats up, both the payback period and the product life cycle are shortened even further. In other words, an ever shrinking product life cycle makes for even more intense competition, which, in turn, compresses the product life cycle even more.

An excellent example of this dynamic is competitive leapfrogging.[48] This is the phenomenon in which new generations of the same product keep streaming out of the marketplace. Firms churn up ever-new features and uses that are substantial and attractive enough to entice consumers to upgrade to the latest versions of the same genre of product or service. Competitors follow suit. As a result, the fight for the same market niche is intense. Take, for example, the competition for personal computers and consumer electronics, such as mobile phones and other wireless devices. There has been an endless flow of ever more powerful wireless phones (e.g., iPhone) that act as a single platform for a variety of functions, such as taking pictures and video streaming, surfing the Web, receiving e-mail, serving as a personal organizer, watching movies, and even storing and playing music. Recall, too, the profusion of services and plans offered by wireless network providers. The same has been true for music downloading and movie rentals. And, of course, we have the confusing cornucopia of different configurations, memory rams, external attachments, drives, and chips that differentiate personal computers. A common feature in all these cases has been the steep drop in the real cost of these products and services once we correct their nominal prices for technological improvements and other intangible, additional benefits.[49] These quality-adjusted prices reflect the higher value that consumers enjoy per dollar spent, given all the additional capabilities and conveniences furnished by the new generation of the product or service.[50] Even more important to highlight is the short life span of many of these new models due to the need to leapfrog to the next generation of technological breakthroughs.[51]

Second-mover advantages also contribute to tougher competition stemming from a shorter product life cycle. The common belief is that economic agents on the cutting edge of developing and adopting new technologies get the choicest benefits from such innovations. There may actually be an advantage to being a late adopter. Because of expected additional advances in quality and the drop in the price of technological improvements as the product is further developed, second movers will be able to avail of the same technologies at a fraction of the cost incurred by first movers. For example, the ICTs purchased by U.S. firms in 1993 at a cost of $143 billion were priced at a mere $15 billion by the year 2000, a mere tenth of the original price and after only seven years. Moreover, second movers can avoid the expensive mistakes of early adopters.[52] Thus, whatever advantages accrue to first movers are quickly eroded. This is not even to mention the pressure on first movers to recover their development costs within the brief period of time permitted by an abbreviated product life cycle.

These second-mover advantages can be verified indirectly by looking at recent economic history. During the second era of globalization (1950–80), Japan and the Asian Tigers achieved within a single generation what took the United States and Western Europe nearly a century to attain. China has even bested the record set by Japan and the Asian Tigers by growing at an even faster rate. Indeed, there has been a telescoping of the development process. This means that there will be tougher competition all around especially for those who are ahead of the development process. Using the image of the ladder of created comparative advantage, this means that follower nations will be increasingly pushing, and perhaps even overtaking, leading nations up the ladder.

"New" Competition

A third factor accounting for the more severe economic rivalry in the information age is the change in the nature of competition itself. The object of the "new" competition is the "minimization of product development and product changeover times."[53] Economic success today means the ability "to innovate rapidly and continuously to develop new products that meet market demands."[54] Winners in today's marketplace must exhibit not merely cost effectiveness and technological competence, but more importantly, the capacity for ceaseless innovation.[55]

On the surface, it would appear that this is the same dynamic described in the shorter product life cycles in the preceding section. But, it is not.

[A]lthough the theory of product cycle retains a certain degree of contemporary validity, . . . it concerns itself almost entirely with the different phases of development in the life cycle of a *given* product, rather than the effect of a *new* product on the comparative advantage enjoyed by developing countries in old (or mature) product varieties.[56]

The new competition is about timely and effective responsiveness to a rapidly evolving marketplace. Thus, competitiveness no longer means just being able to produce a commodity or a service at the lowest price. Even more important, it is about round-the-clock innovation that improves all facets of a firm's operations—its products, organization, and processes—with an eye toward developing an agility superior to that of the competition in filling or, better yet, in anticipating the market's new demands.[57]

Workers at three knowledge-intensive businesses (environmental engineering, accountancy, and architecture) were surveyed on their perceptions of their respective business environments in the knowledge economy. When asked about the sources of competitive advantage, more than 50 percent of accountants, architects, and environmental engineers surveyed from different-sized firms ranked the following as either critical or important: speed of response, competitive prices, respected name, quality of core service and adaptability to client.[58] It is important to highlight the similarity in the factors they flagged as essential for remaining competitive in the knowledge economy.

Competitiveness in the knowledge economy is about being the most responsive to change, the quickest to adapt, and the fastest at product development. The goal is to be ahead of the curve, to enjoy first-mover advantages, despite the ability of second movers to subsequently whittle down these initial gains. Unfortunately, this is yet again another self-feeding phenomenon because all competitors will be forward-leaning and will be bent on reaping first-mover rents. Everybody else will be accelerating their efforts in order to beat others in an ever-ratcheting race to be the first to reach the market. As a consequence, the bar will be continually raised for all market participants.

Furthermore, competition in the knowledge economy does not always follow the product life cycle or the flying-geese pattern to development.[59] In fact, nations at the bottom of the ladder are able to leapfrog the queue and end up being at the head of the line competing with the bigger, more advanced economies. India is an excellent example. With the advent of international vertical specialization even in the field of R&D, India has gained entry into the tightly knit networks of research centers initiated by transnational firms and largely based in the major industrialized nations. India conducts a wide variety of cutting-edge research ranging from improving basic consumer goods, to computer hardware and software design, avionics, microelectronics, and biomedical products.[60] According to the flying-geese pattern of international trade and the product life cycle model, these are activities that are supposed to come much later in India's development path. However, ICTs have made it lucrative for advanced nations to collaborate with India's small but growing cadre of highly skilled scientists and engineers. The rise of Bangalore as a major hub of IT-related industries is an example of such leapfrogging.

Or, consider the quick rise of China in overshadowing even its neighboring Asian Tigers and Japan in certain activities, such as research in mobile phone technology. Not even the cutting edge of R&D has been spared the phenomenon of outsourcing in which scientists and engineers in emerging nations are subcontracted by first world multinationals to do first-rate research. Indeed, "[o]utsourcing is climbing [the] skills ladder."[61] All these underscore how this new competition, based on the creative invention and commercialization of new products and processes, is progressively rendering the traditional models of comparative advantage obsolete. With human capital, rather than industrial capital or natural resources, as the new basis for creating value in the knowledge economy, the playing field for comparative advantage is a little more level compared to what it used to be.[62] This makes for even more intense competition.

Consumers are more time-conscious and, consequently, expect expeditious service. For example, note the growth of fast foods and take-out counters, precut vegetables, precooked meals, online grocery shopping, and many other convenience services. Business itself has also become even more time-conscious in an effort to trim costs and respond rapidly to consumer needs. Improvements both in business organization and in ICTs have made coordination and communication much easier. Together with the continued decline in transport costs and more reliable service, ICT advances have made it possible to reduce inventories to a minimum level and to rely on "just-in-time inventory management." This is true across the board, from car manufacturers that have trimmed their stocks of automotive parts to a bare minimum, to retail chains that have drastically reduced their inventories.[63] Manufacturers have adopted "post-Fordist" production methods that stress flexibility, responsiveness, quality, and lean cost structures.[64] The savings from post-Fordist production techniques and from new methods in merchandising are substantial, especially for high-value intermediate and final goods (e.g., computer chips and cars). Capital no longer needs to be set aside or borrowed to keep stocks of expensive intermediate or final goods sitting in storage. Moreover, warehousing costs are also minimized. The practice of just-in-time inventory control is a consequence of the more intense competition occasioned by globalization, for a variety of reasons. It is a direct outcome of the pressure on manufacturers and retailers to cut costs. Moreover, just-in-time inventory is a good example of creatively using ICTs and transportation technologies to get an edge on the competition.[65] In addition, observe that the costs and risks of inventory management, which used to be borne by manufacturers (for intermediate goods) and retailers (for final goods), have in effect been transferred to their respective suppliers. Today, suppliers have assumed responsibility for ensuring that their goods get to their customers on time. It is now the suppliers who have to bear the costs and risks of occasional supply disruptions. The stakes are particularly high when we speak of manufacturing high-value and complex goods, such as cars, airplanes, and consumer electronics, in which the right parts have to be on hand at the right time, in the right place, and in the right sequence for assembly, lest entire production lines and plants stand idle. To make such organizational change work, timeliness and reliability have become even more important qualities in distinguishing competing suppliers from each other. On occasion, expensive air freight has to be used for heavy or bulky goods in order to get supplies to manufacturers or retailers on time. The ability of manufacturers and retailers to shift such costs and risks upstream to their suppliers is evidence of the intense competition among the latter; it is a buyer's market. Moreover, the foresight and intricate planning required by such tight scheduling are indicative of the higher level of human capital required by the knowledge economy.

Suppliers have responded to this tougher competition with their own organizational changes. In particular, they are moving their operations closer to their customers in order to get better feedback and to monitor, firsthand, developments and changes in the marketplace.[66] Proximity to customers is especially important in industries that are extremely time-sensitive, such as fashion apparel, or in economic sectors that are heavily reliant on just-in-time inventory, such as automotive manufacturing.[67] This need to be close to final markets reflects both the faster pace and fiercer market rivalry in the knowledge economy.

The more intense competition inaugurated by ICTs is also evident in the manner in which businesses are compelled to keep investing in new technologies even as most of the benefits from such expenditures are reaped by their customers and not by the firms themselves.[68]

Why then will firms invest and make increasing use of the Internet if they cannot permanently enjoy the extra profits? Very simply, because they will have no other choice. If they do not stay at the cutting edge, then someone else will. Andrew Grove of Intel could not have put it any better than in his famous book title *Only the Paranoid Survive.*[69]

ICTs ensure that businesses keep investing in such technologies. The savings from ICT adoption is then passed on from businesses to consumers by a buyer's market. The "new competition" is characterized by competitive leapfrogging, competitive organizational innovations, competitive strategic alliances, and competitive R&D. Competitive innovation has taken a life of its own in the knowledge economy.

More Frequent Adjustments

The greater flux in the marketplace is a fourth factor behind the stiffer competition in the information age. The economy tends toward allocative efficiency through marginal adjustments in the decisions of market participants, precipitated by changes in the relative prices of the goods and services they buy or sell. As we will see in chapters 4 and 5, these price changes have a twofold allocative and distributive dimension. Moreover, they spawn both beneficial and adverse unintended consequences (pecuniary externalities) across the entire economy. These never-ending readjustments in the marketplace and their sporadic shocks give rise both to new risks and to fresh profit opportunities. People reap rents or incur unexpected losses from these ceaseless price shifts depending on their human capital and sociohistorical location, in addition to the chance and contingency intrinsic to economic life. Thus, the relative standing of firms constantly changes in extremely competitive industries.

These disruptions and readjustments require appropriate responses from market participants, especially from those in highly contested sectors. In fact, some people even welcome these pecuniary externalities and their attendant shifts as occasions for changing the status quo and perhaps even gaining an edge on the competition. We expect to experience even greater flux as a result of market widening and deepening. The global economy is not only moving much faster, but it will also encounter even more bumps along the way. In other words, competition will be even more severe as market participants scramble to respond appropriately to unexpected market demands and pecuniary externalities. And, as each of these episodes is potentially redistributive by reshuffling burdens and benefits within the industry, each must be taken seriously. Economic actors respond as best as they can to ever-shifting market conditions with the goal of improving their position relative to their peers.

An indirect measure of the intensity of competition in the wake of the knowledge economy is the fragility of relative standing within industries, even for the biggest firms. In the past, industry leaders easily maintained their market standing at an impressive rate: 90 percent in the 1950s and 85 percent in the 1960s. In contrast, only 20 percent of market leaders in 1985 still held that position by 1995.[70] A third of the Fortune 500 companies in 1980 were eventually absorbed in mergers and takeovers by 1990 and an additional 40 percent were gone by 1995.[71] Not even the biggest and the strongest firms are immune to the discipline of the marketplace.

Unrelenting competition in the knowledge economy has led to a spate of mergers and acquisitions in a wide variety of sectors, such as banking, household appliances, computer hardware and peripherals, computer software, and entertainment. Many of these mergers and acquisitions were driven by rapidly changing conditions in the global marketplace. Every economic disruption is either an opportunity for gain or a threat of reduced revenues and lost market share.

Another indicator of the cutthroat competition inaugurated by global economic integration is the swings in corporate profit margins. Global inflation has been minimal since the early 1990s partly because firms have been unable to pass on to consumers increases in the price of their essential inputs, such as labor and energy.[72] Businesses have been compelled to simply absorb these cost increases out of fear of losing their market share.

Larger Potential Profits

The size of potential profits is a fifth factor behind the more severe competition in the knowledge economy.[73] As the marketplace expands in scale and in depth, the potential gains are correspondingly much greater. For example, corporate profits as a proportion of national income in the United States, United Kingdom, Canada, and the 13 euro-zone nations are at an historical high at 15.5 percent in 2006 compared to 11 percent in 2001.[74] For the United States, it was 8.5 percent in 2001 rising to 12.3 percent in 2005.[75]

Competition is most pronounced in markets with a huge purchasing power either through the size of the population (e.g., China) or through high income or wealth (e.g., United States, Japan, and EU), or both (possibly China in twenty years?). The United States, for example, has for many years been the biggest recipient of foreign direct investments. Or, note the rush of investors into China, eager to set up a presence in anticipation of the rise in the purchasing power of its huge domestic market (e.g., automotive manufacturers). Problems, such as a murky and still evolving legal infrastructure to protect and enforce property rights, are considered minor compared to the future profits in such a large and lucrative market. The same phenomenon can be said of the U.S. market. Manufacturers have no choice but to accede to Wal-Mart's "suggested" price because of the huge volume it commands and its long list of suppliers eager to fill its merchandising requirements. Both the Chinese and the U.S. markets are paradigms of what global economic integration is all about. The larger the purchasing power in a particular market, the more it will be contested terrain.

There are also larger potential gains because of the nature of knowledge-based activities. Traditional industries exhibit diminishing returns; unit costs go up as output expands because of limitations in fixed inputs (e.g., managerial talent). However, ICT-related industries may be subject to increasing, rather than decreasing, returns because their upfront, fixed investments (e.g., R&D and product development) are high, but their variable costs are minimal. Moreover, there is the phenomenon of network externalities in which the value of the product increases as more people use it. The most well-known example, of course, is software. Duplicating the software after the first copy is practically costless compared to the expense of writing and developing the computer program. Furthermore, more people would be enticed to use the software if it becomes the industry standard that everyone else uses. Thus, expanding sales may not lead to an increase in unit costs at all. There are huge rents that can be reaped, with the possibility of even gaining monopoly power for the particular product.[76] Microsoft, eBay, Google, and Apple are simply some of the many examples that can be cited.

The liberalization of capital markets since the 1980s is another indicator of the larger potential gains inaugurated by the digital age. Investors freely roam the globe competing with each other for the highest returns both from portfolio and foreign direct investments. Finally, the larger potential rents made possible by global economic integration is also evident in the change in the scope of firms' R&D. Research that used to be only for local use is now being scaled up and targeted at the global marketplace.[77]

Outsized Returns

A sixth factor behind the increase in competition in the knowledge economy may have to do with the manner in which top performers are compensated. In the face of a shorter product life cycle and more intense competition, gains are increasingly subjected to the same "winner-take-all" phenomenon observed in sports and entertainment.[78] The pace is hectic in an economy of creative destruction because the first to commercialize technological innovations is believed to be the one that generally gets the credit and the rewards, despite some of the second-mover advantages we examined earlier.[79] Others who may have arrived at the same technological discoveries independently neither get credit nor reap the rents. Second place is not good enough, as in sports and entertainment. The first-place holder is rewarded handsomely and disproportionately relative to second placers. This gap in rewards and credit leads to even more acute competition for the next generation of innovations. Again, the success of Microsoft's operating system, eBay's virtual auction market, Google's search engine, and Apple's iPod come to mind. Other success stories that have created overnight multimillionaires include YouTube, MySpace, and Infosys.

Government Aid

Governments have played a role both in speeding up change and in escalating competition.[80] Their most notable contribution to globalization to date has been their liberalization of goods and capital markets. However, despite their seeming greater openness to trade, some governments have, in fact, directly or indirectly intervened in the marketplace to give their domestic companies an edge in international competition. For example, national innovation policies have subsidized domestic firms in mastering new technologies with an eye toward building an insuperable lead over foreign competitors and locking in their global market share. Other forms of assistance include exchange rate undervaluation, formal or covert protective trade barriers such as antidumping tariffs, and licit or illicit aid to selected "winning industries" deemed to be the most promising incubators of the next technological breakthroughs. The Japanese and European subsidies to develop high-definition television (HDTV) are examples of the latter.[81] "National champions" are groomed and supported in strategic sectors.[82] All these provoke countermoves on the part of other governments who are compelled to protect the interests of their own domestic companies. This eventually leads to occasional trade wars and even more intense rivalry in the global marketplace. The disputes before the WTO on a broad range of products, from cotton, lumber, and bananas, to airplanes and steel, are indicative of how government interventions have turned the global marketplace into a heavily contested domain.

Mutually Reinforcing Synergy

Various attributes of the knowledge economy mutually reinforce each other to stoke competition even further. This is particularly true in the case of three of its properties, to wit: the need for more frequent and substantive adjustments, an accelerating pace in economic exchange, and intensified economic rivalry. A constantly shifting economic terrain can shake up the relative standing of competitors within an industry, depending on the nature of the disturbances and firms' reaction to them. They provide opportunities for gains when firms take advantage of the missteps and the slow or inadequate response of their competitors. Thus, firms are compelled to be alert to industry trends, to be vigilant with their competitors' progress, and to weigh their own adjustment accordingly.[83] The accelerating pace of economic life fuels competition even further by raising the tempo of these moves and countermoves. Such sharp competition, in turn, increases the vulnerability of these firms and the industry as a whole to even more exogenous shocks, even as the speed of economic decisions and readjustments increases. Thus, the pace of economic life, sudden market shifts, and intense rivalry feed off each other.

The mutually reinforcing dynamic of all the aforesaid factors responsible for an intensifying competition in the information age is best described by the *Economist* in its editorial on the occasion of the tenth anniversary of eBay.

> The commercial opportunities presented by an expanding global web seem almost limitless. But *the pace of change is rapid, and so is the ferocity of competition.* To succeed, firms need agility, an open mind and the ability to reinvent themselves repeatedly. Most of all, they need to listen carefully to their customers, paying close attention to what they do and don't want.
> *Such qualities . . . are not a luxury, but necessary for mere survival . . . .*
> The Internet is not only growing, but changing rapidly—which, in turn, changes the rules of the game for any business relying on it.[84]

Indeed, e-business is a paradigm of how ICTs and globalization have jointly transformed the traditional marketplace into a fiercely competitive, unforgiving, and slippery terrain with an insatiable appetite for pushing the technological envelope.

Competitive Networking

Types of Knowledge

New fields of competition have emerged with the advent of the learning economy. But first, we must make some distinctions regarding knowledge. There is a difference between data, information, and knowledge.[85] Data are the observations and measurements recorded in numbers, words, sounds, or images. Information is the end result of organizing these data together in a digestible, coherent, and usable format. Knowledge is the outcome of analyzing and synthesizing disparate information with the goal of drawing inferences, forecasting, and making sense of divergent events. Knowledge affords a descriptive account and understanding of why natural and social phenomena are the way they are. It is the productive use of information.

There are two types of knowledge: explicit (codified knowledge) and implicit (tacit knowledge). These two types of knowledge are different in terms of their codifiability, acquisition, and potential for aggregation.[86] First, codifiable knowledge is that which can be completely preserved in written format; it can be fully documented. Because of the four technological breakthroughs in microelectronics described in chapter 2, this kind of knowledge can be readily reduced to a binary code and be easily stored, replicated, and transmitted in whatever media desired. Hence, codifiable knowledge can be fully separated from its subject (i.e., owner, author, source); it is altogether transferable (e.g., through textbooks and operating manuals). In fact, it is distinctive because of the ease with which it can be shared and communicated. Tacit knowledge, on the other hand, pertains to all other kinds of learning that cannot be fully documented as they are internal to the person.[87] It "cannot be communicated, understood, or used without the 'knowing subject'."[88] Examples include the competence in skills and technical proficiency that come with experience. This is the kind of knowledge that is not articulated but is manifested only through action.

Second, with respect to acquisition, codified knowledge lends itself to complete appropriation via book learning. After all, it can be altogether abstracted, documented, and then transmitted separate from a "knowing subject." It can even be embedded in capital equipment, as in numerically controlled machine tools and custom-made integrated electronic circuits. Tacit knowledge, on the other hand, can only be acquired through actual experience or through extensive interaction with the author or source of such knowledge. And even then, it cannot be fully transferred, even for the closest master-apprentice relationships, because it is a knowledge that is not completely alienable as it is inseparable and indistinguishable from its subject. It can be shared, but not in its totality. It cannot be gained simply by purchasing new equipment that embodies the latest technological innovations. Tacit knowledge is unavoidably conditioned by experience and can only be attained hands-on in a process of "learning by doing."[89] Hence, tacit knowledge has even been called "context-dependent knowledge," "sticky information," "experience-based and socially embedded knowledge," and "craft knowledge."[90] The transfer and diffusion of tacit knowledge is both expensive and time-intensive.

Third, with respect to aggregation, codified knowledge can be easily collected and even concentrated at a single site. The extent to which it can be amassed in one location is circumscribed only by the current limits of technology (e.g., chip memory and speed, available bandwidth). Moreover, there are no restrictions to replicating such concentrations of data at different sites simultaneously because the use of codified data is nonrival in consumption. In contrast, tacit knowledge cannot be easily aggregated at a single site because such knowledge is firm- or person-specific. The only way to accomplish such a concentration is to gather "talent" physically at a single location. This also means that, unlike codified knowledge, it cannot be replicated in its exact form at multiple sites concurrently. Thus, tacit knowledge is described to be distributive in nature, that is, it does not lend itself to easy aggregation.[91]

Another helpful, complementary set of distinctions for knowledge is know-what, know-why, know-how, and know-who.[92] Know-what refers to facts (e.g., cookbook, almanac), know-why pertains to the principles behind observed phenomena (e.g., scientific knowledge), know-how encompasses skills in doing things, and know-who is about personal contacts and connections. Know-what and know-why are codifiable; know-how and know-who are context- and experience-dependent. Know-how is intuitive, rather than explicit, and deals with competencies that are learned only through effort and practice over time. Playing a musical instrument, swimming, driving, skiing, skating, and riding a bicycle are examples of practical skills and aptitudes that cannot be communicated or transferred to another subject. Know-who is about social skills or the ability to effect collaborative ventures with others; it is sometimes called the firm's or person's "networking capital." It is knowledge of "who knows what and who knows how to do what."[93] Both know-how and know-who are gained through hands-on interactive learning.[94]

Indispensable Networking

As knowledge now holds the key to value creation, one would expect competition for the social and human resources essential to knowledge creation. This gives rise to what I would call *competitive networking*, for a number of reasons.

First, even as the price of information has gone down due to ICTs, the requirements of the marketplace for information have gone up. Economic decision making in the information age demands even more and better data be made available in a timely fashion. A more interdependent world generates more consequential ripple effects to which economic agents must react with even greater preparation, agility, and adaptability. Consequently, economic actors have banded together in networks both in production and in research. Such collaborations are much more cost-efficient in searching, sharing, and using information. Thus, as we will see in the next chapter, international vertical specialization is a shift away from the centralized, hierarchical, Fordist organization to a more decentralized model with economic agents interacting directly with each other.[95] The need for a prompt and accurate sifting, analysis, and utilization of a burgeoning amount of data makes collaborative work unavoidable.

Second, for all the possibilities and opportunities inaugurated by the knowledge economy, globalization is, nonetheless, still fraught with considerable risks. For example, take the case of semiconductors. Their manufacturing process is said to be so complex that it requires over a hundred different steps that are still not well understood.[96] Unexpected market events can easily render obsolete expensive equipment and technologies that had been painstakingly developed from years of costly R&D. In such an unpredictable setting, strategic partnerships with other firms are rational ways of spreading risks.[97] This applies just as well in nonmanufacturing concerns, as in the scramble for strategic alliances we have seen in the past five years among software, telecommunications, entertainment, and Internet-based firms.

A third reason for competitive networking is the pivotal role of tacit knowledge in all facets of market participation, from developing and commercializing technological innovations, to appropriating rents. Technological change and production processes are ever more dependent on a composite knowledge base.[98] They are increasingly complex and require a multidisciplinary approach.[99] Highly specialized expertise is necessary for many of the cutting-edge business ventures. As implicit (tacit) knowledge is person-, firm-, and context-specific, there is no substitute to relying on experts.[100] One is compelled to work jointly with people whose talents and experience are needed for particular projects. Thus, there is a race among firms to line up cooperative ventures with others in particularly promising industries or market niches before competitors can get to them.[101] Firms pool their respective experts in networks for specific projects. As a result, the "know-who" component of tacit knowledge takes on greater importance, especially in an increasingly "networked" society.[102]

In a 1999 survey of Canadian firms on why they pursue collaborative work with other firms, the top two reasons given were (1) "accessing R&D" and (2) "prototype development." Among biotechnology firms, the top three reasons given in descending order of importance were (1) "R&D/Access to Specialized Inputs," (2) "Access Knowledge/ Skills/Critical Expertise," and (3) "Prototype Development/ Production/Manufacturing." These responses and their order of importance were similar across firms regardless of size.[103]

Such competitive networking is also evident in science and technology. There has been an increase in shared research, joint ventures, consultancy, licensing agreements, data sharing, and other informal exchanges.[104] This is especially true when it comes to ICTs and biotechnology. Individuals and firms reap rents either by accumulating specialized, proprietary knowledge or by accessing networks that own them. In a Canadian survey of innovative manufacturing firms, industries with the highest rates of collaborative work with others were: pharmaceuticals (61 percent), semiconductor/electronic equipment (57 percent), computer equipment (53 percent), and aerospace (51 percent). The average across all industries was 33 percent. Clothing manufacturers had the lowest rate (16 percent).[105]

The days of "self-contained and self-sufficient" R&D are over, and firms are constantly searching for new ventures and networking partnerships, especially as fresh opportunities are opened up by ICTs. By one count, there has been a 100 to as much as a 300 percent increase in the annual number of new international strategic research partnerships from 1980 to 2000. From 212 partnerships in 1980, the number of new international strategic research partnerships has grown to around 400 to 800 per year.[106]

Note, for example, how Boeing and Airbus have been forced to reach out across the globe to solicit the participation of different stakeholders in designing and manufacturing their next generation of planes.[107] There are sizable savings in development costs and time, not to mention economies of scale in production. These arrangements have been called "corporate strategic alliances" in which large corporations collaborate on high-tech projects and products, even while competing against each other in many other arenas.[108] This is true even for small- and medium-scale firms that have increasingly found it necessary for their survival to form ties with companies in countries with lower manufacturing costs.[109] These smaller players engage in technical collaboration to the same degree as their larger counterparts.[110] In the aforesaid Canadian survey, two-thirds of the data set were small firms (50 employees or less) [411 out of 638]. The average number of collaborative arrangements for small firms was 2.7 compared to 3.4 for midsized firms (51–150 workers) and 2.9 for large firms (over 150 workers).[111]

Fourth, there is also the bandwagon effect animating competitive networking. We have already seen that responsiveness and agility are important qualities for market participants in the face of the digital age's accelerated speed and frequent shifts. In pooling their resources and expertise, firms collectively stand a better chance of coming out ahead in such a fluid environment. This being the case, other competitors will also be driven to seek their own business alliances and networks. Firms can no longer go solo even if they wanted to because their competitors are tapping into strategic alliances. There is no choice but to follow suit in order to level the playing field. In fact, some have gone so far as to break old and longtime alliances in favor of new strategic partnerships, even with their erstwhile competitors. Recent examples include the collaboration of Microsoft and RealNetworks, and Apple's surprising termination of its relationship with its long-standing chip supplier, IBM, in favor of a former competitor, Intel.[112] Collaborating with competitors seems to be counterintuitive and, therefore, appears to be the exception rather than the rule. However, it turns out that such arrangements are more common than is generally believed. In a 1999 survey of innovative Canadian manufacturing firms, as much as a third of the firms surveyed (34 to 36 percent) were collaborating with their competitors![113] Indeed, severe competitive pressure gives rise to the most unlikely tie-ups. There are many more examples of such competitive networking.[114]

Fifth, competitive networking has arisen because outsourcing is now an essential venue for the transfer of technology. Prior to contemporary globalization, import substitution was a channel for acquiring technology. We now know that this protectionist, inward-looking strategy to development causes more harm than good and is not appropriate for the knowledge economy. Today, offshore outsourcing has replaced import substitution as a vehicle for technology transfers.[115] Unfortunately, there is an operative zero-sum phenomenon in most cases of international outsourcing because such jobs are subject to rival consumption and there are only a limited number of them to go around, at least in the short term. We would therefore expect a scramble among firms and nations to become part of the more lucrative supplier networks.

Finally, networking is also partly due to the self-feeding dynamic of hypercompetition. The greatly expanded revenue base from market widening and deepening more than compensates for the huge upfront fixed investments in ICTs, organizational changes, R&D, and other technologically related expenditures.[116] Because of this augmented customer demand, these large front-end overhead investments are no longer a deterrent from entry by newcomers. This leads to even greater competition, especially for the most promising industries. Moreover, there has been a downward pressure on prices as a result of ICTs, their accompanying organizational changes, and the freer flow of goods and services across borders. This squeezes firms' profit margins even further and makes the fight for market share all the more important. This requires much leaner cost structures that can only come about through even more profound technological and organizational innovations. These, in turn, precipitate another cycle of competitive changes leading to even further drops in prices, thereby completing the cycle.[117] The global textile, automotive, microelectronics, services, and distribution sectors illustrate this self-feeding dynamic.[118] For example, the U.S. domestic automotive industry has become so competitive that the "Big Three" American automakers have been pushing their parts suppliers for further cost cutting measures using Chinese prices as a benchmark for comparison. The target prices have been set so low as to compel these parts suppliers to go overseas themselves and outsource.[119]

In sum, global economic integration has led to a more collaborative approach in ensuring a continued supply of technological innovations. This need for competitive networking is a constitutive element of contemporary globalization and has been described in various ways: as "alliance," "relational," "collective," or "collaborative and associational" capitalism.[120] Firms, no matter how big or dominant, have been compelled to join networks or to get together with their peers given the increasing complexity of the science-technology nexus, the tremendous expense of failure, the need to share scarce and highly specialized personnel with unique skills, and the speed with which such innovations and inventions have to be commercialized in order to beat competing, parallel efforts. Whether it is in processing data better or in sharing risks, the response of firms has been one of organizational change (such as networking) with the goal of "intensifying internal information and knowledge exchange."[121] Procuring the right information and expertise quickly has not only been vital to surviving in a highly dynamic economic environment, it has also been the means to get ahead of the competition.

Increasing Value of Time

At a much deeper level, the new competition described earlier is ultimately about the increasing value of time. Time has always been important in economic theory and practice, but timeliness takes on even greater significance in the globalized knowledge economy. In regards to both the consumer and the firm, time and place utility pertain to having what we want or need at the right time and at the right place. Time and its economic dimensions have received much attention in the wake of Becker's (1965) and Lancaster's (1966) groundbreaking household production model (described in chapter 5). This analytical framework explicitly incorporates time as a key variable in traditional consumer theory. An insight that emerged from this household model is that economic development raises the value of time. As the economic freedom of market participants expands, so does the opportunity cost of using such liberty and, by extension, time. Hence, observe the greater demand for labor- and time-saving tools, products, and services as per capita incomes rise.

This appreciation in the value of time will accelerate even further as a direct and indirect result of contemporary globalization. First, as already mentioned, a central feature of our current economy is the shift in the source of value creation to knowledge. Tacit knowledge is the essential factor input in a learning economy. However, the acquisition of tacit knowledge is extremely time-intensive because it is founded on "learning by doing." Moreover, it entails a roundabout process of investing in human capital formation. No amount of spending on tangible assets can substitute for tacit knowledge because it is embodied in the human subject. Thus, the knowledge economy is exacting in its demands on personal time.

Second, the process of discovery, invention, and innovation is itself a lengthy, all-consuming undertaking. Despite the possibility of networking and collaboration with others in breaking down complex problems into manageable parts, there is nonetheless still no substitute for personal time as a critical input in developing and implementing technical change. The more central the role of technical change and innovation, the greater will be the demands on personal and collective time. Both the formation and application of human and social capital are extremely time-intensive.

Third, key characteristics of the knowledge economy impose additional demands on the use of time. The faster pace of economic life, the more intense competition, the greater frequency and abruptness of change, and the deeper and wider impact of pecuniary externalities all require constant attentiveness and effort on the part of market participants, thereby increasing the value of time. The knowledge economy has led to an even faster and more substantial expansion of the opportunity set of economic actors than would have otherwise been the case as part of the normal process of development. The downside to this, of course, is that it also leads to an increase in the opportunity cost of time. This makes human capital formation and use all the more important.

Higher Requisite Human Capital[122]

Relative to the industrial era, the human capital requirements for effective market participation in the knowledge economy is much more stringent and will continue to get even more so, for a variety of reasons. First, the superfluity of data requires numeracy in addition to literacy. The deluge of data provided by ICTs encumbers market participants with a heavier threefold task of sifting, analyzing, and then using relevant data. This entails having to go through an extensive amount of materials, separating helpful from trivial data, discerning their importance and urgency for decision making, turning them into coherent information, and then producing knowledge.

And, as if this were not enough of a challenge, one must remember that this entire exercise will have to be done repeatedly in a prompt and competent fashion in view of the constant stream of new information, the accelerated pace of economic life, the shorter time-frame for decision making, and the stiffer competition inaugurated by globalization. Some argue that the distinguishing feature of the digital economy is not the volume of data available, but the revolutionary improvement in our ability to manipulate the resulting information.[123] If so, this changes the nature of competition to one of making sense of information and acting on it before anybody else. Competitors have access to the same kind of data, and it is the nimble and competent market participants, who are able to turn data quickly into usable information and act upon it, who will profit handsomely from the enormous rewards of the knowledge economy. Economic agency has turned into a race against competitors in transforming data into actionable information for the purpose of reaping rents.[124] This requires a well-developed and well-trained human capital. This is reflected in the progressively rising level of skills and education required for employment in the leading developed nations, such as the United States, Germany, and the United Kingdom.[125]

Second, the aforesaid dynamic (coping with a superfluity of data) becomes a self-reinforcing cycle in the subsequent rounds of economic activity as even more market participants become adept at using codifiable knowledge and as more decisions are based on it.[126] In other words, there will be an increased reliance on codifiable knowledge. As the price of data acquisition, storage, processing, transmission, and application drops precipitously, economic operations will demand even more and better information. After all, the market not only dispenses information via its price mechanism, but it also uses immense amounts of information so that its participants can make appropriate and timely adjustments in their economic decisions. Consequently, even the dynamics of market operations make information increasingly more significant as a source of wealth creation compared to earlier periods in economic history. The R&D undergirding the financial markets and their many new products (e.g., derivatives and hedge funds) is an excellent illustration of this increased demand for information management. Of course, this comes with a corresponding need for advanced human capital. Not surprisingly, Wall Street has been hiring Ph.D.s in physics or mathematics for their research departments.

However, even more important than codifiable knowledge is tacit knowledge. Codifiable knowledge is useless if it cannot be employed to good effect. In fact, it even turns into an obstacle if it unnecessarily uses up scarce time and resources. It is tacit knowledge that sifts through codifiable knowledge and recognizes what is relevant and what is not.[127] It is tacit knowledge that assigns an order of importance in going through the superfluity of data coming out of a wired, globalized economy. It is tacit knowledge that makes the necessary connections between various fragments of information and the profit opportunities they present. And most important, it is tacit knowledge that provides the know-how and the know-who in marshaling the necessary resources to act upon such information and to reap gains for oneself, or at least to protect one's interests from economic disturbances.

It is paradoxical that even as the price of information has dropped sharply and even as microelectronics has greatly expanded our capacity to deal with information, contemporary market participants are confronted with more, not less, demanding requirements in the ICT-driven economy. This is because of the increased complexity of the knowledge base and the much faster speed with which such knowledge has to be internalized.[128] Tacit knowledge is getting to be even more vital. Far from reducing the role of tacit knowledge because of the greater ease and the lower cost of codifying data, ICTs have ended up expanding both the scope and the role of implicit knowledge even further.

A third reason for requiring more advanced human capital comes from the constant need to adjust in the knowledge economy given its greater dynamism. By its nature, creative destruction brings everyone, even the innovators themselves, into unknown terrain.[129] No one can foresee the full extent and significance of the ripple effects of technological discoveries. Recall, for example, how the carrier inputs of earlier long-wave cycles had been fraught with chance and contingency. Furthermore, given the more intense interdependence of economic agents and in light of extensive market widening and deepening, shocks can emanate from anywhere at anytime in the global marketplace, and each of these disequilibria brings its own share of exigencies. Recall how the 1997–98 Asian financial contagion started with a banking and financial crisis in Thailand and ended up hurting the entire region, including some of the stronger economies like South Korea and Malaysia. As a consequence of being "wired" to each other, local communities are more vulnerable to events halfway across the globe. This is not even to mention the quicker transmission of these ripple effects because of linkages through markets and international vertical specialization. In addition, the faster pace of economic life means a constantly shifting terrain requiring constant readjustments. Moreover, an ever shortening product life cycle leads to faster creative destruction, leaving its own trail of disruptions. All these highlight the central role of education and human capital in building market participants' capacity to deal with disequilibria.[130]

Fourth, there is an operative "cumulative circular causation"[131] in which developing human capital in earlier rounds of economic activity pushes the minimum requisite human capital even further in the later rounds. Firms are compelled to hire personnel with superior human capital in response to the demands of the knowledge economy. However, these highly qualified personnel will, in turn, most likely push for even greater change and technological innovation. This speeds up the rate of transformation even further, requiring an even quicker adjustment from everybody else. Moreover, ever more sophisticated technologies require ever more creative organizational changes and networking. In both cases, the resulting faster pace of technological innovation and the increasing demands of the workplace call for a well-honed capacity for learning, initiative, flexibility, and tacit knowledge that only well-developed human capital can provide. But this is only half the story as there is a domino effect.

In order to keep up with their competitors, businesses are obliged to follow suit in upgrading their own stock of human capital. As knowledge is now the critical factor behind value creation, getting ahead of rivals means having a better pool of human capital than the competition. There is a cascading effect in which competing firms set ever higher expectations in hiring their personnel. Thus, it is not surprising to see a widening wage gap between "the best and the rest" as businesses lavish their top performers with sizable merit pay increases.[132] Earlier we saw that the "new" competition is no longer merely about low-cost production, but is currently about speed in product development and changeover times. This requires better human capital. Thus, there is a "cumulative circular causation" in which a rising entry cost to participating in the knowledge economy calls for a constant improvement in human capital, which in turn raises the entry cost even further for subsequent periods. The firms' collective response to the new exacting demands of the knowledge economy ends up raising the bar even higher. There is an ever-ratcheting standard for human capital formation. Competition often takes a life of its own.

Fifth, market activity is by its nature a repeating "game" of endless rounds of economic exchange. Such an endless iteration raises the challenge for tacit knowledge in two ways: Successive rounds of economic activity will keep raising the standards, and the ability to learn and adapt swiftly becomes an even more critical element of tacit knowledge. This need for speed and flexibility in learning new areas means that economic agents must simultaneously specialize even as they accumulate breadth of knowledge.

> [I]n a wide set of activities what constitutes success is not so much having access to a stock of specialized knowledge. The key to success is, rather, rapid learning and forgetting (when old ways of doing things get in the way of learning new ways). Narrowly defined skills may actually even hamper rather than support economic success.[133]

The capacity for lateral thinking cannot be overemphasized, especially in a rapidly evolving economic environment. Moreover, there is always the risk of skills being rendered obsolete overnight. Nonetheless, some degree of specialization is still important if one is to be good at performing tasks that are themselves becoming ever more complex. This is especially true not only for the more technically demanding segments of the marketplace, but for all activities that are highly competitive. Excellence requires some depth in one's field. New scientific knowledge is a public good, but it will be of limited use to economic agents or firms if they do not have the necessary competence to understand it to the point of adapting it for their own use.[134] This observation applies not only to the natural sciences but to all the other fields of scientific knowledge, including the social and management sciences.

Thus, in general, the most successful market participants in the knowledge economy are those with the necessary human capital that enables them to specialize even while having breadth of knowledge, in other words, a Renaissance person. Both specialization and lateral thinking require a sharply trained capacity to learn quickly and well even under different and difficult circumstances. Thus, a more accurate description of our current globalization is not the "knowledge-based" economy but the "learning" economy.[135] It could also be aptly called a reflexive economy because it changes and develops as it internalizes fresh information.[136] Rapid changes in processes and new products leave producers (and for that matter, any economic agent) "perpetually high on a shifting learning curve."[137] Market participants in the knowledge economy must have the capability and staying power to climb this steep and ever-changing learning curve.

Sixth, specialization and ever-finer divisions of labor push minimum requirements ever higher. Path dependence in knowledge creation means that a constantly improving technical competence is needed to maintain and build on existing technologies that are increasingly complicated. Climbing further up the ladder of created comparative advantage requires ever-greater depth and breadth in human capital. Furthermore, ever more powerful information-processing tools keep raising the benchmark of performance for everyone.

In sum, many of the features of an information-driven globalization call for more advanced human capital formation. The empirical evidence presented in chapter 2 attests to this shift.[138] Transforming a deluge of data into actionable information and knowledge requires skill and experience. Market widening and deepening demand an even greater breadth of outlook as there are more factors to consider in economic decision making. Value creation is dependent on a robust tacit knowledge. The accelerating pace of economic life needs a matching agility and responsiveness. More frequent shifts in the economic terrain invite a greater capacity for mobility. Stiffer competition leads to ever improving inventiveness and resourcefulness. Closer collaboration between science and technology calls for ever more sophisticated competencies. Thus, it is not surprising that most scholars agree that knowledge has become the basis for value and wealth creation in contemporary globalization.

In all this, note that there is an operative "cumulative circular causation" because as human capital rises up to the occasion and provides the necessary tacit knowledge to meet all these new requirements, it produces fresh tacit knowledge in the process. This augmented and even more advanced tacit knowledge raises the standards and expectations for the next rounds of economic activity. Hence, the knowledge economy becomes even more demanding of its market participants, and the envelope of human capital formation is pushed outwards constantly and at an accelerating pace.

Summary and Conclusions

Now to conclude these two chapters on the knowledge economy. Contemporary globalization has been impressive in the rapid expansion of the international exchange of goods and services, cross-border financial flows, and the penetration of trade in domestic economies. Even more consequential than market deepening and widening, however, is the shift of the primary source of value creation from natural resources and industrial capital to knowledge. This fifth Kondratieff cycle is different from the four earlier long-wave cycles because the key carrier input is information. Thus, besides inducing extensive changes in society just like the earlier carrier inputs, information (better, inexpensive, and plentiful) has also greatly improved the market's core process itself. ICTs have made the market more efficient at being efficient in allocating scarce resources to their most valued uses. After all, information is the lifeblood of the marketplace.

It has been said that Kondratieff cycles are properly called techno-economic paradigms because technological change gives rise to low-cost carrier inputs that end up radically altering the economic terrain.[139] I submit that in our contemporary Kondratieff cycle, the term "techno-economic" is even more appropriate because of the manner by which microelectronics has profoundly upgraded the efficiency of the marketplace. And, as we will find in the next chapter, this is not a one-time transformation in efficiency, but a self-perpetuating dynamic that constantly expands the limits of the market's efficiency.

Part II

Efficiency as a Criterion of Distributive Justice

Chapter 4 claims that efficiency matters, and it matters even more in the digital age. Moreover, the market is an essential vehicle for attaining such economic efficiency. Thus, critics of globalization ought to be cautious in being dismissive of the market as they may be inflicting more harm than good on the very people whose welfare they are supposed to be championing. Chapter 5 examines the literature and empirical evidence on the central role of institutions and social norms in market economies. Efficiency does not arise in a vacuum. It requires wide-ranging socioeconomic preconditions if the market is to work properly and produce its much-touted economic benefits. Besides, efficiency cannot be the sole economic goal of nations because the distribution of its gains is often so skewed as to make unfettered market operations unsustainable in the long term and ultimately self-destructive. It is a paradox that seemingly unconstrained market operations are in fact undergirded by extra-market interventions and much unseen preparatory work. They require an extensive web of social and human capital patiently and deliberately accumulated over time. The knowledge economy highlights both the importance and the limitations of economic efficiency as a criterion of distributive justice.

Chapter 4

Efficiency Matters Even More in the Information Age: Considering the Allocative Dimension of Price

It is rare for many neoclassical economists to come close to a consensus. The superior ability of market exchange to promote economic welfare compared to autarky is one such unusual point of near agreement. The claim that more open economies perform much better than closed economies over the long haul is supported by both theory and evidence. At the dawn of the discipline of economics, there was already an appreciation for the value of specialization, division of labor, and exchange in Adam Smith's *Wealth of Nations*.[1] For his part, David Ricardo (1817) formulated the theory of comparative advantage in which nations benefit themselves and their trading partners by producing that which they do best and then buying all their other needs from nations that can supply these at a much lower price. The Atlantic economies of the nineteenth century thrived and converged in their economic performance during that first era of global economic integration as they permitted the free flow of goods, capital, and migrants across their borders.[2] Moreover, the stark contrast in the anemic growth of nations during the interwar years, when markets were closed to each other, compared to the post–World War II period of more open markets also attests to the value of international trade. Note, too, the numerous regional and bilateral trade agreements negotiated and ratified during this period (e.g., European Common Market, NAFTA, MERCOSUR, ASEAN, APEC). These international commitments would not have been sought to begin with if nations did not see any value at all to cross-border trade.[3] And, of course, we are now well aware that the import-substitution strategy to development was a mistake. The export-promotion strategy of Japan and the Asian Tigers has proven to be the better path to development compared to the inward-looking policies pursued by Latin America and other Asian nations that languished from the 1950s to the 1980s. The literature in development economics has long accepted the tenet that cross-border trade is an important venue for self-sustaining growth, especially for small and developing countries.[4]

Indeed, market exchange has been instrumental in improving the lives of people who would have otherwise wallowed in destitution. International trade has given opportunities for economic advancement and upward social mobility to many millions more, indeed even entire nations and regions of the world. Dollar and Kraay (2001b) underscore the glaring difference in the impressive economic performance of the NICs compared to the lackluster growth, if growth at all, of nations that have kept their markets closed. Bhagwati (2004, 51–67) points to the overwhelming empirical evidence on the role of globalization in reducing poverty in the developing world and in narrowing global inequality. While recognizing the difficulty of quantitatively measuring the benefits of trade and even after acknowledging that cross-border exchange is not a guaranteed cure for developing countries' ills, Irwin (2002, 67–69) nonetheless concludes that nations give up not merely a few percentage points in their growth rate by foregoing international trade, but they risk impoverishing entire generations of their own citizens. Wolf (2004, xvii) argues that there is, as yet, no rival to the market as the "most powerful institution for raising living standards" and that the problem today is not too much globalization but too little.

The common thread in the arguments of this sampling of advocates of globalization is that fully functioning markets can greatly improve economic well-being, and in a self-sustaining manner, to boot.[5] Economic efficiency matters. This chapter maintains that economic efficiency and markets, by extension, matter even more in the information age because of a self-feeding dynamic between market operations and technological-organizational innovations in producing even greater subsequent efficiencies.

In what follows, different types of efficiency are examined. I follow this up with a brief outline of the institutional and dynamic preconditions of the knowledge economy based on the preceding chapters' findings. I then make the case for why the market is an effective societal vehicle for meeting these requirements. The chapter concludes by presenting international vertical specialization as an excellent illustration of how (1) ICTs greatly improve market efficiency even while

(2) markets, in their own turn, facilitate further ICT technological advances. International vertical specialization is an organizational innovation made possible only because of ICTs and markets. International vertical specialization, ICTs, and markets mutually strengthen each other.

Efficiency

Different kinds of efficiency have been proposed in the literature. Dosi et al. (1990, 240, 248–54) and Kuttner (1997, 24–27) propose three types: microeconomic/Ricardian, Schumpeterian, and Keynesian. Microeconomic/Ricardian efficiency is the textbook allocative efficiency in which the right goods in the right quantities and the right quality are produced with the right methods and the right inputs in the most cost-effective manner, and then brought to the right markets at the right time. There are no unsold inventories and all markets clear. Consumer preferences are satisfied within people's budget constraints and societal resources. This is the much-heralded power of unrestrained markets to put scarce resources to their most valued uses.

Schumpeterian efficiency is the ability to keep pushing the technological frontier as far as possible given the current state of knowledge. These technological leaps fuel the famous "perennial gale of creative destruction" that Schumpeter (1942, 84) describes as the defining feature of the capitalist economy. Keynesian efficiency pertains to a proper rate of growth in demand that ensures full employment of the key factor inputs in the economy. In graphical terms, Keynesian efficiency is concerned with being on the production possibilities frontier, Schumpeterian efficiency is about constantly shifting the production possibilities outward as far as possible, and microeconomic efficiency is about being on the highest possible indifference curve.[6]

Shipman (1999, 32) proposes a different taxonomy. He lists five kinds of efficiency. The first is "static efficiency" that is comprised of productive efficiency (least-cost production) and allocative efficiency (putting resources to their best use). The second type of efficiency is that which fully employs resources. The third is "dynamic efficiency" in which an optimum and sustainable growth is attained within the limits of a nation's natural resources. The fourth is the efficiency that comes from the cross-border exchange of goods, services, and factors of production between nations. Finally, there is the efficiency in which income inequality is no greater than that which is necessary to bring about the preceding four types of efficiency.[7]

There is a substantial overlap between the above-mentioned lists, and for this study, I propose that we can reduce these to three kinds of efficiency. First, we have the microeconomic/allocative efficiency in which scarce resources are employed to their most valued uses given people's preferences and the finitude of available resources. However, unlike Dosi et al. (1990) and Kuttner (1997), I will not call this "Ricardian efficiency" because David Ricardo is better associated with the gains that flow from international trade given his classic work on the theory of comparative advantage. Moreover, unlike these authors, I will subsume Keynesian efficiency, that is, the full employment of resources, under allocative/microeconomic efficiency. After all, resources are put to their most valued uses only if they are fully employed to begin with; unemployment and underemployment are indicative of an economy operating below its full potential given its available resources. Furthermore, productive (engineering) efficiency is a necessary condition of allocative efficiency.[8]

Second, I propose a Ricardian/Smithian efficiency that comes from nations specializing in their respective comparative advantages. As any introductory text in microeconomics shows, sizable gains are produced when nations trade with each other. They buy some goods and services at a much cheaper price overseas than if they were to produce these themselves, while at the same time specializing in the production of other goods and services that they then sell at a much higher price abroad. Compared to their autarkic position, nations reap mutual benefits when they produce according to their comparative advantage given their technologies or factor endowments. This type of efficiency is properly called "Ricardian" because of David Ricardo's (1817 [1929]) seminal contribution to the notion of comparative advantage. It is also aptly called "Smithian" because of Adam Smith's (1776 [1937]) insight into the gains that arise from a division of labor and specialization.

The third kind of efficiency we will be using for this study is Schumpeterian efficiency. This is equivalent to the aforesaid optimal and sustainable growth given a nation's resources.[9] One can truly call this "dynamic efficiency" because it involves the continued outward shift of a nation's production possibilities frontier in the face of technological change and innovation.

Note some common features in these three distinct efficiencies. In the first place, they all ultimately deal with the effective and sustainable use of scarce resources. This means that efficiency must, at a minimum, employ the least-cost means to reaching predetermined goals and lay the groundwork for self-sustaining growth. To put it in another way, economic efficiency, no matter how it is defined, is in the final analysis about attaining the highest level of economic well-being possible over the long term given the limited resources available.

Second, these three efficiencies are not mutually exclusive and should, in fact, converge in the ideal case of perfectly competitive markets. Let us take globalization as an illustration. Free trade across nations induces Ricardian/Smithian efficiency. As nations liberalize their domestic markets and as they move toward their comparative advantage, they put their resources toward their most valued uses (allocative/microeconomic efficiency). The resulting specialization and competition engender technological change and innovation (Schumpeterian efficiency). Thus, in the ideal market, these three efficiencies mutually reinforce each other and converge into a single harmonious dynamic.

Finally, a common characteristic of these efficiencies is the central role played by the market. For example, Shipman (1999, 32) lists his five efficiencies in the context of his discourse on the "advantages of markets as a social organising principle." Kuttner (1997, 24–27) explains his three efficiencies within his exposition on the "virtues and limits of markets." Dosi et al. (1990, 240, 248–54) consider efficiency in the course of their treatment of technological change in the wake of international trade. Indeed, the market can be viewed as the milieu or the overarching framework within which economic efficiency is achieved. In fact, one can make this claim even stronger by noting that the market is a necessary, though not sufficient, condition for economic efficiency.[10] It is the only social institution, to date, that can best approximate the ideal economic state described by the above-mentioned efficiencies. If economics is indeed about putting scarce resources to their most valued uses,[11] then the market is an incomparable social institution that generates such a disposition. The market and economic efficiency are inextricably linked to each other. The market is the means to attaining efficiency, even as efficiency, in its own turn, is an end for which the market exists.[12] We examine this linkage in greater depth in the next section.

Institutional and Dynamic Requirements of the Knowledge Economy

Institutional Preconditions

As we will see in chapter 5, the market neither arises nor operates in a vacuum. There are structural preconditions to the smooth functioning of the market. Having seen some of the salient features of the knowledge economy in the preceding chapters, we can infer some of its requisite institutional foundations.[13]

First, because of the major breakthroughs in ICTs, the knowledge economy must provide market participants with the infrastructure with which to access, organize, and use the resulting deluge of data in ever-new ways that create value. After all, the market is not merely a producer of information, but it is also the major user of information, and immense amounts of it. Second, ripple effects are expected to be even more frequent, unpredictable, and disruptive in a more interconnected global economy. The resulting greater uncertainty requires even greater vigilance. The knowledge economy must provide the means by which economic agents are able to respond and adapt to these constant changes. Moreover, it must also furnish even better methods of risk management.

Third, globalization has made economic activity even more complex and has highlighted the even greater importance of collaborative work. Thus, the knowledge economy must give rise to institutions that facilitate networking among economic actors. Fourth, the increasing transformation of the international community into a single economic unit characterized by a global division of labor requires even greater goods and factor mobility. Specialization entails nations moving toward their comparative advantage and then simply procuring their other needs from the international marketplace. This greater cross-border movement of finished and intermediate goods and factors of production will require mechanisms that facilitate and enhance such mobility.

Dynamic Prerequisites

The aforesaid institutional prerequisites are critical for maintaining market operations. In contrast, the dynamic requirements of the knowledge economy are the essential preconditions for keeping the economy forward-looking. These are the necessary building blocks of Schumpeterian efficiency.

First, as we have seen in chapter 2, ICTs have been a proximate cause of global economic integration. Given the central role and importance of technology in the knowledge economy, there is need to encourage and support economic agents who are willing and able to undertake the risks attendant to technological change. Moreover, just as a bicycle has to keep moving forward to avoid tipping over, an economy has to keep moving up the ladder of created comparative advantage, if only to keep up with peers or with follower nations that are quickly moving upwards.

Second, since tacit knowledge is now the source of value creation in the digital age, it is all the more important for the economy to provide market participants with hands-on learning opportunities that build their know-how and know-who. Third, given the accelerated pace of economic life, there is need for the economy to develop two qualities in market participants, to wit: (1) timely responsiveness and (2) flexibility and adaptability to change. The knowledge economy should be one that breeds a disposition to change and openness to discovery. It must also develop economic agents' personal and collective capabilities to deal with pecuniary externalities.

Fourth, the knowledge economy has been aptly called the "learning" economy[14] since adjustment to ceaseless change is a characteristic requirement of our contemporary era. There is a self-feeding interaction between change and learning. Learning is a function of change. However, learning, by itself, also provokes even further changes down the road. A knowledge economy must strengthen this nexus between change and learning. Moreover, it must also systematize and institutionalize the means by which human and social capital are continuously developed through such an interactive process.

Fifth, the knowledge economy needs to build the capacity for discovery and provide an appropriate climate for creativity.

> [T]he "economic problem" is fundamentally different from that depicted in contemporary orthodox theory. The latter views choice sets as known and given. The economic problem is to pick the best possible production and distribution, given that set of alternatives. The function of competition is to get—or help to get—the signals and incentives right. In evolutionary theory, choice sets are not given and the consequences of any choice are unknown. Although some choices may be clearly worse than others, there is no choice that is clearly best *ex ante*.[15]

Indeed, it has even been suggested that the market process is ultimately about discovery and creation.[16]

The aforesaid institutional and dynamic preconditions of the knowledge economy do not work independently of each other. In fact, these are interlocking requirements. For example, more frequent and disruptive market shifts require even better goods and factor mobility, an enhanced capacity to deal with risk and uncertainty, and improved information and price signals. Moreover, there is need for even more daring, more responsive, and better informed private initiatives. Individual autonomy and liberty take on even greater importance, especially in an economic environment in which the acquisition of tacit knowledge has become extremely important. In other words, the institutional and dynamic preconditions of the knowledge economy produce a synergy of prerequisites that are much greater and more stringent than the sum of their individual requirements. And it turns out that the market is able to match these exacting conditions with an impressive synergy of its own.

Efficiency-Market Nexus

The unique qualities of the market, especially in contemporary globalization, neatly dovetail the aforesaid institutional and dynamic requirements of the knowledge economy. The market is an ideal, in fact *the only*, social institution to date that is effective in bringing about economic efficiency.[17] Here, I will limit myself to only some of the more significant properties of the market relevant for my thesis:

1. its potential for internalizing information and for discovery,
2. its capacity for fostering private initiative,
3. its ceaseless competitive pressure,
4. its management of risk and uncertainty,
5. its networking web,
6. its sensitivity and responsiveness to change.

Market Operations as Discovery

The economic problem entails deciding what to produce, in what quantities, when, how, and for whom. Moreover, recall from the preceding discussion of efficiency that these questions must be resolved both in a timely fashion and in a manner that fully employs available scarce resources in an optimal fashion. Thus, Hayek (1944) is emphatic that economics is largely an informational problem because economic agents are constantly pressed to make informed decisions. It turns out that the economic problem is, in fact, a nested, twofold allocative exercise in which the need to put scarce resources to their most valued uses is preceded by the need to distribute information properly to their intended users. In other words, information makes the economy work.

The informational needs of this twin allocative task are truly staggering. In the first place, data about goods, services, factors of production, technologies, household preferences, and business decisions in both the product and input markets must be generated, collated, and then digested. Second, this wide diversity of requisite data is compounded by a constantly shifting economic terrain. In other words, data have a very short half-life and must be continuously updated. Third, economic agents have very different informational requirements depending on their role, activity, and location in the marketplace. Correct and well-timed decision making is entirely dependent on sorting through a tremendous volume of data and then getting the relevant information to the right people at the right time in an expeditious and cost-effective manner.

This is a formidable and demanding informational environment, and the market is "uniquely capable" of meeting these requirements.[18] In the first place, the market is an efficient information processor because it internalizes huge quantities of data and condenses them into a simple and easily understandable form: price. Thus, the market price saves people time and effort by synthesizing for them the economic impact of disparate factors. Take the case of the global market for sugar. This industry has been buffeted by a wide variety of events, such as the impressive technological and productivity advances of Brazil in sugar production, oversupply, French export subsidies, and U.S. quotas. The implications of these developments are conveniently summarized in the resulting weak price of this commodity. Sugar beet growers in the developed world and inefficient sugar cane growers in emerging nations do not need to go into an extensive analysis of their industry to know what is going on. All they have to do is to look at the chronic low price of sugar to get the message that it is time for them to shift to another crop. Of course, this has not happened in the United States and the EU because of government coddling that insulates their sugar beet and sugar cane growers from the discipline of international prices.

Second, shifts in economic conditions are immediately internalized by the market through price changes. The upward or downward movement of prices and their trends are signals for economic actors to modify their decisions and to plan accordingly. Thus, observe the speed with which current events, even noneconomic news, are reflected in the volatility of prices in the stock, commodity (especially crude oil), and foreign exchange markets.

Third, viewed as an input or as a commodity itself, price is nonrival in consumption and can be easily disseminated, especially in the digital age. It can be read and used by as many people as are interested and have access to it. The unparalleled strength of the marketplace lies not merely in its swiftness in processing information but also in its expansive geographic reach. The market is the venue by which widely dispersed economic agents communicate and exchange relevant information indirectly via prices. ICTs have made this feature of the market even more potent.

Finally, price reveals relative value and, therefore, the opportunity cost of people's choices. Not all events or commodities are readily commensurable relative to each other. Price serves as a convenient tool for economic actors by providing a common measure with which to weigh competing choices.

In sum, the market is more than a match for the daunting informational requirements of the economic problem of determining what to produce, how, when, how much, and for whom.[19] The marketplace is a cost-effective vehicle for synthesizing voluminous amounts of data and then disseminating the appropriate information to the right economic actors, even over a widely dispersed geographic area. And it accomplishes this swiftly and within an ever-shifting economic terrain. Thus, the market process has been described as one of using information for discovery.[20]

The Market as an Incubator of Private Initiative

A basic difference between the economy of precarious subsistence in the feudal era and the economy of flowing abundance in the modern period is the separation of the economic and political realms in the latter.[21] Recall the restrictive nature of the feudal economy in which peasants and artisans were bound respectively by the rules of the manor and by the guilds. The medieval guilds curbed or regulated product innovations and improvements in sales practices to prevent undue competition within the craft. In contrast, note the technological vibrancy of the Industrial Revolution. Despite the efforts of the Luddites, the English parliament refused to halt or slow down the move toward mechanization. Indeed, in separating the economic and political spheres from each other, the modern economy has served well as an incubator of private initiative. This is, in fact, the hallmark of the capitalist market, the single most critical factor behind Schumpeter's (1942, 81–86) "creative destruction." There are a number of reasons why thriving individual autonomy has been both a foundation and a consequence of the market economy.

First, the market has a "thin" notion of the good. In other words, besides its goal of allocating scarce resources to their most valued uses, it does not require any philosophical commitments from market participants.[22] A wide diversity of ends can be pursued in the marketplace.

Second, the market affords people wide personal freedoms. Market participants are free to set their own objectives, to choose a variety of means to reach their goals, and to transact with whomever they wish. They have the liberty to decide the extent to which they participate in the marketplace. As I argue in part III, the market is a public good and cannot exclude anyone with the necessary purchasing power from availing of its services. There is full freedom of entry or exit from *particular* transactions whenever or however people choose to do so.[23] Thus, some go so far as to argue that a normative case can be made in favor of the market on the basis of the autonomy and liberty it affords individuals.[24]

Third, such expansive personal freedoms have unleashed the creativity and energy of economic actors. In making economic decisions on their own, people can explore and be more daring in taking risks. They have a better sense of responsibility for their own economic well-being. Market participants have the possibility of improving their lot and moving upward in the social order. Both socioeconomic and geographical mobility afford people ease of entry or exit in whatever economic activity or sector they choose. Thus, it should not come as a surprise that the wealthiest and most productive countries are the ones with the most enlivened private sectors. These economies are imbued with dynamism and energy. In economic history, observe how the modern era of technological change and innovation coincided with the emergence of a relatively freer market economy in the nineteenth century. In our own time, note the positive correlation between the freedom index (a measure of the freedom accorded to private initiative) and material well-being.[25]

Fourth, the market rewards initiative. Entrepreneurship can pay off in terms of considerable rents.[26] In giving economic agents their due according to their contribution, the market encourages even further private initiative in the succeeding rounds of economic activity because people have both the incentive and the means to apply themselves in effort and striving.[27] Thus, private initiative ensures vigorous competition. There is no room for complacency in an economy with an unfettered private sector because profits can be easily whittled away by the ease of entry and exit from markets. Economic agents are compelled to work assiduously just to keep up with their peers or to prevent their competitors from catching up. As a result, there is a built-in mechanism and momentum to be forward-looking. Market participants are always on the prowl for the least-cost method of accomplishing ends. A free private sector is foundational for the market's capacity for disciplined economic behavior. Recall our earlier example on the anemic economic performance of countries that had pursued the import-substitution strategy to development (such as Latin America and India from the 1950s to the 1980s) compared to those that had embraced an export-promotion strategy to development (such as the Asian Tigers). The import-substitution strategy to development curtailed private initiative with excessive government restrictions in an effort to protect selected sectors. In contrast, the export-promotion strategy to development encouraged private initiative to compete in the global marketplace, thereby creating a pool of lean and seasoned entrepreneurs.

Fifth, the market is an incubator of private initiative because of its lightning ability to internalize information in decision making owing to its decentralized structure. There is no single person or government agency that sets price levels. In a truly functioning market, allocative decisions on the proper disposition of scarce resources to their most valued uses are not left in the hands of just a few people but are the result of the collective impact of a multitude of private choices spread throughout the entire market. Market participants are price-takers at the personal level, but they are ultimately price-makers in their aggregated effect in the economy. The market is impressive in its ability to digest information because it leaves it up to individual market participants to read and interpret price signals on their own and to make the necessary adjustments to their respective economic behavior. Furthermore, economic actors observe each other's market reaction and respond accordingly. Moreover, people reveal their needs and preferences through their economic choices. Indeed, the market is an excellent example of both a decentralized decision-making and information-disseminating mechanism. It is individual economic autonomy that enables the market to discharge this twin function.

Three consequences of the market as an incubator of private initiative must be highlighted. First, the market plays a pivotal role in economic development. Economic development is a process of self-sustaining growth.[28] Advances achieved within the economy cannot be imposed exogenously, from the outside. If it were so, such growth is not genuine development. Schumpeter (1955, 63) states it well when he limits the definition of economic development only to "such changes in economic life as are not forced upon it from without but arise by its own initiative, *from within*" (emphasis added). In other words, self-sustaining growth is possible only to the extent that the economy has the capacity to continually rejuvenate and re-create itself. The market develops such a requisite capacity for endogenous change because it is itself animated by vibrant private initiatives.

Second, in fostering private initiative, the market, in effect, also nurtures diversity. This is a necessary condition for the market's much-vaunted "creative destruction." Recall the earlier observation that contrary to the neoclassical school's view of economic agency as an exercise in finding the optimum solution to a known set of alternatives, the economy is, in fact, more in line with the evolutionary school of economic thought.[29] In this latter view, the economy is in a continual state of evolution, characterized by unknown sets of choices that are discovered in an iterative process of trial and error. The vigor of the search and the probability of discovery are dependent on the diversity of effort, which in its own turn is determined by the state of private initiative within the market.

Finally, in strengthening private initiative, the market, in effect, also fosters redundancy. This is important for risk management. Private initiative may, on the surface, appear to be wasteful of resources given the duplication of effort. However, this seeming waste is more apparent than real. There are long-term benefits from competition that are instrumental for innovation and technological change. For example, consumers have reaped astonishing gains from ICTs in the past twenty-five years given the parallel private initiatives to develop ever more advanced chips and consumer electronics.[30] Or, recall the 5,000 railway firms and the 2,000 car manufacturers in the nascent stages of these industries in the United States.[31] The market eventually corrects itself by pruning down such "duplication" to the bare minimum that can be sustained and is necessary for competition (within the limits, of course, of antitrust legislation). A similar phenomenon is currently at work in the U.S. airline and global auto industries. Besides the disciplining effect of competition, a duplication of effort imbues the economy with the pliability to respond rapidly to sudden change. Redundancy in a thriving private sector makes for a flexible economy in the face of severe shocks and disequilibria.

> There is a requirement for variety in capabilities, behavioural rules, and allocative processes which allow for greater adaptability to uncertainty and change. . . . To put it in another way, one of the greatest strengths that capitalism has shown is its capability of continuously producing redundant resources, of exploring an "excessive" number of technological/organisational "genotypes."[32]

Numerous examples illustrate the resilience of the market economy: the overnight conversion of the U.S. and U.K. peacetime civilian economies into wartime manufacturing powerhouses during World War II, West Germany's absorption of a failed East German economy during its reunification, the quick recovery and minimal disruption to the global oil markets in the wake of the 1990 Kuwait invasion, the strong rebound of Kobe after its devastating earthquake in 1995, the ability of the U.S. transportation system to continue moving goods and people around the nation on 9–11 and the following days, and the minimal impact on U.S. GDP of devastating natural disasters such as Hurricane Katrina in the Gulf Coast (2005) and Hurricane Andrews in Florida (1992). Indeed, the redundancy that emerges from the disparate, spontaneous initiative of autonomous economic actors provides a valuable hedge against the chance and contingencies of life. It cushions the disruptiveness of both man-made and natural disasters. It makes for a supple system.

In sum, the ascendancy of markets observed in the past thirty years[33] is in large part due to governments' newfound appreciation for their most valuable and often untapped resource—the ingenuity and initiative that come with an unimpeded private sector.[34] The market not only respects private initiative, but it also rewards it, nurtures it, and provides it with the breaks and the opportunities that allow it to be tested, to make mistakes, to learn, and then to grow and develop. Even as the market is lauded as an efficient information processor, the market is even more remarkable as an incubator of private initiative. It is, after all, ultimately powered by personal striving and effort.[35]

Market Competition

The market weeds out weak and inefficient players and allows the proverbial cream to rise to the top. This feature of the market is an indispensable mechanism by which efficiency is attained. The market can indeed be generous in rewarding correct decisions (e.g., Google, Microsoft, eBay) and be harsh in punishing mistakes or subpar performance (e.g., the failed Time-Warner and AOL merger). In so doing, the market sends out the necessary signals and incentives that change people's economic decisions and behavior. Technological dynamism is a function of market pressure. Industries that are characterized by extremely competitive environments tend to be the most innovative.[36]

Management of Risk and Uncertainty

Technological change is said to be fraught with at least five kinds of uncertainties, to wit:[37]

1. The yet to be discovered properties of new technologies.

Lasers and electricity are excellent examples. They were outcomes of pure scientific research and were not innovations meant to replace an existing or failing technology. Consequently, it took decades for the manifold uses of electricity to be slowly discovered. The same phenomenon is happening to lasers today as we see a gradual expansion in their use.

2. Improvements in complementary technologies or inventions that may enhance the subsequent impact or utility of innovations.

Once again, lasers can be cited as an example. It was not until the advent of optic fibers that the full benefits of using lasers for telephone communications were reaped. Similarly, recall that the idea of computers is not recent. Computers were already used as early as World War II to calculate the trajectory of artillery shells. However, it was the invention of the microchip and the miniaturization it permitted that turned the computer into an all-purpose technology.

3. The possibility that innovations and inventions may actually be harbingers of a completely new technological system instead of merely replacing small parts of existing systems.

Railroads in the 1830s and 1840s are an example.[38] They were meant to serve merely as feeders for the canal system, but later came to overshadow the canals altogether. Using the taxonomy[39] we have seen earlier, we can describe the railroad as more than just an incremental innovation or radical invention; it turned out to be a techno-economic paradigm shift. It is only with the benefit of hindsight that one gets to appreciate the full impact of a particular invention.

4. Unanticipated solutions to problems that the innovation or invention was not originally designed to address.

The most famous example of this, of course, is the steam engine. It was invented to pump water out of flooding mines due to the increasing depth of mining operations in the eighteenth century. It turned out to be the invention that revolutionized both land and sea transportation (railroads and steamships, respectively).[40]

5. The uncertainty of whether or not new technologies are economically feasible.

The Concorde is an illustration. It was a technological marvel but was not cost-effective as a means of transportation. Hence, it ultimately failed as a commercial venture.[41]

The market is an ideal mechanism for dealing with these uncertainties for a number of reasons. First, technological development and change are generally extremely expensive endeavors that often fail. The networking that the market facilitates is an effective way of spreading risk.[42] Moreover, market widening and deepening mitigate the risk of huge upfront, fixed-cost investments by providing a much larger potential customer base from which to recover these expenditures within a shorter payback period.

Second, the market provides essential forward and backward linkages that facilitate diffusion, further improvement by end users or competitors, discovery of fresh applications, and the creation of synergies by combining new and existing technologies. Take the case of microelectronics. The different components of ICTs mutually reinforced each other and eventually gave rise to the next generation of technological innovations.

> [T]he microprocessor made possible the microcomputer; advances in telecommunications . . . enabled microcomputers to function in networks, thus increasing their power and flexibility. Applications of these technologies to electronics manufacturing enhanced the potential for new design and fabrication technologies in semiconductor production. New software was stimulated by the fast-growing microcomputer market, that, in turn, exploded on the basis of new applications and user-friendly technologies.[43]

In all this, it was the market that facilitated the combined use of these different components of ICTs. End users gave innovators and inventors feedback through the market on the kinds of capabilities that truly added value to the product. Take a look at the consumer-driven development of ever more powerful and convenient features in wireless devices and laptop computers that combine functions from different equipment into a single unit. The market is a potent tool not only for discovering profitable ways of interfacing technologies, but it is also extremely effective at nurturing demand-driven innovations.

Third, as we have seen earlier, the market consists of a diverse cacophony of private initiatives. This wide variety of approaches and efforts to problem-solving is clearly superior since more options are explored and tried simultaneously, making technological breakthroughs more likely. It is a distinctive strength of the marketplace.[44]

Finally, the market is a ready-made laboratory for test-runs of technological change and innovation. Because it is an efficient information processor, the market is effective at reducing exogenous and endogenous uncertainties.[45] It provides quick, clear, and reliable feedback from end users on what changes and innovations work and what do not.

[A] further considerable virtue of the marketplace is that it also provides strong incentives to terminate, quickly and unsentimentally, directions of research whose once-rosy prospects have been unexpectedly dimmed by new data, by some change in the economic environment, or by a restructuring of social or political parties.[46]

Indeed, recall that the price system of the marketplace is an expeditious and cost-effective manner of gathering and conveying information. One advantage of this laboratory is that no one can be excluded from it. Innovators can keep on fine-tuning their alterations by going back to end users for feedback for as many times and for as long as it takes to perfect the changes. Thus, the market is an ideal testing ground for inventions and innovations because it provides free access, is always up-to-date with the most recent developments, and is swift in rendering judgment. Test marketing can minimize some of the uncertainties listed above as it reveals technological complementarities, unforeseen uses, and significant properties of inventions or innovations. The history of technological development in the modern era is eloquent proof of this market strength in fostering technological revolutions.[47] The development of the Web and its growing manifold uses are prime examples.

The Market as a Networking Hub

It has been suggested that "chaos theory" is descriptive of the joint work between the biological sciences and the ICT sector in pushing the scientific frontiers. Proponents of this theory see the "emergence of self-organizing structures that create complexity out of simplicity and superior order out of chaos."[48] I submit that this is an apt description of the market as well. The market can be likened to a highly integrated, organized chaos.

The history of technology shows that an invention or innovation is not an isolated event.[49] It is an endogenous phenomenon built up in a cumulative fashion over time and is dependent on previous rounds of investment, production, and economic exchange.[50] It does not arise in a vacuum.

[Technology] reflects a given state of knowledge, a particular institutional and industrial environment, a certain availability of skills . . . an economic mentality to make such application cost-efficient, and a network of producers and users . . . learning by using and by doing . . . [an] interactivity of systems of technological innovation and their dependence on certain "milieux" of exchange of ideas, problems, and solutions . . .[51]

The market provides just such a milieu with all the necessary ingredients for continued innovation, and more.

The market turns out to be a very responsive mechanism in dealing with complexity. It fosters change because of its promise of substantial gains and the fear generated by its unforgiving logic of "survival of the fittest." It is excellent at searching, finding, and completing mutually advantageous exchanges. It enjoys an unparalleled ability in matching widely dispersed economic agents with like interests. Equally important, the market is a dynamic setting in which new ideas are hatched, tried, refined, or combined with existing knowledge given its fluidity and the multiplicity and redundancy of its private initiatives.

Volume and diversity of use and applications are essential for vibrant technological development.[52] The market satisfies both of these conditions. In addition, empirical evidence suggests that the market is particularly good at diffusing the benefits of technological change and R&D across borders through international trade.[53] Foreign direct investments are another venue by which the market disperses these technological spillover effects.[54]

The market is an excellent vehicle for technological diffusion because of its "demonstration effect." The general types of innovations are technical, service, financial, managerial-organizational, marketing-distribution, and institutional. Only the first one (i.e., technical) is patentable.[55] The intellectual-property features of the four other types of innovations are nonpatentable because they are unenforceable. Market participants can readily observe others' improvements and simply imitate them. For example, one cannot patent or prevent others from emulating one's innovative management practices, such as off-shore outsourcing or a just-in-time inventory system. The market provides an excellent terrain for a constantly unfolding demonstration effect in which industry best practices can be readily observed and copied. Because of its open and interactive nature, the market is a fertile ground for learning from others' triumphs or travails.

The Market as a Catalyst and Medium for Change

As we have repeatedly seen, the market, by its nature, is dynamic. It is in a ceaseless state of flux as economic actors constantly improve the disposition of their resources in reaction to changes and to their peers' or competitors' responses to new information as it becomes available. This incessant process of adjustment is further intensified by the faster and larger flow of information and by the accelerating pace of economic life described in the preceding chapters. This presents both dangers (because of shocks and adverse pecuniary externalities) and opportunities (because of potential rents to be reaped).

The textbook model of markets in equilibrium is more of an aberration than a norm. In reality, markets never quite reach their equilibria; they are more accurately described as equilibria-in-the-making, or equilibria-in-progress as many have claimed. In economics, an equilibrium is a condition in which economic actors are satisfied with the status quo; they have no cause or incentive to change their decisions. This is an idealized description of economic life, just like the model of perfectly competitive markets. Disequilibria and change are the constant parameters of the market economy; they also imbue the market with some of its strengths and weaknesses.

> Contrary to common beliefs, any advantage of contemporary mixed economies as compared to centrally planned ones, reflects the fact that the former do not achieve an equilibrium of the Arrow-Debreu kind, but are highly imperfect and always characterized by allocative inefficiencies and technological slacks.[56]

These slacks and inefficiencies become the occasion for the market's process of constant adjustment. After all, recall that the market is both a producer and a user of considerable amounts of data and information. Because economic agents fine-tune their decisions and behavior in response to new information, the market never stands still. This market attribute is extremely important for attaining its much-vaunted economic efficiency for a number of reasons.

First, the open-ended nature of market operations provides the means for responding swiftly in an extremely dynamic knowledge economy. This permits quick correction or reaction, either to avail of profit opportunities or to minimize damage. Moreover, the fluidity of the market allows for ongoing marginal alterations, as needed, and prevents distortions from becoming so severe as to require major corrective action later. The value of the market as a mechanism for steady incremental modifications is best illustrated in the case of foreign currency exchange rates. Countries that insist on overvaluing their currencies end up paying an enormous cost when they are ultimately forced to devalue their foreign exchange rates. In contrast, nations that adopt a flexible exchange rate policy allow markets to make the necessary corrections gradually and as early as possible, thereby avoiding any further distortions within the economy. Necessary adjustments can be accomplished easily and in an orderly fashion. Equally important, their attendant costs can be absorbed in small increments.

Second, the market is a catalyst for change because of its fluidity. The information furnished by an unimpeded price mechanism is fresh and up-to-date. This permits a corresponding up-to-date decision making on the part of economic agents. Third, a fluid market has the advantage of a quick learning cycle. Innovations and inventions can be refined rapidly given the instant feedback provided by the marketplace.

Finally, the market is central to the development, diffusion, and then maturity of the Kondratieff carrier inputs. Recall Freeman and Perez's (1988) description of how techno-economic paradigms evolve. Earlier carrier inputs are eventually unable to meet the changing needs of the marketplace and cause bottlenecks that induce a search for new, alternative technologies. It is the market that provides the signals on the kind of innovations and inventions needed through the structural crises that it provokes. In the end, this leads to the next techno-economic paradigm and a new Kondratieff cycle. The market is the milieu that facilitates the transition from one long-wave cycle to the next. This changeover is seamlessly achieved through the market's price mechanism. Prices constantly adjust economic actors' behavior and decisions, and these collectively shape the form and uses of the next carrier input. We have seen this in the Industrial Revolution and we are witness to it again in the case of ICTs.

To sum up, the proper operation of the knowledge economy requires the satisfaction of manifold institutional and dynamic preconditions. The market is more than a match for these requirements. It is an information-processing institution; it nurtures the requisite private initiative; its unforgiving competitive environment fosters disciplined economic behavior; it is effective at managing risk; it facilitates networking and collaborative work; and it is a catalyst and medium for change. There is a mutually supporting dynamic between the knowledge economy and the market. ICTs have irreversibly transformed the market to be even more efficient at being efficient. In their own turn, ICTs are ever more dependent on the market for their continued development. This mutual dependence is best illustrated in the set of market-generated technological and organizational innovations that jointly make up what is now known as international vertical specialization, a hallmark of the knowledge economy. It is to this that we now turn our attention.

International Vertical Specialization

Technological or organizational improvements do not arise by themselves but are, in fact, a function of their immediate milieu.

Technology is a socially and institutionally embedded process. The ways in which technologies are used—even their very creation—are conditioned by their social and their economic context. In the contemporary world this means primarily the values and motivations of capitalist business enterprises, *operating within an intensely competitive system*. Choices and uses of technologies are influenced by the drive for profit, capital accumulation and investment, increased market share . . .[57]

Put in more succinct terms, change and innovation (whether technological or organizational) respond to price signals. This price sensitivity is at the heart of the efficiency-market nexus.

Technological and organizational innovations are price-sensitive; they are engendered by and mediated through the marketplace. But the causation also runs in the opposite direction. Organizational and technological innovations, in their own turn, also transform the marketplace. In other words, there is a feedback cycle with the market and technological-organizational innovations mutually shaping and improving each other. This is the dynamic that generates capitalism's self-sustaining gales of creative destruction. International vertical specialization, a constitutive feature of contemporary globalization, is an excellent illustration of the role of the market in satisfying the requirements of the knowledge economy. In fact, this organizational change can be aptly described as both a cause and effect of late-twentieth-century global economic integration.

Nature and Types of Networks

Networks are important and ubiquitous in economic life. Note their various forms:[58]

1. Supplier networks: These are clusters of providers of intermediate inputs or merchandise. An example is the current network of East Asian ICT component manufacturers supplying parts for the consumer electronics that China is assembling and exporting to the West.[59] Wal-Mart, Home Depot, Target, and all the other major retailers are dependent on similar supplier networks.
2. Producer networks: These are firms pooling together their production facilities and resources (financial and human) in order to expand their respective geographical coverage and product lines. Examples of this are the alliances and the code sharing that airlines have formed to avoid the duplication of equipment and to provide seamless connections between international and domestic flights.

3. Customer networks: This involves cementing forward linkages with end users, distributors, and customers. This is standard practice for many firms even before the age of ICTs. Beverage firms like Coca-Cola and Pepsi-Cola have had long-standing marketing arrangements with restaurants and retail outlets for exclusive use of their products or for preferential supermarket shelving of their drinks in exchange for price breaks and equipment.
4. Standard coalitions: This is the phenomenon of getting as many firms as possible to use a particular proprietary product with an eye toward making it the industry standard. Microsoft's operating system for the personal computer is an example of the importance of such a lock-in. Microsoft Windows continues to dominate the field despite the availability of free alternative operating software such as Linux.[60]
5. Technology cooperation networks: These are the collaborations in R&D and product development and design. The international partnerships lined up by Boeing and Airbus for the design and manufacture of their most recent models, the 787 and the A380 respectively, are examples of such technological cooperative ventures.

Two common threads run through this variety of networks. First, these networks are mutable, with independent entities constantly searching for collaborative work with other firms that share similar ends.[61] This leads to joint ventures in areas in which autonomous economic units have a coincidence of interests, even while remaining competitors in other areas.[62] Thus, the network enterprise has the best of both worlds because it can belong to any number of alliances and be even heavily dependent on them, while maintaining its independence in many other areas at the same time. One could aptly describe such networks as cooperative endeavors of convenience and expediency.

Second, ICTs and the market are pivotal in undergirding or enhancing these networks. ICTs provide the technological means to overcome the physical constraint of geographic separation. Moreover, they have also reduced erstwhile indivisibilities within firms. Given the speed and the safety with which data can easily be transmitted with the click of a mouse, R&D, product design and engineering, data entry and management, and many other functions that used to be centralized in the home office can now be broken up into separate components and farmed out to different parts of the world. Human capital–intensive functions can be differentiated from low-skill labor processes as in the case of the textile, apparel, and consumer electronics industries.[63] This has been described as the slicing up of the value chain into ever-thinner and ever-more specialized segments in order to squeeze more cost savings out of the firm.[64]

The market, in its own turn, provides the "highway" for the resulting long-distance interaction made possible by ICTs. Both ICTs and the market provide the two key attributes of networks.

> The performance of a given network will then depend on two fundamental attributes of the network: its *connectedness*, that is its structural ability to facilitate noise-free communication between its components; its *consistency*, that is the extent to which there is [a] sharing of interests between the network's goals and the goals of its components.[65]

Both *connectedness* and *consistency* are supplied respectively by ICTs and the market. The market provides consistency through its unceasing service of matching economic entities with a coincidence of goals and needs.[66]

From Manufacturing to Information Processing

The nature of the firm has changed in a highly dynamic business environment of continuous innovations, falling prices, accelerated pace, and complex products and services. Prior to the technological breakthroughs in ICTs in the 1980s, a "Fordist vertical integration" was the appropriate business model. In his classic article "The Nature of the Firm," Ronald Coase (1937) observes that it made rational economic sense for firms to integrate their operations vertically given the high transaction (searching, bargaining, and enforcing contracts) and coordination costs of farming out their requirements to outside subcontractors through the market. It would have been a very tedious and expensive process to monitor the manifold transactions they would have had to negotiate and complete through the marketplace. It was much cheaper for firms to consolidate their operations and supply their needs from in-house facilities. For example, in the early days of the automotive industry, General Motors and Ford manufactured most of the critical components of their vehicles.

Such Fordist vertical integration no longer makes business sense in the current economic climate. What is needed is the exact opposite—horizontal integration (international vertical specialization).[67] This entails extensive subcontracting and networking with other firms, even for its core competencies.[68] Furthermore, trends indicate a further rapid pace in offshore outsourcing and trade in parts and components.[69] The IMF (2002, 129) lists three proximate causes behind this phenomenon, namely: the improvement in services links, market liberalization, and product standardization. To this, I add a fourth factor: hypercompetition. I examine each of these in what follows.

First, a vastly improved global transportation and communications network due to ICTs has provided a "virtual link" to far-flung sites. Distance has increasingly become irrelevant or less important in most firms' sourcing or location decisions because of the technological breakthroughs in microelectronics.[70] Indeed, this is yet another example of how technological changes induce complementary organizational changes.[71] Recall, for example, how the telegraph expanded the scope of the marketplace. The electric motor permitted smaller-scale production enterprises, led to greater flexibility in the layout of plants, and transformed the machine tool industry. The steam engine altered the industrial base and the transportation network of the nineteenth century in a dramatic fashion.[72] And, of course, electricity and the automobile left their indelible mark as they shaped twentieth-century society in the way people lived, worked, and interacted with each other. These organizational innovations precipitated by technological changes spawned productivity gains that rippled throughout the economy. For example, gains from the adoption of electricity ultimately came from the organizational changes it engendered, accounting for as much as 70 percent of electricity's contribution to U.S. economic growth for the period 1919–29.[73] We see the same dynamic at work in our contemporary Kondratieff cycle. Today, technological changes due to microelectronics have given rise to the "networked society," the signal organizational innovation of the digital era.[74]

Organizational changes have been instrumental in reaping the full benefits of ICTs. Numerous empirical studies show that the computerization of business functions without accompanying organizational changes may in fact hurt, rather than boost, productivity. Firms with a decentralized organizational structure garnered a higher productivity as a result of ICTs.[75] Moreover, the full gains from ICTs come, not from controlling work processes, but from creating innovative organizational structures that make firms even more responsive to change and learning. A critical benefit of ICTs is that they "provide options for designing work and business processes."[76] This flexibility is important especially in a knowledge economy characterized by so much flux and unexpected events requiring a swift response. The combination of ICTs and their attendant changes in business processes and structures has led to increased productivity, cost reduction, and improved product quality.[77]

A second cause of international vertical specialization is governments' liberalization of their respective domestic economies. This greater openness has facilitated the cross-border exchange of components, intermediate goods, and final products. Trade barriers and restrictions would have made international vertical specialization very difficult, if possible at all, given the substantial additional costs involved in having to deal with bureaucratic red tape and tariffs.

Third, the microchip and other technological changes have led to the standardization of parts for a wide variety of products, from simple computer electronics to even the most complex products like cars and airplanes. For example, despite their fierce rivalry, Boeing and Airbus use the same suppliers for some of their key components.[78] Such standardization has resulted in huge economies of scale. It makes more sense for firms to subcontract with specialist manufacturers who produce these parts at volume prices instead of fabricating them in-house. Outsourcing these parts is no longer merely an option; it is an imperative of business survival.

To these three main drivers of international vertical specialization enumerated by the IMF, I add a fourth factor—the hypercompetition inaugurated by globalization. Recall from the preceding chapter's section on *Competitive Networking* that current market conditions have compelled firms to collaborate with each other in order to respond faster in a highly dynamic environment, minimize losses from ever-riskier ventures, access highly specialized skills, match their competitors' networking, and secure technology transfers.

Transforming the Firm

These remote and proximate factors (improvement in service links, market liberalization, product standardization, and hypercompetition) account for the unfolding metamorphosis of the global economy into a single integrated workshop in which parts are made in a variety of continents for eventual shipment and assembly in designated sites. Nyholm et al. (2001, 256–67) describe the mechanics of this shift in business organization at the microeconomic level. In the pre-ICT era when transaction, transportation, and coordination costs were high, firms supplied their own requirements through a division of labor along functional lines (e.g., marketing, engineering, etc.) and with multiple manufacturing facilities at different locations. There were clear lines of decision making characterized by a top-down approach to management. Such a hierarchical organizational structure made sense in view of expensive coordination costs; it was essential to minimize the number of communication nodes. The process of innovation was sequential and predictable. Innovations within the firm followed a traditional linear trajectory: from the R&D crew that developed the technology, to the manufacturing engineers, to the marketing experts, and then to the sales staff.

In contrast, contemporary globalization requires a model of networking in which people pool together their knowledge and expertise. Instead of a hierarchy, the firm is organized in flexible work teams that freely interact with each other without any formal channels of communication or protocols. The difference is most clearly evident in the manner in which innovation is pursued in the knowledge economy. Instead of the aforementioned linear and sequential approach to innovation, all departments are immediately involved in the design of the product. R&D personnel, brand managers, sales staff, and production engineers are brought on board early in the project. Innovation is understood to be nonlinear, interactive, and intensive in the use and sharing of each other's tacit knowledge. Moreover, speed in product changeover is of the essence in the "new competition" as we have seen in the preceding chapter.[79] "Flexible specialization" is an essential strength in which producers respond quickly to market opportunities as they arise.[80] For example, in reaction to the end of the textile and apparel quotas on January 1, 2005, major retailers and Chinese subcontractors consolidated their operations to lower costs and speed up the supply chain. As part of this shake-up, fashion designers, trend spotters, fabric suppliers, button manufacturers, and anyone else who has a critical role in the design, manufacture, and sale of apparel are brought to one place, close to the factory floor. Such reorganization (the "supply-chain city") has avoided a duplication of effort and personnel and has greatly reduced the time it takes to launch new designs.[81]

Observe the subtle, but significant, change that has occurred in the nature of the twenty-first century firm. In the industrial economy, the focus of business was to produce goods or services and then to get them to the consumer in the most cost-effective manner. In contrast, firms in the knowledge economy aim at handling and using information creatively and expeditiously. Business in the knowledge economy is no longer concerned merely or primarily with manufacturing, but with managing information.

> The factors determining a firm's competitiveness have changed over time. Today it is not necessarily the cost of traditional inputs that determine whether a firm is competitive or not, *but its organizational*

competence, its ability to understand and adopt new knowledge, to read market signals, and to adjust to customer needs.[82]

The bottleneck is no longer the cost of computation but the capacity to innovate and use available information nimbly and profitably.[83] Thus, the key constraint is human capital, and collaborative work with others is one way of getting around this limitation.

The digital age has inaugurated a new basic unit of economic organization—the network of firms working together on overlapping goals.[84] What binds these networks together is their mutual need for each other's proprietary abilities and resources for advantage and gain. The importance of networks rises in direct proportion to the complexity and centrality of information management in the economy.[85]

If twenty-first-century business is, indeed, more about the administration of information than manufacturing, it makes sense for the firm not to operate its own production facilities but to subcontract with specialists who can produce each segment of the value chain reliably and competitively. Outsourcing allows for a much quicker response compared to having to worry about the overhead expenditures (plants, equipment, and personnel) that come with relying on one's own manufacturing facilities. Thus, the model of networking, supplier networks in particular, makes sense for major retail chains and brand names. Unpredictable changes in fashion and tastes require responsiveness and agility.

There is a similar phenomenon regarding consumer electronics and computers. Take the case of the major PC laptop brands. As of 2004, Dell, Apple, Gateway, and Acer were outsourcing 100 percent of their laptops. Other major companies were not too far behind with their outsourcing ratios, such as HP (95 percent), NEC (60 percent), and Sony (50 percent). The comparative advantage of these firms is no longer in manufacturing but in product development and marketing. As we have seen from earlier anecdotes, the same dynamic is true even for the garage or mom-and-pop start-ups that run "virtual" businesses and simply rely on overseas subcontractors and local warehousing and transportation specialists to handle all the facets of their operations except for design and sales.[86]

To appreciate the full extent of the transformation of the contemporary firm, one only has to look at the changes in the automotive industry, which has long been the paradigm of what manufacturing is all about. In fact, the fourth long-wave cycle is called the "Fordist mass production Kondratieff."[87] We have come a long way since then. Today, not only have the automotive makers embraced international vertical specialization, but they are even seriously considering transferring to smaller contract manufacturers the responsibility for making the entire car. This would permit the major car makers to concentrate only on design, engineering, and marketing.[88]

Impact

It is best to conclude this section by illustrating the potency and the self-reinforcing dynamic of these networks.[89] Take the case of the supplier networks undergirding the ICT sector and their stunning impact in reshaping East Asia. Between 1990 and 1999, IT goods as a percentage of regional exports for Asia[90] increased from around 16 to nearly 25 percent. Japan showed a comparable gain from around 13 to 20 percent. These figures are in sharp contrast to Europe's that hovered around 5 percent during this period and that of the United States and Canada, which had a modest increase from 8 to 10 percent.[91] The importance of ICTs for Asia is reflected in the impressive share of net exports of electronics as a proportion of GDP for the individual countries of Asia.[92]

What is noteworthy about the ICT industry is its high degree of international vertical specialization. It is estimated that anywhere from 50 to 75 percent of Asia's ICT production and exports are from imported intermediate goods, coming from within the region itself. In other words, intra-industry trade in the East Asian ICT sector is intense.[93] In the period from 1996 to 2000, intra-industry trade accounted for 75 percent of the growth in the total trade of East Asia. This is at least twice that of the other developing regions.[94] In fact, it has even been suggested that the label "made in China" is inaccurate for many products because China has increasingly been used merely as a final assembly point with parts coming from all over the world.[95]

International vertical specialization is not pursued as an end in itself. In fact, there are enormous upfront overhead investments that must be incurred to facilitate coordination and communications in a "fragmented" production structure. Moreover, additional inventories-in-transit, longer lead times, and transportation costs are incurred to get parts and components from one overseas site to another. That vertical specialization is nevertheless still pursued despite these hurdles and added costs is testimony to the sizable cost savings that it generates in slicing up the value chain into ever-finer segments. It is also reflective of the economies of scale brought about by market deepening and widening.

It is estimated that in the early 1990s, around 30 percent of global trade in manufactures involved some kind of production sharing arrangement. Note that this phenomenon is not limited only to high-technology goods such as the transport and machinery sectors. Production sharing was also found to be prevalent in labor-intensive manufactures such as textiles and clothing, leather goods, and footwear.[96]

What difference has international vertical specialization made for efficiency? First, the continued precipitous drop in prices for micro-electronics and information processing described in chapter 2 is partly due to the fierce rivalry between these ICT supplier networks. The resulting competitive innovation and competitive networking lead to ever more radical product-quality improvements.

Second, ICT-producing nations have acquired even more hands-on experience in trading in the global marketplace; they have augmented their already considerable tacit knowledge as seasoned international traders. This intangible trade-enhancing impact of international vertical specialization is noteworthy because empirical studies point to the importance of trade as an engine of growth[97] and as a vehicle for technological transfers and diffusion.[98] In other words, trade occasions large and expansive spillover effects in the domestic economies.[99]

Finally, the unrestrained drop in the price of microelectronics and information processing has been responsible for the ubiquity and the pervasive impact of ICTs since the 1980s. Despite the difficulty of measuring the productivity gains from ICTs at this early stage, studies already indicate that there are appreciable benefits reaped by ICT end users.[100] Gains have already been comparable to those of earlier carrier inputs at much later stages of their cycles. It is very likely that these early payoffs are merely a small part of much larger forthcoming returns. Further advances in ICTs will have substantial externalities on market processes, such as international vertical specialization. These resulting organizational changes and innovations, in their own turn, will make ICT producers leaner, nimbler, more responsive, more intensely competitive, and more creative. In other words, the efficiency spawned by international vertical specialization is self-reinforcing and ripples through not only the ICT sector but the rest of society as well. The biggest winners, thus far, have been the end users, courtesy of the efficiency-market nexus undergirding international vertical specialization.

Summary and Conclusions

The efficient use of a nation's scarce resources matters because (1) it maximizes the collective welfare and (2) it is a necessary condition for the long-term viability of the community. Economic history provides abundant empirical evidence to support this claim. The glaring contrast between the Soviet-style economies and Western-style capitalism was in large part due to the productive efficiency of the latter. The breathtaking economic performance of China in the past twenty-five years, unparalleled in modern history, can be attributed to the more market-oriented, efficiency-enhancing policies it adopted from 1979 onwards. The same can be said of India and Vietnam since they similarly embraced market reforms. The move by many other nations toward a more market-friendly political economy in the last half of the twentieth century reflects an appreciation for the central importance of economic efficiency.[101] There is a stark difference between nations that reaped the full benefits of liberalization (e.g., the NICs such as the Asian Tigers) compared to the failed states in sub-Saharan Africa. The latter have even regressed in the past thirty years due largely to their inability to use their natural and human resources productively. Economic efficiency matters, not only in the textbook model of the perfectly competitive market, but in practice as well. History and empirical evidence suggest that nations ignore economic efficiency to their own detriment. The judicious and productive use of scarce resources, especially in the face of rival consumption and finite means, is a pragmatic goal that reasonable people would want to achieve.

The market creates value whenever it combines information in ever-new creative ways or whenever it brings people together to collaborate in networks, thus pushing the technological frontier even further. Globalization promotes both of these, and there are significant opportunity losses to curtailing the smooth functioning of the market. As we have repeatedly seen in the last few chapters, ICTs have made markets even more efficient at creating value. ICTs have led to more, better, and timely information. ICTs have made powerful data-handling tools readily available and affordable. This has greatly enhanced economic agents' access to and use of information (e.g., the Internet), leading to improved and quicker decision making and adjustment. By extension, this also makes the market an even better information-processing institution. We have also seen how ICTs have been responsible for incorporating even the most isolated communities into the global marketplace, for increasing the volume of trade, for creating new forms of market exchange (e.g., eBay, B2B), for organizational innovations such as international vertical specialization, for easier collaborative and strategic networking, for an accelerated economic pace, and for even greater market access and opportunities for small- and medium-scale enterprises and farms. All these changes have led to greater productivity, leaner and more creative firms, decentralization, an empowered private sector, faster growth, and a telescoped development process. Indeed, the fifth Kondratieff cycle is different from all the earlier technological revolutions because it is the core process of the market itself that has been transformed, thanks to our current long-wave cycle's carrier input: cheap information.

But this is not the end of the process; it is only half of the entire story. For, the market, in its own turn, feeds back and strengthens the infrastructure and the mechanisms that ensure technological dynamism. The market has been described, aptly, as the milieu for innovations. As we have seen, the market is an excellent vehicle for discovery and information processing, for nurturing and unleashing private initiative, for weeding out poor outcomes and rewarding performance, for facilitating change, for managing risk, for accumulating tacit knowledge via "learning by doing," for pairing complementary technological and organizational innovations, and for bringing together economic agents with like interests and matching needs—all the critical ingredients for even more profound techno-economic paradigms in the next rounds of economic activity. And, the market does all this in a swift, seamless, and cost-effective manner. International vertical specialization is an excellent illustration of the synergy between technology and the marketplace; better economic efficiency has been the product of such a synergy.

The knowledge economy is characterized by a self-reinforcing dynamic. ICTs strengthen the market further as a "milieu of innovations."[102] Microelectronics strikes at the heart of the market process itself and has made it even better and faster at producing the next generation of ICTs or like technologies. It has been a "market-led speed up of innovation."[103] After all, technological and organizational innovations are price-sensitive. Indeed, the knowledge economy can truly be said to have a self-feeding momentum, that is, self-sustaining gales of "creative destruction."[104] Efficiency and the attendant institution that brings it about, that is, the market, matter even more in the digital age.

Chapter 5

Preconditions and Limitations of Efficiency: Considering the Distributive Dimension of Price

The price mechanism has an allocative dimension because it induces economic agents to put their scarce resources to their most valued uses. This lays the groundwork for sustainable long-term growth and, thus, economic efficiency is unavoidable as a criterion of distributive justice and as a proximate end of market operations. However, efficiency can be neither the only nor necessarily the primary goal of economic life. After all, the price mechanism also has a distributive dimension. The same price movements that lead to the most efficient disposition of resources have the collateral effect of redistributing burdens and benefits within the economy.

For example, the gentrification (urban renewal) of rundown sections of a city is a boon to local merchants, property owners, and the city as a whole. It enhances property values, brings new business to the area, and expands the tax base of the city. However, all these may come at the expense of the more vulnerable property tenants such as the elderly and the retired who may be living on fixed incomes. The rise in property values from gentrification is generally accompanied by a corresponding rise in property and residential rental rates. Longtime residents may be forced to seek affordable housing elsewhere. In other words, the allocative function of price is only one side of the coin. It is always accompanied by redistributive ripple effects. There are always winners and losers in price adjustments; there are always both beneficial and adverse pecuniary externalities.

This chapter calls for extra-market interventions in rectifying the harmful distributive ramifications of market operations. It makes this case by arguing that each economic actor faces a different, indeed unique, set of "full" prices in participating in the marketplace. Moreover, it is the poor who often face the steepest entry cost to market participation, a disadvantage that only worsens over time because of the phenomena of bounded rationality and path dependence. The market is unable to correct its deleterious outcomes on its own and requires assistance from without. I discuss each of these in the sections that follow.

The Market as an Effective Price Discriminator

The price mechanism is the core process that makes the market what it is. In the textbook model of the perfectly competitive market, economic welfare (measured in terms of preference satisfaction) is maximized by allocating goods and factors of production according to their respective price ratios.[1] Prices are essential to market operations because they provide the information that guides economic actors in the allotment of their resources. It is the common denominator that permits the exchange of what would have otherwise been incommensurable goods and services; we know how many apples to exchange for shoes because of their relative prices. Unfortunately, the marketplace can sometimes be regressive in the manner by which it sets these prices. This phenomenon has already been examined at length elsewhere,[2] but I would like to extend the discussion further in this chapter by showing how these regressive instances may in fact be self-reinforcing, especially in the knowledge economy.

First, let us quickly review the nature of the market as an effective price discriminator. Becker (1965) and Lancaster (1966) have offered an alternative approach to consumer theory by incorporating time in the traditional model. Each economic actor is no longer viewed merely as a consuming agent, but as a "micro-firm" producing commodities using goods, services, and time as inputs. In the traditional model of consumer theory, the maximization exercise facing *homo oeconomicus* is as follows:

Maximize: $U = f(y)$

subject to:

Income = Price x Inputs of goods/services

where:

U = utility
y = goods and services (such as food, clothing, books, etc.)

Becker (1965) and Lancaster (1966) recast this model as:

Maximize $Q = f(y, t)$

subject to:

Full income = Expenses
Wage × 24 hours = (Price × Inputs) + (Wage × Time input)

where:

Q = Beckerian-Lancasterian commodities (such as nutrition, learning, rest, fellowship, etc.)
y = goods and services (such as food, clothing, books, etc.)
t = time expended in producing Beckerian-Lancasterian commodities

Consumers do not consume goods and services (e.g., food, books, theater tickets) for their own sake, but for the qualities and characteristics that they provide (e.g., nutrition, learning, recreation). The latter are what we call Beckerian-Lancasterian commodities, and it is these that are maximized, not the goods and services consumed as per traditional consumer theory.

The inclusion of time in the model and the reformulation of the exercise from one of mere consumption to one of production-consumption have the collateral benefit of explicitly recognizing the pivotal role of human capital. Thus, we can rewrite the household production model as:

Maximize $Q = K f(y, t)$

where:

K = human capital (reflected in skills, talents, aptitudes, etc.)
y = goods and services (such as food, clothing, books, etc.)
t = time expended in producing Beckerian-Lancasterian commodities

Let us now examine in what manner the market is an effective price discriminator on the basis of these Beckerian-Lancasterian household production functions.

First, each of these "household production functions" is unique because it is person- or household-specific. After all, human capital is embodied in economic actors who/that are different from each other. Personal and collective capabilities are critical because they determine how efficiently and effectively economic agents allocate, use, and benefit from purchased goods and services. This is not even to mention the critical role of human capital in seeking, interpreting, and using information in the marketplace. The higher the human capital (K), the more efficient is the household production function and the less inputs of time, goods, and services it requires.[3] For example, the empirical literature shows that more educated mothers tend to have healthier children even after correcting for the effects of their higher incomes.[4]

Second, sociohistorical location also matters. The social position of people determines the market prices they have to pay, the obstacles they face, and the degree to which they are subjected to volatility and disequilibria. For example, farmers face greater risks and uncertainties compared with industrial manufacturers by the nature of their trade and their social status. Both social location and personal/collective capabilities shape the ease or difficulty with which market participants are able to access social goods. Both also influence the market's valuation of these economic agents' endowments and, by extension, their purchasing power. The more advanced their human capital and the better their sociohistorical location, the higher is their wage rate.[5]

Third, the "full" price that people pay for the commodities they produce-consume is comprised of both the market price of the inputs (goods/services consumed) and the time that it takes to complete the task. The more inefficient or ineffective the human capital, the higher will be the "full" price paid in terms of the person's time and effort.[6] And, as people have widely divergent human capital, these "full" prices will also be unique across different economic agents. This has important ramifications in any discussion of distributive justice because the poor often end up paying a much higher "full" price for certain commodities. They are not likely to have the requisite skills and education. For example, with the advent of the knowledge economy, gaining computer competency would be much easier for the well-educated compared with those who have had minimal schooling or job training. In fact, high-level computer skills may even be out of the latter's reach. Thus, not only does the marketplace assign economic agents different "full" prices, it may even be regressive by charging those with minimal human capital (most likely the poor) a much steeper entry cost to market participation than it does those who are computer literate.

Fourth, Becker and Lancaster's household production model can be extended to collective economic agency at any level of aggregation. Hence, we can easily employ the model, as I do in what follows, as a national production function, in which case K stands for the country's social and collective human capital.

Fifth, this all-important human or social capital is endogenous as it is a function of previous periods' consumption of these Beckerian-Lancasterian commodities. In other words, the past is important because human or social capital formation is path dependent in its development and growth. The adverse impact of the market as an effective price discriminator is aggravated by this path dependence.

In sum, there is a price to participating in and availing of the benefits of the marketplace. These prices differ across economic agents depending on their human capital and their sociohistorical location within the community. Moreover, these prices can often be regressive wherein the poor pay much more in terms of time, effort, and money compared to the wealthy and the middle class.

Path Dependence

Economic changes generally occur in increments; marginal adjustments are typical in economic life. To this we can add that the economy is autocorrelated, which is to say that it builds on itself and works with what it has to begin with. The market is characterized by path dependence in which later outcomes are partly a function of what had transpired in the earlier rounds of economic exchange. This is not to say that the market is incapable of accommodating revolutionary changes or of moving in a new or opposite direction. The five long-wave cycles we have had since the advent of the industrial age are proof of the adaptability of the market to new conditions. All I am claiming is that future economic outcomes are influenced by, indeed even a product of, previous and current economic transactions. In other words, just like a moving train or ship, the market has a momentum deriving from operations in the preceding periods. This inertia will build on itself unless altered by a major force or transformed gradually by changes at the margin, as is the case in regular market operations. Thus, even for the Kondratieff cycles we have had, the later techno-economic revolutions were the result of the accomplishments, inadequacies, and bottlenecks of the preceding carrier inputs.[7] There are at least three proximate causes for this path dependence that should be examined: the institutional preconditions of the marketplace, bounded rationality, and the market as a network externality.[8]

Institutional Preconditions

The market often operates so smoothly that we take its services for granted; we have come to expect it as a normal part of community life. Indeed, we would be lost without it. But its ubiquity and impact have not always been this way. In fact, it took centuries to slowly develop and perfect the various institutions that underpin the modern marketplace: property rights and their attendant legal infrastructure, contract law, limited-liability corporations, double-entry bookkeeping, insurance, banking, capital markets, letters of credit, and risk-diffusing financial instruments.[9] This is not an exhaustive list, and there are surely many other business practices and institutions that make economic exchange not only possible but also cost-effective and enforceable. Institutions have been defined as the formal and informal constraints that shape the content and the quality of interactions within a nation. Examples include organizational entities, established procedures, and regulatory structures.[10] The requisite institutional preconditions for the smooth functioning of the market have also been described as those that establish "an incentive structure that reduces uncertainty and promotes efficiency" and those that foster "better policy choices."[11] The IMF cites examples such as central bank independence, balanced budget amendments, properly designed and executed international trade agreements, and regulations that give rise to appropriate labor, product, and financial markets. Concrete measures to gauge the presence and quality of such institutions include the degree of transparency, political rights, the extent and enforceability of laws protecting private property rights, and public sector efficiency.[12]

This immediate, enabling, environment is itself enveloped within an even larger, overarching moral and cultural framework.[13] Despite all the institutional checks and balances, not all possible contingencies of economic exchange can be anticipated. These gray areas, and there are many of them, must ultimately be covered by trust, moral norms, and personal honesty. Take the simple case of accepting checks, of prepayment for later deliveries, of buying or selling on eBay, or of employees whose work output and performance are impossible to supervise. There must be a minimum level of trustworthiness on the part of economic agents if the market is to work at all. Otherwise, the transaction costs (e.g., monitoring and enforcement) would be prohibitive.

In the final analysis, market participants have to accept each other's word at face value. Culture influences economic performance.[14] Moral norms are a necessary condition for economic efficiency and viability, and they are integral to the social capital that shapes market outcomes and processes.[15] Nations facing the same market conditions and opportunities end up with widely divergent results because of differences in the quality of their respective institutions.[16] The market may appear to be a simple straightforward operation, requiring minimal maintenance and supervision on the surface, but in reality it is shored up by an intricate web of legal, epistemological, ontological, organizational, corporate, and financial foundations that took time to build, refine, and maintain.[17] And because economic life is, by its nature, dynamic, especially with the advent of the knowledge economy, these substructures are constantly evolving. In other words, the marketplace neither arises nor operates in a void; it has institutional preconditions. Not surprisingly, economic processes and outcomes are materially affected by the quality of these underlying foundations. The market can accomplish only as much as its overarching framework permits. The presence and quality of these institutional preconditions take on even greater importance in the information age because of capital mobility. After all, investments flow to nations whose institutions create a friendly and stable environment.

Bounded Rationality

Herbert Simon (1976) doubts that the process of maximization according to neoclassical consumer theory is an accurate description of how economic agents behave in practice. Market participants face so many choices that it would simply tax human computational capacities to have to weigh available alternatives for every decision they make. Besides, economic actors would have very little time left for anything else if they had to do all these calculations for every choice.[18] Such instrumental rationality is simply impractical and unworkable. Thus, Simon proposes that economic agents employ procedural or bounded rationality in which choices are made on the basis of rules of thumb. People do not maximize; rather, they "satisfice," that is, they settle on choices that may not necessarily be the optimum or the maximum but are nonetheless satisfactory enough. Thus, economic agents are spared the tedious task of having to spend most of their time in an interminable computational exercise.

These rules of thumb and preset procedures are gradually accumulated as custom, law, and usage. People are rational and learn from their mistakes. They observe what works and what does not under different circumstances and adjust their behavior and subsequent decisions accordingly. Market participants learn not only from their own mistakes but also from others' as well. In other words, the convenience provided by bounded rationality is built up over a long period and is based on time-tested formal and informal conventions that are continually refined.[19] In fact, such custom, law, and usage are part of the market's foundational institutions described in the preceding section. Thus, the past unavoidably influences current economic affairs. Where people are and where they have been matter both for the opportunities open to them and for how they make their choices. There is a path dependence even in the manner people arrive at their decisions.

If markets truly operate according to bounded rationality, this means historical experience (path dependence) takes on even greater significance. This is so because the regressive nature of past disadvantageous rules or outcomes can take a life of its own and perpetrate the same cycle in subsequent rounds of economic activity. Moreover, later market outcomes reinforce this bounded rationality further. This is a vicious cycle that can be broken only through extra-market remedies that reshape and recast some of the norms and established practices embedded within the market's formal and informal conventions.

The Market as a Network Externality

Chapter 8 examines the phenomenon of the market as a network externality in greater depth. For now, it is sufficient to note that the market becomes even more valuable to its participants as more people partake of it. Such a market expansion benefits all its participants by providing an even wider menu of choices and trading possibilities. An excellent example of this phenomenon is eBay. People use this "virtual" market because of its critical mass of buyers and sellers. The larger this critical mass, the better it is as a venue for locating and completing mutually beneficial exchanges. A similar dynamic works for malls. The more numerous their stores and restaurants, the more enticing they are for the choices they offer. Note that the attraction of Wal-Mart and other giant retailers is not just their low prices but also the wide variety of items they stock.

An expanding marketplace also facilitates a further division of labor with beneficial economies of scale and an even more cost-effective production of goods and services. A wider market, better specialization, economies of scale, and lower costs all lay the groundwork for more technological and organizational innovations. These innovations, for their part, expand and improve the market even further, thereby completing a self-reinforcing cycle as we have seen in the last chapter. We also saw how technological and organizational changes are not isolated events but are shaped by their economic environment. Moreover, they are autocorrelated, that is, they build on existing techniques in ever-new and creative ways. In all these cases, observe how the market's vitality is a function of its past. There is a path dependence in the manner by which the market grows and by which it generates the gales of "creative destruction" that imbue it with such vitality.

Why Should Path Dependence Matter for Distributive Justice?

The market's institutional preconditions, its bounded rationality, and its dynamic as a network externality are chiefly responsible for economic life's path dependence. But why should path dependence matter? Why should we be concerned about it as we evaluate efficiency as a criterion of distributive justice? The economy's path dependence matters for distributive justice because it makes it that much more important to address the market's adverse effects, and to do so promptly, especially in the information age.

As we have seen in chapter 4, the market is particularly good at creating value if it is allowed to operate with economic efficiency as its proximate goal. However, we have to be cautious because the allocative function of price has unavoidable, unpleasant distributive ramifications. As discussed before, these are often regressive because it is the poor and those who are unable to fend for themselves who eventually bear the brunt of these adverse pecuniary externalities. A strength of the market, especially with the knowledge economy, is the real possibility of geographic, social, and even virtual mobility that it permits. This is a major improvement from the organic, hierarchical structure of the premodern era in which people were often locked into their social status and occupations based on birth. However, this modern mobility may, in fact, be more apparent than real for many who find themselves unable to keep up with the rising entry cost to meaningful market participation. Path dependence means that people's sociohistorical location shapes (1) the scope and quality of their opportunities and (2) their personal and social means to pursue these possibilities for advancement. Path dependence becomes even more important in the digital age, which requires ever more advanced human capital, better tacit knowledge (know-who and know-how), and greater agility and responsiveness in the face of an ever faster economic pace marked by unexpected turbulence. The information economy provides bountiful economic rents, but only for those who can navigate its dangerous shoals with speed and finesse.

The entry cost to meaningful and successful market participation has been rising, and at an accelerated pace, as a consequence of the exacting demands of the knowledge economy described in chapter 3. In other words, the bar for what constitutes adequate social and human capital keeps getting higher and higher. Path dependence means that it will be difficult for those who are trailing to keep up with the rest of the economy. The gap will widen even more as those who are endowed with the necessary human and social capital reap much and develop their capital even further, while those who have little to begin with find it difficult, if not impossible, just to keep their heads above water. We run the risk of giving rise to a permanent underclass. A market that is left on its own to pursue efficiency as a proximate goal will not correct this situation because it is not designed to do so. Recall that an unfettered market gives full vent to the allocative function of price and is not concerned with its distributive consequences.

The Coase (1960) theorem[20] succinctly illustrates why the market's pecuniary externalities are left unaddressed in neoclassical economics, unlike technological externalities. In the Coase theorem, "the initial allocation of legal entitlements does not matter from an efficiency perspective so long as they can be freely exchanged."[21] To this observation we can add that the final allocation is not considered either; it is irrelevant to the theorem. This is a glaring weakness of the Coase theorem as it disregards the distribution of the costs and benefits of the parties' bargaining. Symmetry in cost and benefits between the parties involved is not of interest to the Coase theorem.[22] In other words, the incidence of the burdens of such a transaction does not count at all; the overriding goal is to achieve Pareto efficiency.

Thus, extra-market action is needed to correct adverse distributive outcomes. More important for our study, path dependence means that efficiency cannot be a sufficient condition for distributive justice. Even as efficiency is indispensable, it cannot be the only goal of economic life because the market is not self-correcting when it comes to its problematic outcomes. By its nature, the market is marked by distributive flaws because its path dependence may prevent sociohistorically disadvantaged economic agents from upgrading their human or social capital to the levels required by a very fluid and demanding knowledge economy. In fact, path dependence may worsen past deprivations and even turn them into insurmountable hurdles for the hapless market participants left behind. Obviously, this exclusion of segments of the population damages long-term allocative efficiency in the knowledge economy because it is depriving itself of vital human capital, the principal source of wealth creation.

Empirical Evidence

The empirical evidence on the negative impact of path dependence on market outcomes is vast. Hence, I will present only a sampling of empirical studies to illustrate the adverse ripple effects of market operations in cases in which poor human capital, a disadvantageous sociohistorical location, and a self-reinforcing path dependence all mutually reinforce each other to exclude populations at risk in the knowledge economy.

Modern market exchange and international trade, in particular, have led to more vibrant and much faster growth.[23] Critics of globalization would be hardpressed to deny the improved standards of living seen in rising incomes, wealth, and social indicators, such as longer life expectancies, higher literacy, and better health care. Nevertheless, we cannot ignore the other side of the coin: There are those who have been hurt by global economic integration. Longitudinal and cross-country studies provide empirical evidence of how path dependence can indeed produce a permanent underclass.

Poverty Traps and Cross-National Comparison

Path dependence in market outcomes is evident regardless of how poverty is measured. Take the case of "income mobility" between 1980 and 2002, a period that coincides with our contemporary globalization.[24] Within a sample of 138 countries for which data for purchasing power parity (PPP)–adjusted gross national income (GNI) are available, there is a mixed record of upward income mobility for some and stagnation and even regression for others.[25] China is the miracle story. With a GNI per capita of less than $710, it constituted 93 percent of the bottom decile (10 percent) of the world's per capita income in 1980.[26] By 2002, China jumped three income categories to be in the $2890–$10,000 per capita income range. However, this is only one side of the coin. During the same period, twenty-six countries, mostly from Africa and many with negative growth rates, lost ground and retrogressed into the bottom income decile. With the exception of China, all the countries in the bottom decile in 1980 were still stuck in the same decile in 2002.[27] In fact, all of them with the exception of Mozambique were below the global economic growth rate. Even more alarming is the observation that 16 percent (nearly one out of every six!) of those who were in the second ($711–$1100) or third ($1101–$2890) income ranges in 1980 fell to the lowest income category (less than $710) by 2002.[28]

This income-class immobility is confirmed by other statistics that also find an increasing polarization.[29] There has been widening inequality both within and across countries, especially in this third era of globalization.[30] In breaking down global income by deciles, we find a consistent pattern in the annual growth rates for two time periods (1960–78 and 1978–2000). The bottom income deciles were not growing as fast the top deciles. For the period 1960–78, the top income decile was growing at twice the annual growth rate of the bottom decile. It was worse for 1978–2000. The bottom group declined by 0.1 percent per year during this period versus an annual 1.9 percent growth rate for the top decile.[31]

From 1960 to 2000, the per capita income of developed countries grew while that of developing nations stagnated. Moreover, compare the increase of GDP per capita in absolute terms: For the wealthiest group of countries, income rose from $16,000 to $43,600 while the lowest income group saw an increase from $102 to $280.[32] The gap in absolute terms widened even further. In addition, there were few countries in the intermediate range ($6,000 to $16,000); most nations had per capita incomes less than $6,000.[33] Even the reduction by 400 million people worldwide of those living under $1 a day between 1981 and 2001 has to be tempered by the deepening poverty in sub-Saharan Africa where the number of people living below $1 a day increased nearly a 100 percent from 160 million in 1981 to 313 million by 2001.[34] In addition, the international goal of cutting the $1-a-day poverty rate of 1990 in half will most likely occur only in East and South Asia.[35] Indeed, these numbers highlight the uneven strides achieved in poverty alleviation in different parts of the world.

To further underscore the persistence of poverty, note the importance of economic growth in accounting for global income distribution. Annual real GDP growth for East Asia and the Pacific increased from 5.5 percent (1960–80) to 8.5 percent (1980–2000). In contrast, sub-Saharan Africa's growth rate was cut in half from 4.4 percent (1960–80) to 2.2 percent (1980–2000).[36] Even as sub-Saharan Africa's annual growth rate is forecast to increase to 3.3 percent for the next two decades (2008–30), it is still expected that most of the poor in the world by 2030 will be in sub-Saharan Africa.[37] Moreover, even as other regions catch up with the per capita income of highly developed nations in the next twenty years, sub-Saharan Africa will remain stagnant. East Asia and the Pacific's per capita income was around 18 percent of wealthy nations' GDP per capita in 2000. This is expected to double to around 35 percent by 2030. In contrast, sub-Saharan Africa's per capita income has been around 5 percent of developed nations' per capita income and is expected to stay at the same level. In other words, even with an annual growth rate of 3.3 percent for the next generation, sub-Saharan Africa will not make any headway in closing the income gap; it is merely running furiously in place just to keep up with the marketplace.[38]

The prognosis for sub-Saharan Africa is even bleaker if tacit knowledge (and therefore, learning by doing) is indeed the key to wealth creation in the digital age as the previous chapters suggest. Compare, for example, the performance of different emerging nations over time with respect to merchandise exports. As a share of total global merchandise exports, developing nations in Latin America held a fairly steady share from 5.5 percent in 1970 and 1980 to 5 percent in 2004. The Asian "miracle" is evident in their share of global merchandise exports that was 9 percent in 1970, increased to 18 percent by 1980, and then to 26 percent by 2004, nearly a threefold increase. In contrast, sub-Saharan Africa began with slightly over 2 percent in 1970, declined to 1.5 percent by 1980, and was eventually reduced further to 1 percent by 2004.[39] These trends suggest that sub-Saharan Africa cannot compete in the tough but rewarding international trade in manufactures. This shuts out sub-Saharan Africa from the most dynamic niches of the global marketplace and prevents it from using the market as a stepping stone to self-help, self-improvement, and development. It is caught in a poverty trap, a vicious cycle in which its lack of market participation leaves it unable to acquire the necessary know-how and experience to compete effectively in the subsequent rounds of economic activity, thereby isolating it even further from the marketplace. The region's poverty is not the result of its global market participation but rather a result of the lack of it.

It is ironic that a fourth world has emerged during the period of the fastest growth rates ever recorded in economic history.[40] In terms of real GDP per capita, share of total world exports, share of total LDC exports, and food production per capita, sub-Saharan Africa has regressed over time. If there is one issue that both pro- and antiglobalizers can agree on, it is on the sad and distressing plight of sub-Saharan Africa. The region is an illustration of a poverty trap.

Two observations immediately come to mind from these statistics. First, the poor are in a precarious state in the highly dynamic and unrelenting environment of contemporary globalization. They run the risk not merely of stagnation but of precipitous decline. Second, they are not doomed to be trapped in such poverty, as China demonstrates. Public policy, social capital, and institutions are vital, and they are critical not only in riding the waves of market turbulence but even in profiting from the opportunities they bring along.

Households and the Intergenerational Transmission of Poverty

Microeconomic data are extremely helpful in shedding light on the mechanisms by which poverty and inequality are transmitted from one generation to the next. There is ample empirical evidence showing that children inherit many of the socioeconomic characteristics of their parents.[41] For example, parental schooling accounts for anywhere from 2 to 20 percent of the variance in the schooling of the next generation. Parents' earnings or wages explain anywhere from 1 to as much as 35 percent of variations in current earnings or wages. The same can be said for other variables in which parental characteristics account for much of the variations in current family income (2 to 42 percent), family wealth (7 to 58 percent), and family consumption (35 to 59 percent).[42] What is striking about these results is the extent of the intergenerational spillover effects. And yet, a study on Brazil shows even stronger links than these figures suggest.

On the basis of the 1996 Brazilian household survey, parental schooling, father's occupation, race, and region of birth are significant predictors of current earnings and inequality.[43] These four variables shape people's socioeconomic opportunities and they are significant factors behind inequalities in current earnings and even schooling. For example, these family background variables account for 8 to 10 percent of the Gini coefficient for individual earnings and as much as 12 percent of the Gini coefficient for household income per capita. Parents' schooling accounts for anywhere from 35 to 47 percent of the variation in the next generation's schooling. This is more than twice that observed in the above-mentioned literature survey in other countries (2 to 20 percent for schooling). For earnings, it is 25 to 30 percent for Brazil (cf. 1 to 35 percent in other countries) and for family income per capita, it is 32 to 44 percent (cf. 2 to 42 percent). Brazil has a reputation for being one of the most persistently unequal economies in the world. These findings of an unusually strong intergenerational transmission of inequality provide one possible explanation for such a record.[44]

Not even a mature, wealthy economy like the United States is exempt from such poverty or inequality traps. The plight of African Americans as a group is well documented. They have much higher rates of poverty, incarceration, morbidity, and mortality. In his book *The Hidden Cost of Being African American: How Wealth Perpetuates Inequality*, Thomas Shapiro (2004) argues that African Americans are at a disadvantage because they do not inherit as much "transformative assets" as whites do. The racial gap for wealth (tenfold) is much greater than the gap for income. This exacerbates racial inequality because inherited wealth has a multiplier effect: Their white recipients enjoy economic and social opportunities beyond what their own education or accomplishment would have provided. And since wealth tends to replicate itself, the marketplace will maintain and even widen this racial divide further for subsequent generations.

Inequality has indeed been on the rise even for a middle-class economy such as the United States. Take the case of household net worth. From 1995 to 2004, the top quintile (20 percent) expanded its share of total household net worth from 63.5 to 69.3 percent at the expense of all the other income quintiles. The lowest income quintile had the largest percentage drop (40 percent), being reduced from 4.2 percent in 1995 to only 2.5 percent by 2004.[45] The same pattern is found when it comes to household income distribution. In 1979, households in the top 1 percent of income distribution received 8 percent of total after-tax income.[46] By 2004, their share had nearly doubled to 14 percent. Households in the top income quintile had 42 percent in 1979 and increased their share to 50 percent by 2004. In contrast, households in the bottom income quintile saw their share of 7 percent in 1979 decline to 5 percent in 2004. Note how the top 1 percent of households enjoyed the largest increase during the period. This same dynamic applies to the increase in real wages between 1979 and 2006. The ninetieth percentile of the wage distribution enjoyed a gain of 34 percent versus those in the fiftieth percentile at 11.5 percent and those at the bottom decile at 4 percent. In 1979, the ninetieth percentile earned 3.7 times as much as those in the bottom decile; by 2006, this gap had increased to 4.7 times.[47] In all these cases, observe that the poor are getting left farther behind by whatever measure we use: wage shares, household income, or household net worth. This is yet another illustration of some of the more regressive consequences of market operations in which the poor make the least headway and are consequently trapped in their destitution.[48]

Sociohistorical Location and Regressive Pricing

The persistence of poverty across generations should not come as a surprise considering that sociohistorical location determines the "entry costs" that people have to pay to participate successfully in the marketplace. In its *World Development Report 2006*, the World Bank examined the relationship between equity and development. Note its principal conclusion after a literature review of recent empirical studies: The life outcomes (health, education, socioeconomic status) of people are a function of their race, their parents' income and education, their rural or urban location, and their gender.

The case of child health is an excellent example. Infant mortality rates (IMR) vary widely among emerging nations. There is a fivefold difference between the lowest (Columbia at 25 infant deaths per 1,000 live births) and the highest (Mali, Niger, and Mozambique at more than 125 infant deaths per 1,000 live births). A common pattern across all these countries, however, is the importance of mother's education. In nearly all cases, a secondary education or higher for mothers dramatically reduces their IMRs manyfold compared to those without an education. This difference is particularly noticeable in countries with the highest IMRs. For example, on average, the infant's risk of dying is more than halved in the case of more educated mothers (IMR of 50). In Bolivia, more educated mothers reduced their IMRs by two-thirds compared to their peers with little or no schooling. The case of El Salvador is even more pronounced with more educated mothers cutting IMRs nearly fourfold compared to their uneducated counterparts.[49] All this should not come as a surprise. In addition to their higher incomes, more educated mothers have healthier children because they have better allocative and social networking skills and are in a much better position to access and benefit from public health programs.[50]

A similar pattern emerges when it comes to childhood immunization, severe stunting, and education. There is a wide variation among developing nations when it comes to their immunization rates. However, a common phenomenon across nearly all of these countries is how wealthier families' immunization rates are many times higher compared to the poorest households. Wealth is a key determinant of inequalities in access to immunization. In the case of severe stunting, there is again a consistent pattern across nearly all these countries: The likelihood of severe stunting among children born in rural areas is clearly many times that of urban children. Place of birth matters when it comes to subsequent growth.[51] Children from the richest income quintile are multiple times more likely to reach upper secondary and tertiary education compared to those from the lowest income quintile: Indonesia (4x), Colombia (2x), Thailand (2x), and Zambia (6x).[52]

Sociohistorical location and family circumstances also determine the price people pay, in terms of time and money, for some of the most basic services. For example, studies repeatedly find that the poor pay more for water. In Niger, households in the lowest income quintile pay three times more than those in the top income quintile. This is not even to mention the difference in the quality of water available to these different groups: tap water for the wealthy and water trucked in by tankers for the poor. In many emerging nations, the poorest do not benefit as much as other income classes from improperly designed and poorly executed government subsidies for water and electricity; the well-to-do gain more from many of these programs. In Africa, while most urban residents are within an hour's travel time to a health center, only half of their rural households have similar access. And, of course, we have the well-known problem of regressive pricing when it comes to credit markets as the Grameen Bank has brought to the world's attention. The poor, farmers, and rural folks pay much higher interest rates, if they can even get credit at all. For example, in India, in the rural areas of the states of Kerala and Tamil Nadu, people in the two lowest asset groups pay interest rates that are anywhere from twice to even four times that of the top asset group. Not even the poor in wealthy countries such as the United States are exempt from this phenomenon. The poor, the elderly, and minorities often pay much more for their insurance, mortgage, and credit card loans, assuming they are even able to access these resources.[53] Despite the great strides that have been achieved in addressing inequality of opportunities, socioeconomic class (i.e., income, education, wealth, and occupation) is still a major determinant of life outcomes (including health) and social mobility in the United States. Class still matters.[54]

Two concerns arise from all these findings. First, most people would find it troubling that "morally irrelevant" factors, such as the aforesaid family and social circumstances, predetermine people's chances of success.[55] It would seem that personal choice, effort, and striving ought to play a much bigger, if not decisive, role in a world of just deserts and fairness. Second, and perhaps even more troubling, is the regressive dynamic of these "morally irrelevant" factors: The poor, the helpless, and those who are most at risk are precisely the ones who are stuck with the most disadvantageous conditions and market prices. Both of these concerns warrant extra-market redress. The market, if left on its own, will not correct these flaws in its operations because it is not configured to do so.[56]

Kuznets Inverted U-Shaped Curve

Kuznets's hypothesis of an initial worsening inequality at the start of economic growth with a subsequent improvement in the later stages of development, if accurate, points to path dependence in market operations. The proverbial rising tide does not raise all boats, only those that are ready for it. This is particularly true if there is an absolute, and not merely relative, decline in the standing of those left behind, as in the preceding examples we have seen on chronic generational poverty.

Besides the United States, numerous empirical studies have found worsening income inequality for many other nations. For example, household budget surveys from 88 countries from 1988 to 1993 show that there may indeed be an operative Kuznets phenomenon.[57] Market openness initially worsens income distribution before improving it. Moreover, the impact of trade and foreign direct investments are largely determined by countries' initial income levels. If accurate, these findings substantiate the importance of short-term adjustment assistance and a better integration of the poor into the market economy.[58] This is particularly true for countries with very low initial income levels, such as sub-Saharan Africa, whose poor are the least likely to benefit from market openness.

The preceding findings are also consistent with another study that distinguishes three types of labor: no education, basic schooling, and highly skilled.[59] When a country opens its domestic market, income inequality worsens because those without any education are left farther behind. However, as a country's economic welfare improves, more people receive basic schooling, and it is then that the earnings gap starts to close. This model provides an explanation for the Kuznets inverted-U phenomenon. It also highlights the link between human capital formation and path dependence in market operations.

The initial rise in poverty or inequality would have been a bit more palatable if it could be shown that it is merely temporary as a necessary rite of passage through the Kuznets inverted U-shaped pattern of growth and inequality. Unfortunately, the expected subsequent amelioration of inequality may remain an unfulfilled hope for many. Data from the 1970s to the 1980s do find an inverted U-shaped pattern, but an odd-shaped one in which inequality worsens drastically in the early stages of growth and gradually improves, but ever so slightly and over a very long period of time.[60] The turnaround may be too far into the future as to be beyond the lifetime of many of the poor.

Many scholars question the existence of the Kuznets curve to begin with.[61] Some empirical studies suggest that growth is distribution-neutral, that is, it does not alter the country's income-distribution profile. Despite the short-term cost of adjustment that most critics of globalization stress, the poor ultimately gain from the stream of long-term benefits from market liberalization.[62] What is important is to provide bridging assistance to the poor during the painful period of adjustment and to ensure that the marginalized are truly able to partake of the marketplace. It is only through such participation that they will be able to reap the gains from economic growth as a result of international trade.[63]

The literature is filled with conflicting evidence for and against the Kuznets hypothesis. Nonetheless, regardless of whether or not this inverted U-shaped phenomenon exists, extra-market assistance will be required. If the hypothesis is true in which inequality worsens at first, only to decrease later during self-sustaining economic growth, then international trade can be used as a vehicle for poverty alleviation for as long as the disadvantaged are provided short-term assistance and are integrated into market operations. If the hypothesis is invalidated, on the other hand, there is nevertheless still a case for such extra-market correctives given the importance of human capital formation, especially for those who are lagging, as will be argued in the next two chapters.

Social Capital

Neoclassical trade theory itself notes that even as the pie grows bigger and even if everybody got a much larger slice of the pie in absolute terms, there will still be losers in relative terms. In other words, there will always be a reshuffling in the relative shares of income as a result of trade.[64] Furthermore, we have also seen that not everyone benefits in absolute terms, as in the case of displaced manufacturing workers in deindustrializing nations. As this chapter has argued, the incidence of these burdens and benefits is heavily dependent on the social and human capital economic agents bring with them to the marketplace. In the case of nations, the depth and strength of its institutions are vital when it comes to reaping benefits or minimizing harms from trade.

The striking difference in the economic performance of globalizers versus nonglobalizers accentuates even more the importance of institutional preconditions, such as a stable political economy with transparency, accountability, and economic freedom.[65] Social development is an excellent predictor of subsequent economic growth.[66] Numerous empirical studies have arrived at the same conclusion: There is a well-established and strong correlation between the quality of nations' institutions and their economic performance measured in terms of growth rate and volatility. The causation has not been definitively established; whether it is institutions that lead to good economic performance or vice versa is not known. It is likely that there is a mutually reinforcing dynamic between these two factors.

For example, nations may enhance and develop even further the regulatory framework undergirding their real and financial markets as they develop.[67] There are practical reasons to agree with such a feedback effect. After all, most institutions are expensive to establish and maintain and can only be financed as nations grow. In addition, staffing these requires both personal and collective tacit knowledge that are slowly built up over time in a process of learning by doing. Moreover, as we have seen in the earlier section on bounded rationality, formal and informal rules of thumb evolve and are strengthened over time by both market processes and outcomes. Thus, the greater likelihood that economic performance feeds back into institutional development is in line with this study's hypothesis on the central role of path dependence in locking nations into either a virtuous or a vicious cycle.

The importance of institutional preconditions is also substantiated in the case of financial liberalization. Unlike trade in goods and services, the free movement of capital across borders has been a mixed blessing. Industrialized countries with deep and stable financial structures have benefited extensively from capital liberalization. In contrast, developing countries have shown either minimal gains or even losses because such cross-border capital movements have brought along greater volatility and financial contagions. The weak financial infrastructure of poor countries has rendered them particularly vulnerable to the vagaries of financial markets.[68] Institutional preconditions are critical; nations that have the necessary financial infrastructure in place gain even more, whereas those that do not end up having even less at the end of the day. The interaction of institutional preconditions and path dependence is clearly operative in financial markets. Thus, the description of capital market liberalization as one of "uneven rewards and risks" is truly apt.[69]

In theory, international trade is a possible venue for closing the wage gap across countries. Recall, for example, the factor price equalization theorem of the Hecksher-Ohlin model of international trade. Trading partners whose relative factor endowments are not radically different from each other should eventually see their relative factor prices equalize over time. After all, trading in goods can be a substitute for factor mobility. In practice, however, the wage gap between countries is a function of their respective institutions and policies. Thus, it has even been suggested that the key to reducing the huge chasm in wages between industrialized and emerging countries is for the latter to implement much-needed institutional reforms and investments in education, infrastructure, technology, and governance.[70] Wage inequalities between nations are subject to the same dynamic experienced within countries. The path dependence intrinsic to market operations may create a vicious or a benevolent cycle depending on economic agents' human or social capital. Nations with the right policies in place and with a functioning economic infrastructure will see their workers improve their lot faster, and those without these requisite institutional preconditions will find their citizens left farther behind.

Finally, social capital is indispensable for technological change. The bulk of global R&D is conducted in the triad comprised of the United States, the EU, and Japan. The same pattern is evident in the distribution of R&D strategic alliances, more than 95 percent of which are between developed countries.[71] Or, consider the ICT-using and ICT-producing nations. The biggest producers and users have been the industrialized countries and the NICs of East Asia.[72] If knowledge is indeed the source of value creation in the learning economy and if tacit knowledge is founded on learning by doing, then one would expect lagging nations to be left even farther behind in the coming years as leading nations internalize the full benefits of an ICT-driven globalization. Jeffrey Sachs (2000) warns that it is no longer ideology that divides the world but the wide disparity in access to technology. Indeed, institutional preconditions and sociohistorical location are potent determinants of successful market participation.

Summary and Conclusions

Both macroeconomic and microeconomic data confirm a path dependence in market operations and outcomes. Sociohistorical location, social and human capital, and institutions determine the socioeconomic opportunities open to economic agents. This means that left on its own, the market will provide even more to those who are advantaged at the expense of those who have little to begin with. This accounts for the intergenerational transmission of poverty both at the household and national levels.

To conclude part II, recall from chapter 4 that efficiency matters, and it matters even more in the knowledge economy. By its nature, the market creates value by putting scarce resources to their most valued uses through the allocative function of price. This feature of the market takes on greater importance in the information age because the resulting efficiency from market operations feeds back into precipitating even more profound technological and organizational innovations that, in turn, reshape and upgrade the market to even greater levels of efficiency. Thus, not only has the pace of economic life accelerated, but the knowledge economy itself has laid the groundwork for self-sustaining "gales of creative destruction." Thus, contrary to the claims of the more radical antiglobalizers, market operations do make a world of difference. Efficiency as a criterion of distributive justice cannot be readily dismissed. To do so would be simply self-defeating and would unconscionably condemn untold numbers of people today and in the future to destitution.

Nonetheless, this chapter has argued that efficiency cannot be the sole criterion of distributive justice. By its nature, the market can create an underclass because of its self-reinforcing path dependence and the pivotal role of people's sociohistorical location in shaping the quality and outcomes of their market participation. The globalizing knowledge economy makes these twin properties of the market even more potent in view of the digital age's various consequences outlined previously, such as the accelerating pace of economic life, stiffer competition, and the higher entry costs to partaking of the marketplace. Thus, it is all the more essential to understand fully the distributive dimension of the price mechanism.

Efficiency requires an array of institutional and dynamic preconditions that the market cannot fully provide on its own. In particular, the price adjustments that are critical for moving scarce resources to their most valued uses also produce collateral distributive effects that are often harmful. These deleterious pecuniary externalities are compounded by path dependence, especially in the formation of human and social capital. Market participants who lag behind in a rapidly moving and highly fluid knowledge economy will be left farther behind and find it that much more difficult to keep up over time. There is an autocorrelated dynamic in globalization in which economic agents who are endowed with excellent human or social capital will find themselves gaining even more, whereas those who have deficient human or social capital will find that what little they have is increasingly inadequate or irrelevant for meaningful participation in the knowledge economy.

Thus, contrary to the claims of pro-globalizers, there is need for extra-market, preparatory and remedial work. The neoliberal call for market liberalization is not a panacea nor can it be applied as a one-size-fits-all solution to global poverty. Nations must be discriminating and disciplined in liberalizing their domestic economies because there are prerequisites and institutions that must be in place if the market is to produce its much-acclaimed benefits. There is need for an intelligent sequencing and calibration of market reforms. Otherwise, an uncritical application of theoretical models may only cause more harm than good, as have been suggested in the IMF's mistakes during the Asian financial meltdown of 1997–98.[73] And, even after liberalization, there will still be need for extra-market vigilance to prevent the emergence of a permanent underclass of economic actors who are unable to keep up with the ever-ratcheting standards of human capital required by the knowledge economy.

Part III

Need as a Criterion of Distributive Justice

The preceding two chapters concluded that (1) economic efficiency matters, especially in the knowledge economy, (2) but it requires extensive institutional groundwork. A balance must be struck between unfettered market operations and the requisite "fine-tuning" that ensures its smooth performance. Such supplemental extra-market interventions must be judicious and strategic, lest the market be impeded from producing its manifold benefits. The next two chapters suggest that the satisfaction of human needs for growth and development is one such judicious and strategic intervention. Chapter 6 argues that need satisfaction is a necessary condition for long-term efficiency because of the foundational role of human capital development in the knowledge economy. Need satisfaction and economic efficiency converge into a pair of complementary criteria of distributive justice in contemporary globalization. In chapter 7 we will find that need satisfaction has the collateral benefit of strengthening the market's technological creativity and stability even further.

Chapter 6

Need Satisfaction as a Necessary Condition of Efficiency

Introduction

In a review of the scholarship on economic justice written for the *Journal of Economic Literature*, Konow (2003) identifies the three criteria of distributive justice considered by many to be the most important, namely: need, efficiency, and entitlement. Unfortunately, his positive theory of distributive justice does not go so far as to provide a rank ordering of these three norms. Most survey respondents concluded that the relative importance of these standards depended on context. Using the features of the knowledge economy described in part I as context, I submit that it is possible to provide a rank ordering of these three measures of distributive justice. For the following two chapters, I compare the principles of need and efficiency. Entitlement is examined in the last part of this study (part IV).

I claim that the knowledge economy narrows the seemingly unbridgeable divide between the economic requirements of efficiency and equity. Since human capital is at the heart of a "learning" economy, long-term efficiency is dependent on how well the community develops its human resources in the earlier rounds of economic activity. Distribution in the earlier periods of market operations determines the degree to which efficiency is attained and sustained down the road.

Need Satisfaction

As we have seen in chapter 5, even as price adjustments put scarce resources to their best use, they also reallocate burdens and benefits among market participants (the distributive dimension of price). In other words, the distributive function of price is an unintended, collateral effect of the allocative role of price. Such de facto redistributions result in the inequalities we see in the economy; they also determine the degree to which people are able to procure the goods or services needed to develop their human capital (need satisfaction in distributive justice). Severe inequalities and the inability to satisfy basic needs often go together, and they are both a reflection of the deficient state with which the distributive dimension of price is managed. All three (pronounced inequalities, unmet needs, and unmitigated distributive ramifications of the price mechanism) adversely affect human capital formation. Thus, the criterion of need in distributive justice, the distributive dimension of price, human capital formation, and income or wealth inequalities (a.k.a. equity) are four distinct but inseparable issues. They have predictable spillover effects on one another and can in certain contexts be used interchangeably.

There are at least two important issues that must be resolved before we can even think of adopting need as a criterion of distributive justice in practice. First, we have to justify why the norm of need satisfaction takes precedence over the other standards of distributive justice. This is the question that the next two chapters address. Second, what is the content of the basket of needs that have to be satisfied, who makes that determination, and on what basis? Answering this second set of questions requires another study in itself. As I had mentioned in the preface, my goal in this work is simply to provide an instrumental justification for need satisfaction as a norm of distributive justice based on its role in bringing about allocative efficiency. Thus, by extension, I am likewise limiting the basket of needs to be satisfied only to those goods and services that are instrumental in developing human capital in the digital age. I do not claim that this is the definitive basket of needs to be satisfied; it is only a suggested preliminary set of requirements that are essential for bringing about economic efficiency.[1]

So, what should be the content of the minimum basket of needs to be satisfied? Most people would agree that this should include the commonly acknowledged necessities of food, clothing, shelter, and medical care. After all, these are the basic requirements of physical survival. In addition to these, it would seem reasonable to include the goods and services that are essential for human capital development— the key requirement of the knowledge economy (part I).

Unfortunately, the notion of human capital is so general and abstract and requires further specification if it is even to be useful at all for practical application. Thus, it is perhaps best to use tacit knowledge (discussed in chapter 3) as a more concrete delineation of human capital in an effort to identify its particular requirements. I would be the first to say that this is still unsatisfactory because tacit knowledge is not identical to human capital. It does not fully exhaust everything that can be said of human capital; it is merely a subset of human capital. Nonetheless, in the absence of a better alternative, tacit knowledge is a good first approximation, a proxy, that allows us to spell out concretely some of the prerequisites of human capital formation.

However, even the notion of tacit knowledge itself is still so broad and will encompass the full range of human needs as to make any talk of a minimum basket of needs meaningless. After all, the life skills afforded by social interaction, culture, friendship, and love are all essential for the tacit knowledge required for human flourishing in community. Thus, in what follows, I limit the use of "tacit knowledge" only to that which is required by economic life, a "market tacit knowledge" so to speak.[2] Empirical studies indicate that, at the very least, this economic tacit knowledge (and human capital by extension) is dependent on formal schooling, work experience, vocational-skills training, and continuing education. These are among the things that must be included in the minimum basket of needs to be satisfied.

Nature of Efficiency

As we have seen in chapter 4, there are three types of economic efficiency, namely: microeconomic, Ricardian/Smithian, and Schumpeterian. These three types of efficiency are not mutually exclusive. In fact, in the ideal economy, they are coincident. Under actual market conditions, however, there are often trade-offs between these efficiencies. For example, the push for full employment in the short run may require heavy government intervention that distorts the economy's microeconomic efficiency. Moreover, governments also often provide assistance to "national industrial champions" or "winning industries" that are groomed to be catalysts for change or engines of growth that pull along the rest of the economy. In such cases, microeconomic efficiency is sacrificed in the short term in an effort to gain a Schumpeterian edge on the competition. Note the long-running feud between Airbus and Boeing over each other's hidden or overt government largesse. In this chapter, I attempt to make the case for how and why a strategy of need satisfaction in the knowledge economy leads to long-term allocative efficiency and results in the convergence of all three kinds of efficiency, even under less than perfect conditions.

The empirical evidence on the market's ability to create value is strong and robust (chapter 4). The strides achieved in the last two decades alone have been impressive both in terms of the reduction of the number of people living under $1 a day and the "telescoping" of the development path. Japan and the Asian Tigers[3] achieved in a generation what took the major developed countries nearly a full century to attain. These newly industrialized economies accomplished this feat by embracing globalization in a full-throated manner. China has even accelerated such a process of catch-up and has broken the remarkable records set by its East Asian neighbors. Of course, this praise for the market is not meant to disregard its ill effects examined in chapter 5. On the whole, however, despite its numerous shortcomings, the market economy has been the most effective vehicle for improving human material well-being in a self-sustaining fashion. Travel, leisure time, education, and apparel that were once luxuries available only to the nobility and aristocrats have become accessible for mass consumption, courtesy of the Industrial Revolution. The market economy is largely responsible for sustaining the largest population base ever, and at a much higher per capita income than at any time in history.

Viewed in the entirety of both its achievements and failures, the record of the market economy speaks for itself. It has been pivotal in improving people's material welfare. This leads me to my first conclusion in comparing need versus efficiency in their relative importance as distributive criteria: We cannot ignore efficiency as a goal of economic life. It is self-defeating to hamper the market from doing what it does best in using price signals to allocate scarce resources to their most valued uses. This is a lesson gleaned from twentieth-century economic history.[4] Thus, *economic efficiency is both (1) an unavoidable reference point and (2) the necessary starting point when talking of distributive justice.* There is no way around economic efficiency if we want long-term viability and self-sustaining economic growth. Put in even more stark terms, there is little point in talking of how to divide the economic pie if we cannot even produce an economic pie to begin with that is big enough to sustain a growing population.

Equity versus Efficiency

The tension between equity and efficiency in economic scholarship is well known. For example, in his classic lecture on the trade-off between equality and efficiency, Okun (1975) calls for caution in designing and implementing redistributive measures as these often spawn distortions and disincentives that adversely affect efficiency.

Recall, too, the disputed inverted U-shaped Kuznets (1955, 1963) curve that shows an initial increase in inequality as a consequence of economic growth. And, of course, we have the counterexample of Taiwan that demonstrates the essential role of equity in attaining efficiency.[5]

Let us examine neoclassical economic theory's positive description of how the economy works. We have already seen that price has both an allocative and distributive dimension. Relative prices are at the heart of the first-order conditions and the three equimarginal conditions that bring the economy to the most efficient use of its scarce resources.[6] The distributive ramifications of these first-order and equimarginal conditions are not of interest to mainstream economic theory. After all, this is an optimizing exercise in maximizing consumer utility and firms' profits. It is merely intent on achieving the most consumer and producer surplus possible in the disposition of resources, and it does not evaluate the division of these gains among market participants. Consequently, in the neoclassical economic theory's descriptive account of how economic agents behave, efficiency overshadows equity as a concern. In maximizing utility or profits in their individual behavior, economic agents in effect collectively, if unintentionally, pursue efficiency as the overriding goal of their shared economic life. Distribution is simply not part of the optimizing exercise of traditional theory.[7]

It is best to cite a second illustration of how efficiency and distribution are separate matters in neoclassical economic theory. Take the case of the Hecksher-Ohlin theory of trade in which differences in nations' relative endowments are believed to be the proximate cause of cross-border exchange. Countries that have plentiful labor end up exporting products that are relatively more labor-intensive, in exchange for more capital-intensive goods from nations that are rich in capital. In other words, nations export commodities that are intensive in using their most abundant factors. Thus, international trade is not necessarily a zero-sum game but a win-win proposition for all trading partners because they are able to fully employ their resources and enjoy the highest income possible. All trading partners end up with a much higher consumption possibilities frontier (the budget line) than would have been the case under autarky; they enjoy a consumption bundle at a much higher indifference curve. Every trading partner's welfare improves and allocative efficiency is successfully achieved.

Unfortunately, this is only half the story, albeit the more important half from the point of view of free trade proponents. Unlike the much older Ricardian model of comparative advantage, the Hecksher-Ohlin theory has the advantage of being able to track the impact of trade on income distribution. One of its axioms is the famous Stolper-Samuelson theorem in which trade leads to an increase in the returns of the abundant inputs at the *relative* expense of the scarce factors of production.[8] In other words, there will be relative winners and losers within the trading countries themselves even if the overall welfare of each trading nation improves.

Two observations can be gleaned from the preceding accounts of welfare theory and the Hecksher-Ohlin theory of trade. First, efficiency and its distributive ramifications are separate issues for mainstream economic theory. Second, there is little attention devoted to the question of whether these redistributive spillover effects facilitate or obstruct the attainment of allocative efficiency in production and exchange. From a basic neoclassical point of view, the allocative and distributive dimensions of price are separate matters.

Beyond economic theory, we find evident tensions between efficiency and equity in actual practice. For example, take the case of petroleum resources, or any other essential commodity for that matter. As emerging nations industrialize, their increased demand for energy translates into a corresponding rise in the price of crude oil. This is as it should be if we are to be efficient because the resulting prohibitive price of petroleum products signals the increasing scarcity of oil. This, in turn, triggers a natural corrective mechanism by encouraging further oil-field exploration and development, better conservation, improved engineering efficiencies, and a more intense search for substitutes. The rise in petroleum prices compels the economy to be sparing in its use of increasingly scarce oil. Unfortunately, more expensive energy becomes an adverse pecuniary externality for poor, non-oil-producing nations. These countries would have to dip deeper into their meager foreign exchange reserves to pay for their more costly energy imports. Many of these nations would have to make the unpalatable choice of either aggravating their fiscal deficits through subsidies or passing on the cost increases to their already impoverished citizenry. A rise in oil prices is a de facto transfer of real resources out of these destitute nations.

Another example of such a tension between efficiency and equity is the dilemma of offshore outsourcing and, for that matter, market liberalization. Long-term efficiency requires more open markets and, by extension, outsourcing. However, we are well aware of the problems such liberalization causes for equity, especially for the displaced workers who do not have the requisite skills for the high-technology jobs replacing those that have been lost.

I argue that in the digital age, the allocative and distributive functions of price converge and must, therefore, be evaluated together. In fact, I will make the even stronger statement that *in a knowledge economy, long-term efficiency has become increasingly a function of the distributive dimension of price in the short run.* In other words, need satisfaction in the earlier periods of economic activity is a necessary condition for allocative efficiency in its later rounds. I propose a variety of reasons for such a claim. This chapter examines four arguments that present need satisfaction as a rational economic response to both the opportunities and the dangers posed by contemporary globalization. Chapter 7 lays out a second set of three claims that highlight need satisfaction as a precondition of an effective and stable market economy. The reasons presented in these two chapters are all instrumental in nature because they are founded on the utility of a strategy of need satisfaction in attaining long-term efficiency in the knowledge economy. They all make a case for why need satisfaction is a necessary condition not only for allocative efficiency but also for Schumpeterian and Keynesian efficiency in the digital age. For the rest of this book, I use "efficiency" to refer to the confluence of the microeconomic-allocative, Ricardian/Smithian, and Schumpeterian efficiencies I had presented in chapter 2.

In what follows, I present four reasons why need satisfaction should be the starting point for building economic efficiency, to wit:

1. Need satisfaction is essential for human capital formation, the wellspring of value creation in the knowledge economy.
2. Need satisfaction safeguards against permanent marginalization in the wake of severe adverse pecuniary externalities.
3. Need satisfaction enhances factor mobility.
4. Need satisfaction is an ex-ante, preemptive measure that is much cheaper than ex-post corrective action.

Need Satisfaction and Human Capital Formation

Need satisfaction is necessary for efficiency because human capital is the source of value creation. The central importance of (market) tacit knowledge in the learning economy necessarily underscores the pivotal role of its mirror image: human capital. After all, it is human capital that actualizes tacit knowledge. A learning economy that is heavily dependent on tacit knowledge ultimately points to the need for human capital development. And, the latter is possible only if market participants have access to the requisite material means for their sustenance and growth. As already noted, information is power, but only if economic agents know how to use it in a timely and appropriate manner. Tacit knowledge is obviously essential for this task, and beyond it, a well-developed human capital. Implicit knowledge is agent-specific. What the subject brings with him or her determines the scope and depth of the resulting tacit knowledge. For this reason, a strategy of need satisfaction that builds up human capital is a constitutive pillar of economic efficiency in the knowledge economy.[9]

There are two problems in making the case for need satisfaction and human capital development. First, it is impossible to list completely what constitutes need satisfaction and human capital formation. Thus, as I had already mentioned at the start of this chapter, I will limit myself only to the tacit knowledge needed in economic life in order to make the scope of this study manageable. The second problem has to do with our inability to actually observe and measure tacit knowledge and human capital. The literature gets around this problem by using proxies for them, such as their requisite inputs like formal schooling, work experience, vocational-skills training, and continuing education. Furthermore, in order to gauge the efficacy of tacit knowledge or human capital in the marketplace, many scholars have simply used their economic returns (e.g., earnings) as an indication of their impact on economic efficiency.

Schooling

Given the twofold difficulty of defining and then measuring human capital, studies have long used returns to education as a convenient shorthand for human capital and its impact on the economy. This is understandable considering that schooling has been one of its more important inputs. This is likely to be even more so in the knowledge economy.

An entire subfield has emerged within the discipline that specializes in the economics of education. Economists have been interested not only in the returns to education, but they have also been keen to study the various channels by which education builds up human capital and the economy. And it is quite an extensive and impressive network.[10]

Education raises individual productivity and, consequently, workers' earnings. It leads to better nonwage compensation (i.e., fringe benefits).[11] In raising people's incomes, schooling also permits them to spend more time in leisure besides providing a wider choice of such activities.[12] Education affords individuals with the basic skills for even faster and better learning down the road. It is self-reinforcing in that it develops the personal means for even more advanced subsequent human capital formation. Furthermore, it enhances the quality of nonmarket household activities, such as do-it-yourself projects, intra-family relationships, and child rearing. The benefits of schooling also spill over into the person's health and that of his or her family through better health knowledge and the improved ability to seek out medical information or benefit from public assistance programs. Education affects fertility by changing people's preferences for family size and by making them more effective at family planning.

Besides its useful effects, schooling is valued in itself because of the intrinsic joy of learning. Moreover, it enhances people's tastes and opens new horizons that permit an even better appreciation for music, art, and culture. In addition, education provides both the information and the ability to seek out the necessary knowledge to make informed choices. Thus, the better educated are supposed to be more efficient in the use of data and their time in arriving at consumption, career, and marriage choices, at least in theory.[13] Schooling has also been found to lead to greater social cohesion, less crime, more vibrant technological change, diminished income inequality, higher savings, and more gen-erous charitable giving. Indeed, education is a fundamental building block of civilization and an orderly community. This is a not an exhaus-tive listing as it includes only those channels of education that have been subjected to empirical testing. There are surely more venues by which education redounds to personal and communal well-being.

All these mechanisms give rise to what we can aptly call the private and social benefits of education that accrue respectively to individuals (households) and the community. The social benefits are notoriously difficult to study because they are hard to pinpoint and quantify, and they have extensive, unseen ripple effects including some that spill over across generations. Consequently, the overwhelming majority of stud-ies have concentrated on the most immediate and well-known contri-bution of education, which also turns out to be the easiest to measure and the one with the most readily available data, namely: the private returns to investment in schooling as reflected in earnings or wage rates.

Based on a recent survey of the literature, the global average private return for an additional year of schooling is believed to be around 10 percent.[14] In absolute terms, world average private returns to investment in education are: 26.6 percent for primary school, 17 percent for high school, and 19 percent for higher education. The private returns for low-income countries are 25.6 percent (primary), 12.2 per-cent (secondary) and 12.4 percent (higher education). An additional year of schooling for these countries provides a return of 10.9 percent.[15]

These high private returns from education are best appreciated in light of another empirical finding. As we have seen in the preceding chapter, the household head's education, gender, and sector of employment are good predictors of whether or not a family is destitute. Using household surveys from different countries, the World Bank estimates that an additional year of primary schooling has a sizable positive marginal effect on the family's private returns to such primary education, in addition to substantially lowering its probability of falling in the lowest income decile. In other words, the poverty reducing impact of primary education is strongest in those areas where there is a high private return to investing in such an education.[16] High private returns to primary schooling and poverty reduction are positively correlated.

Some further notes. To appreciate the size of these returns to education, recall that the long-term returns in the U.S. stock market is around 8 percent. Furthermore, observe that all these are merely private returns. Social returns are even much higher than these, if they can only be properly identified and measured. We are reaping far more benefits than scholars are able to track and measure. In other words, education is about one of the best investment opportunities there is, even in the high-income countries.

On-the-Job Training

Forming (market) tacit knowledge calls for roundabout investments that involve intelligent planning and lengthy lead times. The process is path dependent and cumulative since it is a process of "learning by doing." Thus, one would expect that those provided with meaningful opportunities for participation in the economy would tend to do well. This is confirmed in a study that examines the returns to work experience and training in Burkina Faso, Brazil, Chile, Indonesia, Mexico, Pakistan, Slovenia, Thailand, and Uganda.[17] For twenty-year-old workers, an additional year of formal or on-the-job training leads to a 6 percent increase in their earnings versus a 3 percent rise for their forty-year-old counterparts. These age-differentiated returns should not come as a surprise because younger generations have more productive years ahead of them with which to use their experience compared to the older cohorts.[18]

Moreover, the importance of job experience for tacit knowledge is also confirmed by the study's finding that workers' peak earnings are on the average 2.5 times that of their initial pay. This means that work experience does improve workers' skills and productivity over time. Furthermore, there is evidence that shows that early labor-market experience shapes workers' subsequent opportunities in terms of pay and type of employment. In other words, on-the-job training and work experience matter for human capital development and later economic success. And the earlier these are provided in their careers, the better it is both for the workers and their communities in terms of higher output and productivity. "Learning by doing" does make a difference for tacit knowledge.

Wage Differential

The impact of human capital formation is also evident in the wage gaps both within and across countries. Skilled workers are paid many times more than their unskilled peers. For example, note the ratio of skilled to unskilled wages in 2001: East Asia and the Pacific (over 3.5), Europe and Central Asia (close to 2), Latin America and the Caribbean (over 2); South Asia (4.5), and sub-Saharan Africa (5).[19] Workers' earnings became more unequal in many countries from the late 1970s to the mid 1990s. Observe the percentage change in the gap between the top and bottom earners during this period: U.S. (nearly 30 percent), UK (over 25 percent), New Zealand and Italy (around 15 percent).[20] Wage disparities in the last two decades have been particularly sharp in the United States. In 1979, the weekly median earnings of workers with at least a college education were 38 percent more than those with only a high school degree. By 2006, the gap had widened to 75 percent. In 1979, the median weekly earnings of high school graduates were 19 percent more than those who had never gone to high school. By 2006, this had widened to 42 percent.[21]

Economists have offered two competing factors behind such inequality, namely, trade and technology. Cheap imports have been the usual suspects for worsening inequality because of their devastating impact on the wages and demand for unskilled or low-skilled workers. Trade with developing countries has been shown to reduce the demand for low-skilled work by anywhere from 2 to 5 percent of the unskilled labor force in the last two decades.[22] Trade is also believed to have made the demand for labor more elastic, thereby compelling workers to bear more of the cost of labor standards and protection that used to be borne by employers.[23] Others attribute anywhere from 10 to 30 percent of industrialized countries' labor-market woes to developing country exports.[24] Data from the U.S. durable goods industries show that trade is a major cause of the decline observed in the real wages of low-skilled workers and the sharp rise in wage inequality in the 1980s.[25]

In contrast to the reduction in East Asian inequality, trade worsened disparities in the Latin American countries. This divergent experience is attributed both to the skill-biased nature of technological change and to the stiff competition from the entry of low-wage nations into the global marketplace as a result of globalization.[26] Furthermore, it is believed that there is a correlation between trade and the size of government because increased social spending, income transfers in particular, has been necessary to cushion the adjustment costs and to make it easier for governments to sell market liberalization to their citizens.[27]

Other scholars believe that trade has had a minimal impact on inequality and that the primary cause of the widening income gap has been the technological advances that are part of this fifth Kondratieff cycle. As new technologies are introduced, the productivity and, consequently, the earnings and the demand for more skilled workers increase. Unskilled workers are left out and see their wages stagnate.[28] Many studies show that the most significant source of inequality is not global market exchange, but the disparities in skills.[29] Equality has deteriorated in the last two decades because of the higher earnings of skilled workers compared to the stagnant wages of the unskilled. This finding is consistent with what we have seen all along regarding the central importance of human capital in value creation in the knowledge economy.

Regardless of whether worsening inequality is due to trade or to new technologies, both point to the same conclusion: Human capital formation is vital. Unskilled workers find themselves at a disadvantage in a globalized economy because they do not have the necessary human capital to work with the new technologies or to retrain for the more advanced technology jobs in the face of cheap imports. Moreover, because of their sociohistorical location or age, these disadvantaged workers may not have the means or the opportunity to improve their human capital. Thus, they find themselves in a poverty trap.

Need Satisfaction and Coping with Disruptive Pecuniary Externalities

Pecuniary Externalities

A strategy of need satisfaction is both a direct and an indirect safeguard against adverse pecuniary externalities. Globalization is essentially a process of greater "marketization" in which ever more spheres of social life are governed by market rules. However, as we have repeatedly seen in the preceding chapters, relying on the market has its downside. It renders economic agents more vulnerable to unintended consequences (externalities).

Pecuniary externalities are intrinsic to market operations, and some of them can cause particularly burdensome ripple effects. Workers who have lost their livelihood overnight due to cheaper imports, offshore outsourcing, downsizing, or the transfer of manufacturing plants overseas are well aware of the havoc that international trade can wreak on personal lives. Market deepening and widening, ever stiffening competition, and the accelerating pace of economic life all compound this vexing problem of unpleasant spillover effects within the marketplace. These adverse pecuniary externalities come with ever increasing frequency, often occur so suddenly as to preclude time to prepare for a transition, and can be severe in altering lifestyles and livelihoods. This is particularly true for developing countries.

In tracking the ten-year per capita income growth rates between 1970 and 2005, the World Bank finds that emerging nations have historically been subjected to so much more volatility compared to the developed world.[30] To make matters worse, these sudden and dramatic economic shifts are expected to be the principal cause of the rise in within-country income inequality in the next twenty-five years. Countries that are expected to become even more unequal are those whose demographic shifts are aggravated by economic volatility.[31] Countries that are expected to be more equal are those that are somehow able to use these economic swings to mitigate inequality due to demographic growth.

The poor and the vulnerable often take a long time to recover from adverse pecuniary externalities, if at all, and often only at a high price. Take the case of financial shocks. Compare the fiscal cost (as a percentage of GDP) of banking crises in the past twenty-five years across different countries: USA (3.2 percent), Argentina (55.1 percent), Chile (41.2 percent), Brazil (13.2 percent), Ecuador (13 percent), Mexico (19.3 percent), Venezuela (22 percent), Korea (26.5 percent), and Indonesia (50 percent). Unlike developed nations, emerging countries do not have the necessary financial institutions and infrastructure to cushion them from the forbidding environment of international financial markets. Moreover, they have less financial reserves to tide them over.

A similar phenomenon is at work at the microeconomic level. In his book *The Working Poor: Invisible in America*, David Shipler (2004) describes the plight of those who have the work ethic and who put in long hours but are nevertheless still stuck in dead-end jobs that do not provide upward mobility or a compensation that allows for savings.

These are the "working poor" who are shadowed by poverty, constantly living on a precarious knife-edge balance between destitute homelessness and just scraping enough to keep fed and warm. Events, such as a car breaking down or a family illness, are enough to knock them off this precarious perch. These are people who are barely able to keep up in the marketplace, and they are the ones most vulnerable to the adverse pecuniary externalities that we are all familiar with: unpredictable jumps in the price of gasoline and home heating oil, unrestrained increases in health insurance premiums, and unaffordable housing. The poor are more exposed to these unintended economic ripple effects because they have minimal financial resources to lean on and, as we have seen in chapter 5, they face much higher entry costs to market participation.

The hyper-dynamism of change in the knowledge economy may be outpacing our ability to adapt to and digest its pecuniary externalities. There is the danger of having an increasing number of people who are unable to adjust and adapt fast enough to keep up with the new demands of a rapidly evolving "learning" economy. The risk of getting left behind by the ever-ratcheting requirements of the knowledge economy, coupled with its unpredictable, frequent, and often disequilibrating changes, looms ever larger. This is a second reason why need satisfaction is a constitutive element of long-term economic efficiency in the information age. If tacit knowledge is indeed the key to creating value and sustaining the postindustrial economy, then need satisfaction is a safety net that prevents market participants from being marginalized by adverse pecuniary externalities and left permanently unable to participate in economic life in a meaningful and productive manner. It is in the self-interest of the knowledge economy to husband its human resources in the face of such economic stress, first by preparing human capital to deal with such disequilibria and second, by providing bridging assistance.

A Robust Human Capital to Deal with Disequilibria

One puzzle in the study of the economics of education has been its fairly steady returns despite the tremendous increase in average schooling over the years.[32] Indeed, if we were to treat education as an input in production, by the law of diminishing returns, we should have witnessed a major decline in rates of return to schooling.

Consider the following summary statistics from a recent survey of updated studies on returns to education.[33] Despite their highly educated populations, note that the private rate of return to an additional year of schooling in high-income countries is 7.4 percent. This is not too far off from the world average of 9.7 percent or the 10.9 percent from the low-income countries or the 10.7 percent enjoyed by middle-income countries.[34] During the past twelve years, average returns to schooling declined by only 0.6 percentage points.[35] The overall rate of return to education in the United States is 10 percent.[36] In other words, the private returns to education have remained high and fairly stable despite the substantial increase in schooling worldwide.

Three possible explanations have been proposed for this phenomenon.[37] First, growth may be occurring in those industries with a very high demand for skilled workers, as is likely to be the case in our digital age. We examine this further in the next section when we account for the increasing earnings gap between highly skilled and unskilled workers. Second, there may be an improvement in the quality of schooling, in which case educated workers become even more productive. Third, technological change may be so dynamic and challenging as to open new opportunities to those who are skilled and educated. It is this third possibility that I would like to develop further for the remainder of this section.

Education is said to be valuable because it expands workers' capacity to process, understand, and then put information to good use. In fact, "education is especially important to those functions requiring adaptation to change."[38] U.S. agriculture is a good case in point. More educated farmers tend to be on the cutting edge of adopting farm innovations because they are better than their less educated counterparts at gathering, understanding, and applying new information. Thus, relative to their less educated peers, these farmers could minimize the risks that come with any change, especially in a sector that is as traditional as agriculture. In fact, it is a rational economic response on the part of less educated farmers to simply let their more educated neighbors take the lead and work out the kinks of new farming techniques. They could then later simply imitate the success of the early adopters without having to pay the cost of mistakes. The upshot to all this is that returns to education will be higher the greater is the dynamism of the technology involved. Put in another way, education is even more important in a highly fluid or turbulent economic environment.

In a test of the preceding findings, another study, also using U.S. agricultural data, arrives at the same conclusion that education is valuable because it develops workers' capacity to deal with change. The impact of education can be disaggregated into a "worker effect" (i.e., the direct increase in productivity) and an "allocative effect" (i.e., the value that comes with better choices in the disposition of resources). It has been found that college education enhances the latter, that is, the ability to make better allocative choices. No similar effect is observed for those who only have a high school degree.[39] In a study using U.S. census and manufacturing data, capital is found to be more complementary with skilled or better educated labor than with unskilled or unschooled labor.[40] This empirical result supports the aforesaid claim that a rapidly shifting technological frontier is associated with high returns to schooling (and skills).

In an article that he appropriately entitles "The Value of the Ability to Deal with Disequilibria," Nobel laureate T. W. Schultz (1975) provides even more empirical examples to support the claim that education is invaluable because economic agents are faced with the constant need to reallocate their resources in response to changing opportunities. Schultz laments that traditional economic theory does not pay attention to how efficiently people adapt to changing economic circumstances. For example, once disrupted out of equilibrium, *homo oeconomicus* is assumed to adjust instantaneously to the new equilibrium. In practice, it takes time and there are real costs incurred in reaching the new equilibrium. In this connection, he lists five different human abilities, namely: to learn, to do useful work, to play, to create, and to deal with economic disequilibria.[41]

Schultz concludes that more educated and more experienced economic actors are better positioned not only to cope with change but to even profit from it. He backs this up by citing empirical studies across a broad range of economic activities. In household production, more educated mothers have been found to make quicker and more effective changes within family life in response to new opportunities, as in the case of family planning. More educated migrants tend to be more successful and daring than their less educated peers. College graduates respond quicker and better to changing labor-market conditions than high school graduates. And then, there is agriculture. Educated farmers are more open to new techniques and products such as chemical fertilizers. Second-generation (and better schooled) migrant farming families in the U.S. and Brazil tend to do much better than their first-generation parents. A common thread through all these examples is that better education and more experience enhance economic actors' skills and confidence not only in coping with changes but in turning them into opportunities.

Observe that Schultz highlights the value not merely of education but also of experience. This is important for our study because what he refers to as "experience" corresponds to what has been said all along about tacit knowledge. In fact, I would go even further and claim that all these insights and conclusions about education can be generalized and applied to human capital as well. After all, it is standard practice in economic scholarship to use schooling as a proxy for human capital.

Thus, while the studies we have just reviewed make a convincing case for the value of schooling in the marketplace, even more important for my thesis is the manner by which these works highlight the critical role of need satisfaction (e.g., education and work experience) in preparing economic agents to better cope with and perhaps even take advantage of the constantly shifting and exacting demands of the knowledge economy. The main point of the preceding literature examined is summarized well in the observation that "education is more productive the more volatile the state of technology."[42] And what can be more dramatic and volatile than the information and communications revolution of our contemporary Kondratieff cycle.

Bridging Assistance

Besides preparing economic agents to cope with pecuniary externalities, extra-market assistance is also necessary in mitigating their adverse effects. Left unattended, these can severely damage the market's own foundations: human and social capital. It makes rational economic sense to ensure that need as a criterion of distributive justice includes the necessary provisions for market participants to recover from the unavoidable chance and contingencies of market operations. This permits economic agents to continue contributing their share to maintaining the common economic life. The goal of this temporary, bridging aid is to get valuable human resources back on stream in the economy as quickly as possible after they have been set back by negative pecuniary externalities. After all, the collective tacit knowledge is dependent on the caliber of its constituent individual human capital from which it takes shape. The larger and the better the quality of such a pool, the greater is the communal synergy produced because knowledge creation is both autocorrelated and interdependent. People build not only on their own knowledge and experience, but also on others' shared knowledge and experience. Consequently, market participants have cause both to come to each other's assistance and to strengthen each other's human capital in dealing with the chance and contingencies of economic life.

Enhancing Factor Mobility

The need to move from one economic sector to another is a common example by which people are personally affected by pecuniary externalities. And it can be an unpleasant, even traumatic, experience. A strategy of need satisfaction improves market efficiency by enhancing factor mobility. The perfectly competitive market's proficiency in allocating resources to their most valued uses is partly due to its ability to respond swiftly to changing economic conditions and to shift the disposition of its resources accordingly. Hence, the assumption of perfect mobility (with its consequent ease of entry and exit and a frictionless economy) is critical for this heuristic model. Ceteris paribus, real markets come closer to attaining the allocative efficiency of the idealized model of perfect competition to the extent that they approximate the latter's perfect factor mobility.[43] I make two claims in this section. First, by their nature, actual markets do not provide propitious conditions for smooth factor mobility. In fact, for the vast majority of economic agents, their lengthening job tenure often leads to ever increasing frictional costs in moving from one sector to another. Seniority at work can turn out to be a liability. Second, the knowledge economy compounds this inherent difficulty by imposing new demands on factor mobility.

Intrinsic Hurdles to Factor Mobility

Introductory classes in microeconomics demonstrate the benefits of trade by comparing the autarky welfare of a nation with its post-trade production and consumption bundles. Key to this process is the ability to change the nation's production mix and move its equilibrium to another part of its production possibilities frontier in which it enjoys comparative advantage. Of course, these are costless and painless alterations easily accomplished on the blackboard. In reality, moving on the production possibilities frontier takes time and entails substantial costs. Moreover, at the end of the day, it is entirely possible for the nation not to even reach the optimum point of comparative advantage. At any rate, I bring this up in an effort to underscore the importance of being able to move factors of production around if we are to achieve allocative efficiency. Both in theory and in practice, the market is a highly dynamic institution and it thrives precisely because it is adept at responding to changes in a prompt and cost-effective manner. The price mechanism provides it with the unique capacity to orchestrate simultaneous changes in the decisions of disparate economic actors spread across wide geographic regions. The ability to respond to evolving needs by shifting the disposition of scarce resources rapidly is a constitutive feature of a fully functioning market.

It is paradoxical, however, that in actual markets, such agility becomes increasingly difficult over time. First, change is generally traumatic for most people. There is a psychic cost to change. Second, there are also the costs of job retraining and relocation. Third, the model for perfectly competitive markets assumes homogeneity in factors and goods. In reality, labor inputs are not homogenous. Besides variations in the quality of skills and work ethic, workers also differ with respect to age. If change entails psychic pain, such costs would most likely increase proportionately with age, perhaps even exponentially. And depending on the schooling or the skills of displaced workers, even the cost of job retraining and relocation may rise with age.[44] To make matters worse, it is the older industries that are most vulnerable to requisite change. Thus, we have numerous anecdotes of people who, after twenty to thirty years of working for an aging industry, suddenly find themselves having to look for another job, retrain in their middle age, and compete in a labor market with new entrants half their age.[45] And indeed, displaced manufacturing workers generally do not get the new, high-tech jobs created. These tend to go to younger labor-market entrants, who also turn out to be more educated.[46]

Markets, by their nature, require flexibility in moving factor inputs to their most valued uses. However, human labor as a factor of production does not readily lend itself to such transfers. There are significant frictional costs to moving labor about, and such costs only increase further with age, thereby making it that much more difficult to bring about the necessary redisposition of resources.

Factor Mobility in the Knowledge Economy

Globalization ratchets up the demand for factor mobility in the marketplace. First, as already seen in chapter 2, the downside to greater economic interdependence is that market participants are faced with constant and ever more substantive adjustments in an extremely fluid environment. Furthermore, the knowledge economy moves at an accelerated pace that requires a correspondingly faster reaction time with not much room or forewarning to prepare for a smooth transition.

Second, globalization has greatly enlarged the pool and the quality of potential competitors, thereby raising the standards for everybody else. In a wired world, geography is no longer a barrier to trade. Besides the availability of cheaper imports and the transfer of manufacturing facilities abroad to lower-cost sites, the digital age has also introduced its own new set of challenges: stiffer competition even in the services sector. White-collar workers have joined their manufacturing counterparts in having to face the real threat of job losses posed by trade liberalization. Cross-border migration is still an important mechanism for a more efficient allocation of resources, albeit on a much more modest scale compared to the nineteenth century. However, ICTs have, to a certain extent, provided a substitute for actual physical migration. In particular, note the phenomenon of offshore outsourcing. While this has been a boon for the overseas recipients of these jobs, it has also raised the bar for domestic workers in sectors that used to be nontradable, until the advent of microelectronics. These service workers have now been compelled to upgrade their skills. Globalization has led to even more stringent requirements for factor mobility. As seen in chapters 2 and 3, there is need for workers in developed countries to move faster and ever higher up the ladder of created comparative advantage.

Need Satisfaction as a Necessary Condition of Factor Mobility

The two aforementioned features of the market pull human labor in opposite directions. While human nature, on the one hand, makes it progressively costly and emotionally stressful to move workers as they age, an extremely dynamic knowledge economy, on the other hand, is increasingly exacting with its frequent, speedy, and hugely disruptive reallocations of labor across sectors. In other words, there is an increasing gap between what the market requires and what human labor is able to provide.

This predicament presents another instrumental justification for need satisfaction as a necessary condition for economic efficiency. Factor mobility in the knowledge economy is heavily determined by people's flexibility and their ability to adapt. Moreover, mobility is no longer merely geographic but increasingly "virtual" and functional in a digital world. It is the ability to move laterally across tasks. "Virtual" and functional mobility are about building the capacity for new endeavors. This requires an aptitude for learning and adaptation that only human capital formation can provide.

In making his case on the central importance of human capital in dealing with disequilibria, Schultz (1975) enumerates numerous empirical studies using data from the 1950s and 1960s on the interaction between schooling and mobility. Data on domestic migration show that more educated workers took better advantage of changes in labor-market opportunities. Within the agricultural sector, wealthier households were more successful in switching to nonfarm occupations.[47] Since wealthier families tend to be better educated, it is believed that this illustrates the value of schooling in both initiating and successfully adapting to change. Numerous other studies of domestic migration[48] confirm a pattern of how more educated migrants and families are much better at recognizing and then taking advantage of opportunities elsewhere.[49]

The same phenomenon still applies today. Low-skilled workers are said to be the most vulnerable to shocks from international trade because they are the least mobile.[50] The costs of adjustments and disruptions due to trade are minimized to the degree "that labor and capital markets are highly flexible."[51] Returns to education are much higher (9.9 percent) in countries with greater economic freedoms and mobility compared to more restrictive countries (6.4 percent).[52]

Market flexibility does not merely involve the absence of rigidities and distortions but also includes factor mobility, especially for labor. Specialized knowledge is no longer good enough in an environment that requires timely responsiveness. Even more important is the ability to learn rapidly and to forget "old ways of doing things."[53] Human capital is at the heart of the highly mobile economic agents required by the learning economy. In paying attention to need satisfaction, we are laying the foundation for efficiency by ensuring the availability of quality human resources that can meet the stringent requirement of the knowledge economy for frequent, prompt, and substantive moves across jobs. Need satisfaction is a necessary condition for factor mobility, especially in a "learning" economy.

Need Satisfaction and Preemptive Action

Need satisfaction is a prudent ex-ante measure against more expensive ex-post correction. It is best for the knowledge economy to be ahead of the curve in heading off damage to its human resources, and this often requires extra-market intervention. For example, as we have seen previously, family and social circumstances heavily determine people's life chances. This has been found to be true as well in the case of the child's intellectual growth. In Ecuador, the cognitive development of three-year-old children from the poorest and the wealthiest income quartiles varied by around 4 percentage points. By age 5, this gap in cognitive development had widened tenfold to around 40 percentage points. The same dynamic is found in examining the role of maternal education. At three years of age, there was a difference of around 10 percentage points in the cognitive development of children of mothers with 12 or more years of education versus those with 0–5 years of schooling. By age 5, this gap had grown fourfold to nearly 40 percentage points.[54]

These figures highlight what we have repeatedly seen in the preceding chapter—that parental education and family wealth (income) largely shape the opportunities open to the next generation. However, there is even greater reason to be alarmed at this particular example and others like it. First, as the authors of these studies observe, inequalities in opportunities are determined early in the life of the next generation. Second, cognitive development is a basic building block of subsequent human capital formation. Without properly nurturing their intellectual capacities at such a crucial age, children from the poorest families and of uneducated mothers would fail to live up to their full potential as adults and would in all likelihood be condemned to low levels of human capital. In the Ecuadorian study, the increasing gap between the different groups of children was not so much from the meteoric rise in the abilities of those from privileged families.[55] Rather, the widening inequality was largely due to the precipitous drop in the capabilities of the disadvantaged children.[56] In other words, less educated mothers and poorer households were unable to provide for the intellectual development of their children. This is a potent channel by which poverty and limited opportunities are passed on from one generation to the next. The children are set up for failure and destitution in their own lifetime.

A third observation is that left on its own, this process will unfold unimpeded. Even in a digital age in which it is in the self-interest of the community to develop the human capital that serves as the wellspring of its wealth, the market will not correct this problem on its own because of its inherent limitations.[57]

Ex-ante planning and preemptive action are often much cheaper than ex-post correction and damage control. This is particularly true when speaking of human capital. Take the case of child labor and child malnutrition.[58] In foregoing an education because of the need to supplement a meager household income, children are condemned to a lifetime of illiteracy and poverty. Malnutrition at an early age often results in irreversible physical and mental disabilities. In both of these cases, the subsequent drain on society and the resulting opportunity losses are immense in view of the foregone human capital that will not be available in future rounds of economic activity. These opportunity losses will be sizable in a knowledge economy characterized by increasing returns, a quicker tempo of economic life, and a path dependence in which those who have more will have even more in later rounds. Moreover, it is much better for people to be productive than to be dependent on the rest of the community for their needs. Both preceding cases are instances of market failures, missing markets in particular. Had there been a market that allowed these impoverished families to borrow from their children's future earnings, it would have been possible to provide the education and the nutrition today that would have actualized such future streams of income. Given the new possibilities for human capital formation inaugurated by the digital age, borrowing from future income not only makes sense but is, in fact, a good investment that would easily pay for itself many times over because of the increased productivity and the enhanced value of human capital afforded by the knowledge economy.[59]

Child labor and child malnutrition are merely two cases that clearly underscore the superiority and cost savings of ex-ante planning and action compared to ex-post correction and damage control in contemporary globalization. The same argument can be made with regard to fighting tropical diseases, such as malaria and river blindness. In addition to the intrinsic value of good health, there is the commonsensical, instrumental justification in preventing tropical diseases: It avoids large economic losses from the ensuing debility, morbidity, and mortality.

It has been observed that the conventional response to social exclusion has been ex post in which governments provide social safety nets, such as unemployment insurance and other forms of transfers. However, such an approach will become increasingly difficult in the years ahead because of the greater numbers of people requiring assistance, the stiffening resistance of taxpayers to further fiscal impositions, and the chronic, rather than temporary, nature of the problem of social exclusion. Sizable income transfers will be untenable given the stricter monetary and fiscal regimes required by globalization.[60] The push for a more market-oriented EU away from its traditional social economy reflects these competitive pressures.[61] There is much sense in the following observation:

> *Social and distributional policies* need to focus more strongly on the distribution and redistribution of learning capabilities. It becomes increasingly costly and difficult to redistribute welfare, *ex-post*, in a society with an uneven distribution of competence.[62]

It is imperative to ensure a more even distribution of competence in the digital age. In the first place, as we have seen in chapter 5, there is

a self-reinforcing path dependence by the nature of market operations. Such a dynamic is strengthened even further in the learning
economy because of the autocorrelated nature of tacit knowledge and
the roundabout manner by which it is accumulated. Those who have
poor human capital to begin with will find it increasingly difficult to
catch up with the fast-rising cost of participating meaningfully in the
marketplace; they will find themselves rapidly isolated. Relative
inequality will most likely deteriorate.

Second, as we have seen in chapter 2, market deepening and widening in the postindustrial economy have produced sizable potential
gains and much faster rounds of economic exchange. This means that
the opportunity losses from having human resources relegated to the
fringes will be much more substantial compared to what we have seen
in the industrial economy. Furthermore, these foregone future gains
represent resources that could have been used in ex-ante action to
develop human capital to begin with.[63] Ex-ante intervention pays for
itself by avoiding ex-post opportunity losses, in addition to the direct
cost of ameliorative measures such as welfare transfers. It is much better to ensure people's continued participation in economic life, according to their skills and potential contribution, instead of pursuing
posterior remedial measures.

The cost of such preemptive action to protect human capital can be
substantial. Take the case of the conditional cash transfer (CCT) programs in Mexico, Brazil, Jamaica, Honduras, Nicaragua, and
Colombia.[64] This is an imaginative approach to breaking the intergenerational transmission of poverty by intervening early and effectively in the lives of at-risk children. Traditional approaches until
recently were "supply-side" in nature because governments simply
concentrated on the public provision of essential services. CCT programs, on the other hand, come with a "demand-side" strategy by
using monetary incentives to induce household demand for essential
services for their children. For example, families receive cash grants for
keeping their children in school or for bringing their children to
health clinics for regular checkups.

As expected, these are hugely expensive programs. Mexico's
Oportunidades program[65] covered 300,000 families when it started in
1997. By 2004, it had expanded to more than 4 million families
(20 percent of the population) and cost $1.8 billion for that year alone.
However, CCT programs are extremely effective just as they are expensive. For example, *Oportunidades* is credited with increasing enroll-
ment at the secondary level by 7.2 to 9.3 percent for girls and 3.5 to
5.8 percent for boys. It is believed to have reduced the likelihood of

child labor for boys aged 12–13 years by 15 to 20 percent. Children less than five years old showed a 12 percent decline in morbidity. Growth monitoring visits to clinics increased by 30 to 60 percent. It is believed that the program had also reduced the incidence of stunting for children less than three years of age. Nutrition for families covered by the program improved with a 14 percent increase in average consumption level, an 11 percent gain in food expenditures, a 7.8 percent rise in median caloric intake, and a greater consumption of fruits, vegetables, and animal products. To top it all, the administrative cost of running the program is only 9 percent of its total budget. Comparable gains have been recorded in other CCT programs in the region.

The benefits of CCT schemes and similar programs are grossly understated because intervening early in the lives of at-risk children and youths has significant long-term effects, many of which may be difficult to pinpoint and measure. For example, Jamaican children who received psychosocial stimulation as toddlers (one–five years old) were more likely to be still in school by age thirteen to eighteen compared to those who did not receive such early assistance. The same phenomenon is true for children whose parents received some training in parenting skills.[66] Or, recall the earlier case of on-the-job training for recent school graduates. Their returns (6 percent) from an additional year of work experience are twice that of older age groups because they can parlay skills acquired early on for much better jobs for the rest of their productive years.[67] Furthermore, there are often unexpected positive spillover effects in many of these programs, as in the case of providing school uniforms in the Bungoma and Butere-Mumias districts in Kenya. This led to a decline not only in the dropout rates but also resulted in much later childbearing. In fact, providing school uniforms turned out to be much more effective than the program that was specifically targeted at delaying childbearing among female teenagers.[68] All these cases merely highlight the point that the true impact of many of these child and youth programs is often unseen or unmeasured in their lingering or unintended effects.

The returns from such types of intervention are significant. For example, the World Bank projects that subsidizing secondary education in Kenya as a way of recouping and rebuilding the lost human capital from the AIDS epidemic provides returns that are anywhere from 2 to 3.5 times the cost of the program.[69] The intervention pays for itself over the long haul. Of course, the problem is providing the upfront investment. In this case, the subsidy required amounts to 0.9 percent of GDP and doubles to 1.8 percent by 2020. This example captures the nub of the problem: Ex-ante corrective action is often extremely expensive and requires a political will with a long-term horizon and the courage to can make hard choices.[70]

Summary and Conclusions

There is abundant empirical and theoretical work underlying the claim that education and human capital, by extension, play a central role in economic development and human well-being. The importance of schooling stands out even more during times of disequilibria and turbulence. It is most productive precisely in moments of great dynamism, change, and volatility. This should not come as a surprise because an education provides essential life, social, and coping skills. Education provides the basic tools for further self-improvement, such as, securing tacit knowledge. This, in turn, makes economic agents even better at allocating resources, networking with others, and initiating change. What we have learned about education can be generalized for need satisfaction as a strategy of political economy.

It is in the self-interest of the knowledge economy to ensure that human needs are satisfied. After all, human capital formation has become the chief source of wealth and value creation. Furthermore, a strategy of need satisfaction prevents valuable human resources from being permanently excluded from meaningful and productive participation in the economy on account of the market's unavoidable adverse pecuniary externalities. Besides, need satisfaction is a sensible policy because it is cheaper ex ante to nurture human capital than to have to correct its deficiencies ex post. Meeting the needs of human capital formation is a necessary condition for sustainable, long-term economic efficiency, especially in the knowledge economy.

Chapter 7

Broader Base for Market Initiative, Creativity, and Stability

A signal accomplishment of the industrial age was its revolution of mass consumption. Goods and services that until then were affordable only for the nobility and the wealthy became common items of consumption for ordinary people, thanks in large part to the massive drop in the cost of producing them. In our digital age, we have the possibility of an era of mass technological creativity. A strategy of need satisfaction ensures a stable source of such economic vitality.

The preceding chapter examined the direct effects of a strategy of need satisfaction in bolstering long-term allocative efficiency. This chapter presents some of its more roundabout, indirect contributions to economic efficiency. In particular, I argue that need satisfaction has the collateral benefit of strengthening the market even further as a vehicle for widespread socioeconomic participation. Not only is the market good at creating value, it is also remarkable in providing people with both the chance and the means to better their lives.

Despite its numerous flaws discussed in chapter 5 in which many are marginalized, we must, nonetheless, never lose sight of the market's accomplishments through history. Contrast, for example, the extensive opportunities of modern economic agents with those of their feudal counterparts. The modern market economy has lavished people with a wide range of economic freedoms that would have been unimaginable in earlier times. And, to the extent that such economic liberties spill over into and spawn freedom in other spheres of society, such as the political realm, the market can be said to be empowering for many. By any measure—GDP per capita, human development index, physical quality of life index, various UN social indicators—there has been a steady improvement in the overall material well-being of most populations when viewed longitudinally across time.[1] People from all classes, races, and backgrounds have enjoyed upward socioeconomic mobility and have seen their lives improved in those instances when the market worked properly. Technological change has undoubtedly been the proximate cause of the major advances inaugurated by the Industrial Revolution, but it has been the market economy that has fostered and unleashed the full potential of such technical breakthroughs. Despite all the evident ills of the market, we also have to be honest in acknowledging its immense capacity to improve material welfare.

The knowledge economy and a strategy of need satisfaction reinforce the above-mentioned market strengths. I present the following three arguments to support this claim:

1. The market is unique in its capacity for nurturing private initiative. A strategy of need satisfaction develops this feature of the market even further by improving the human capital undergirding the private sector.
2. A "learning" economy can aggravate relative inequality because of the autocorrelated nature of knowledge creation. A strategy of need satisfaction minimizes such relative inequalities and provides the means for even reversing such a widening gap.
3. By shifting the source of wealth and value creation from industrial capital and natural resources to knowledge, the learning economy reduces the scope for rival consumption. This makes a strategy of need satisfaction relatively more sustainable and less contentious compared to other means of reducing relative inequality.

Each of these three mechanisms is discussed in the following sections.

Broader Technological Creativity

Opportunities

Contemporary globalization has given rise to the network society in which people are drawn to each other in ever expanding but tightening webs of communications. Thus, there are even claims on the "death of distance."[2] A different point of view, however, suggests that the emergence of this network society reflects an even more profound phenomenon—*the democratization of technological change and use*.[3] I agree. Just examine the impact of technology in the everyday lives of ordinary people, even of the most impoverished nations. For example, sub-Saharan Africa and other LDCs have leapfrogged the more expensive, traditional, electromechanical switching telecommunication systems in favor of wireless ICTs.[4] There are accounts too of Indian farmers who have been empowered by ICTs. In informing themselves about prices through the Internet, these farmers are no longer at the mercy of middlemen who used to profit from the rural population's ignorance of larger market conditions beyond the village.[5] Indeed, mass technological use holds enormous possibilities that have yet to be fully exploited as part of the knowledge economy.

Slow Down and Sheltered Industries

Various proposals have been advanced on how to foster the knowledge economy, including a deliberate slow down of change and a national innovation policy. First, the pace of change in the digital age can be so rapid to the point where such "hyper-acceleration" becomes self-defeating. For example, the rate of obsolescence can be so fast as to discourage people from adopting new technologies until absolutely necessary. It is often better to simply wait for the next generation of technological changes instead of investing time and effort in mastering current software or technologies that will soon be replaced anyway.[6] Companies find it difficult to recoup the cost of their investments. Recall the earlier case of Japanese automakers voluntarily slowing down changes in car models in an effort to ensure that technological advances are digested in a cost- and time-effective manner.[7] Of course, an additional benefit to slowing down change deliberately is that it buys time for lagging nations to catch up.

A second proposal is the establishment of "sheltered industries" as part of a national innovation policy.[8] One should not exaggerate talk of mass technological change and use. A look at the empirical evidence provides a quick reality check. For example, the use of ICTs is still limited in the underdeveloped world.[9] Moreover, R&D is still heavily concentrated in the triad comprised of the United States, the EU, and Japan.[10] This should not come as a surprise considering the special requirements of R&D. Schumpeter (1942) argues that monopoly power provides firms with the necessary resources to take risks in pushing the envelope of technological change. It is these firms that provide capitalism with its capacity for "creative destruction."

Many scholars and policymakers agree with Schumpeter's position on the utility of some monopoly power for technological change. Recall, for example, that a long-standing rationale for copyrights and patents is to provide inventors with exclusive control over a limited period of time to permit them to recoup their development costs and reward them with rents for their risk-taking. Change is not only risky, it is also expensive. Moreover, firms must also have the means to pay for some of the adjustment expenses as a result of technological innovation, such as the disruption in operations and the replacement of equipment suddenly rendered obsolete. Some monopoly power is needed to accumulate the profits that are used to fund the next generation of revolutionary inventions. This ensures a constant supply of techno-economic paradigm shifts in the pipeline, with more Kondratieff cycles lined up down the road when the current round of innovations eventually lose their vigor and force.

Schumpeter's insight has been learned well by governments. To this day, even in the face of widespread economic liberalization, governments sidestep the marketplace and provide support for "national industrial champions" or industries that show promise in taking the next great technological leap.[11] A goal of these market interventions is to facilitate Schumpeterian efficiency.[12] Some believe that such an active government role is not merely an option, but a necessity in the learning economy.[13]

An Alternative, More Radical, Proposal

The aforesaid proposals to slow down change intentionally or to create "sheltered sectors" are reminiscent of the restrictions of the medieval guilds and the Luddites of the Industrial Revolution. They are antithetical to the market liberalization that is at the heart of globalization. Such protectionism often ends up creating pockets of vested interests and stifling much-needed technological change. Furthermore, a strategy of purposely slowing down technological innovation may entail significant opportunity losses, especially for future generations. I suggest a different approach: a genuine and even more aggressive expansion of the primary source of technological change.

The knowledge economy has heralded a twofold revolution: a revolution of expectations and a revolution of technological creativity. The revolution of expectations is already well on its way because of satellite television and radio, the Internet, and twenty-four-hour news coverage. One only has to look at recent events in world affairs to appreciate both the greater transparency that ICTs have precipitated and the speed with which news and information travel. People have access to a wide variety of news sources, and national governments have been increasingly clipped of their ability to restrict or to shape the information their citizenry gets, except of course for the most totalitarian regimes. Easy access to different media and better knowledge of how the rest of the world lives have raised expectations, especially among the poor. The digital age has led to rising expectations, a phenomenon whose full consequences have yet to unfold.

The second revolution (mass technological creativity) is still nascent. The nineteenth and early twentieth centuries had their share of industrial titans like Andrew Carnegie and Henry Ford who had the daring, vision, and entrepreneurship to pull together labor, money, machines, and materials to produce essential goods at prices ordinary people can afford. The knowledge economy also has its own icons: men and women who have labored in garages and tiny labs to produce the likes of Microsoft, Intel, Hewett-Packard, Dell, eBay, Google, and Yahoo. The list could go on and continues to lengthen. What is remarkable about this era is that Silicon Valley and Bangalore are most likely not the high points but only the precursors of a revolution of mass technological creativity. Besides the big-name technological firms, note, for example, the proliferation of many tech start-ups whose failure and turnover rates reflect the vibrancy of private initiative.

The key factor that allowed us to move from being a feudal economy of precarious subsistence to our current industrial and postindustrial economies of mass consumption and accelerating growth was the separation of the economic sphere from political control.[14] In transferring allocative mechanisms from the fiat of governments and sovereigns to the price mechanism of the market, the creativity and energy of ordinary economic agents were let loose. The modern economy blossomed under the lead of the private sector once it was liberated from feudal political restraint and given full vent. We see the same phenomenon unfolding in the transitional economies; we witness exactly the same process at work in the newly industrialized economies; and we see it repeating itself again in China, India, and Vietnam today. The market economy and private initiative are a perfect match for each other; they have a proven track record of the synergies they can spawn.

Thus, unlike the aforementioned practices of slowing down change or of sheltering selected industries, I propose that the main thrust of a national innovation policy ought to be nurturing the very foundation of technological creativity: human capital formation. This holds the key to ensuring the quality and continued vitality of the knowledge economy. Furthermore, such an approach dovetails the market's characteristic strength of providing people with the chance and the means to improve their lives. We get a glimpse of the value of a broadened technological base in the role that the pool of well-educated workers, engineers, and professionals have played so far in China and India.

The same dynamic was at work when Great Britain benefited from the availability of mechanically savvy people who provided much-needed skills for the Industrial Revolution.[15] And, again, it was true for Germany when its supply of scientists helped forge the second, more scientific, Industrial Revolution. Despite its much-touted strengths, the contribution of ICTs has yet to appear in a major way in our measures of productivity.[16] Nonetheless, it is clear that a better educated workforce is a necessary condition if ICTs are to result in better economic performance.[17]

Human capital formation across the entire community is a much more potent national innovation policy. In going beyond "sheltered" firms, national industrial champions, or winning industries, nations can build their innovation policies on the people themselves and their private initiative. This is a much more forward-leaning response to the accelerating pace of the knowledge economy than is creating protected sectors or slowing down change.[18] Human capital development has inherent worth on its own; it is an inalienable right to be educated. Besides this intrinsic justification, however, the information age can make a strong case for universal education on utilitarian grounds.

In summary, the market, a strategy of need satisfaction, and the knowledge economy mutually reinforce each other to produce a synergy. On the one hand, a strategy of need satisfaction enhances the market by strengthening private initiative through an improvement of its fundamental building block: human capital. On the other hand, the knowledge economy opens up new and significant opportunities for personal enterprise through the wider access to advanced technologies made possible by ICTs. Schumpeter's (1942) toleration of some monopoly power for the sake of fresh technological initiatives is intended to assist firms to finance their R&D and undertake risks. The varied proposals for "sheltered industries," for slowing down change, and for a coherent national innovation policy are targeted at shoring up both social and firm-specific capital.[19] I suggest going beyond these proposals and going all the way down to the individual market participant. In particular, building human capital at the level of every economic agent provides the most secure and stable foundation for a national innovation policy.[20] It is also likely to be the most rewarding. Only in forming a pool of qualitatively superior human capital, individual by individual, can we ensure continued "gales of creative destruction" into the future. A genuine "democratization" of technology lies not merely in the widespread use of ICTs or in the intensity of networking across society.[21] Rather, a true and effective mass technological creativity in a knowledge economy lies with providing every economic agent with an authentic opportunity to develop and then use his or her human capital. The phenomenon of globalization has just begun and still has a long way to go. Both its beneficial and adverse effects have yet to be fully felt. Thus, there is urgency to human capital formation.

Need Satisfaction and Relative Inequality

Why should relative inequality matter as long as people's basic needs are met? Should we not focus exclusively on absolute measures of poverty rather than on relative standing as well? I submit that severe relative inequalities are detrimental to economic efficiency. If this claim is correct, then, one could also conclude that a strategy of need satisfaction contributes indirectly to attaining efficiency by keeping relative inequalities within reasonable limits.

There are a variety of reasons why severe relative inequalities impede economic efficiency. First, as we have seen in chapter 5, there is an entry cost to market participation.[22] These requirements to market participation are not static but change over time as new standards are set. For example, in contrast to their counterparts a generation ago, office secretaries today are expected to be well-versed, at a minimum, with various word-processing, spread-sheet, and presentation software programs. The same is true for many other professions in view of the heavy use of ICTs. Or take, for example, the need for further graduate or professional degrees for the current generation of college students as a condition for continued employment or advancement. MBAs, law degrees, master's degrees, and even Ph.D.s were not common in earlier times, but are increasingly the norm rather than the exception today. In other words, there has been a continued rise in the required level of education, skills, and training for successful market participation. This is confirmed by numerous empirical studies that point to an increasing gap in the wages and opportunities of skilled or degree-holding workers versus unskilled or nondegree workers.[23]

The same phenomenon is true at a macroeconomic level in the economic relations of nations. The minimum standards for success in selling in the global marketplace are much more demanding today than they were just a decade ago. Normal industry expectations today include high quality products at a low price with superior packaging and assured delivery times to replenish just-in-time inventories. And, the standards for what constitutes high quality, low prices, superior packaging, and timely deliveries are constantly revised upwards as the technological frontier for what is possible to achieve is pushed even further by leaders in the field. A strength of the market economy is the discipline and the drive for further excellence it instills through competition. The best industry practices today are imitated by everybody else, thereby making them standard norms for the next rounds of competition.[24] Anecdotal stories of never-ending improvements in manufacturing processes among Chinese firms scrambling for export market shares illustrate the ever tougher standards of cutthroat competition.[25] As a result, leaders in the field are compelled to improve much further and faster in order to distinguish themselves from the pack, thereby pushing the envelope and expectations even more. Of course, those left behind are forced to follow suit or at least adopt these innovations, lest they find themselves completely shut out of export markets.

It is the leaders of the field that break new ground and set ever higher industry standards; in effect, the leading edges of the market constantly raise the bar for successful market participation by the nature and logic of competition. Firms that lag too far behind will find it that much more difficult to keep up with these rising industry expectations that eventually become the minimum required. In other words, widening or extreme relative inequalities in capabilities among market participants would most likely mean that those who are trailing badly will find it increasingly difficult to participate in the market in any meaningful way. Take the case of sub-Saharan Africa or the nonglobalizers of the past two decades. Without major assistance from the rest of the world and without a massive infusion of technical help, it is highly unlikely that these nations will be able to meet the ever rising standards of the global export markets for manufactures or services. Not even developed countries are exempt from such market discipline. The constant pressure on U.S. and EU manufacturers, service providers, and farmers from competitors overseas is an excellent illustration of the ever-changing prerequisites to participation in the marketplace, even for the wealthiest nations.

In sum, relative inequalities should matter because the severity of the gap in endowments and capabilities determines the degree to which weaker actors are able to keep up with the ever rising entry costs to successful market participation. The leaders of the pack keep on ratcheting standards upwards and, in effect, raise the expectations for everybody else. Those who are too far behind may not be able to catch up, much less thrive in these new exacting requirements, and simply drop out.[26] This is a phenomenon that is true at all levels of market competition: global, national, industrial, corporate, and personal.

A second reason for why relative inequality ought to matter has to do with the importance of bargaining power in market exchange. The perfectly competitive market assumes ease of entry and exit thereby precluding monopoly control. It is a level playing field for all market participants in which everyone is a price-taker. In practice, however, many economic actors often exercise varying degrees of influence and are, consequently, able to shape market outcomes in their own favor. Such market power is a result of disparities in economic agents' relative bargaining strengths, which, in turn, are heavily determined by their endowments and capabilities. In other words, wide relative inequalities in what economic actors bring to the marketplace become the occasion for monopoly power, which is widely acknowledged to be ultimately detrimental to long-term allocative efficiency. This dynamic is true at all levels of market competition down to the individual economic agent. A wide relative inequality in the resources or powers that truly matter is simply too tempting not to be used to one's own advantage. Such wide disparities in bargaining power are believed to be the proximate cause of economic coercion in which weaker parties are compelled to make choices they would normally not take under ordinary market conditions.[27] For this reason, even the most capitalist of nations have instituted antitrust legislation to safeguard against undue market concentration. Such antitrust measures are a de facto cap on the extent to which relative inequalities in corporate market power will be permitted.

Third, relative inequality matters because of the insidious consequences of the demonstration effect of consumption. There is consensus in economic scholarship on the importance of mutual trust as an essential precondition of market operations.[28] There must be a sense of fairness if the market is to function at all and if economic exchange is to be viable into the long term. However, such trust and sense of fairness are eroded by extreme inequalities.[29] This should not come as a surprise as fairness and trust presuppose mutual advantage in market exchange. Unfortunately, this poses significant challenges for our current global economic integration. ICTs are the heart of our current Kondratieff cycle, and the "death of distance"[30] they have precipitated has made interpersonal interaction and the exchange of information so much easier. The poor of the world are now ever more aware of how the wealthy live and consume luxuries. This has brought about a "revolution of rising expectations" that is escalating faster than the global marketplace's ability to satisfy these new claims.

For individuals in poor nations, this situation occasions a perception of increasing inequality, even if their standards of living are rising in absolute terms. It has been argued that despite improvements in the absolute consumption levels of citizens in lower-income countries, they will nonetheless end up frustrated and disappointed at not being able to emulate the lifestyles they witness in other parts of the world.[31] Traditional consumption theory is inadequate because it assumes that preferences are fixed; it fails to account for people's changing preferences in accordance with the demonstration effect of others' consumption and way of life.[32] This has been described as adaptive preference formation.[33] Relative equality matters to the extent that trust and a sense of fairness—critical preconditions to smooth market operations—are eroded by wide disparities across economic agents. Relative equality is important if a perception of mutual advantage among market participants is an essential foundation for continued economic exchange and, by extension, economic efficiency. Socioeconomic harmony and stability will be difficult to maintain for as long as people feel aggrieved.[34]

Empirical studies find a positive correlation between the quality of nations' institutions and their economic performance. The IMF suggests promoting "social cohesion and stability" partly by "guarding against extremes of poverty, reducing civil conflict, and muting the adverse consequences of economic dislocation and change."[35] Relative equality matters because it is indirectly foundational for economic performance by contributing to the maintenance of harmony and collaboration without which no nation can truly develop.

A fourth reason why relative inequality ought to be kept within reasonable limits has to do with the ripple effects of market participants' economic decisions. This point is best explained with examples. Take the sudden jump in tortilla prices of around 40 percent within a short span of three months in early 2007 in Mexico. Many analysts attribute this to the increase in demand for corn from its northern neighbor, the United States, to make ethanol fuel.[36] While hardly causing a ripple in the huge U.S. economy, this rise in demand for ethanol and corn inflicted real costs especially on the poor in the much smaller Mexican economy. Or, take the case of the end of the Multifiber Agreement's quota system as of January 1, 2005. China's overwhelming efficiency in textile and apparel manufacturing has put in peril such industries in many poor developing countries that are heavily dependent on these exports (e.g., Bangladesh). And, of course, we have the well-known and well-debated case of European, Japanese, and U.S. agricultural subsidies to protect a small segment of their respective populations at the expense of inflicting widespread economic hardship on the rural populations of developing nations.[37]

In all these cases, observe how economic events set off by dominant nations and relatively inconsequential to them often spill over into poor developing nations as adverse, even life-and-death, pecuniary externalities. Given wide relative inequalities in national endowments and capabilities, minor decisions in leading economies can cause major economic disruptions or crises in lagging market economies, often the ones that are least able to deal with such disequilibria to begin with.[38] Relative inequality among market participants ought to matter because such disparities determine economic agents' ability to inflict or cope with adverse pecuniary externalities.[39] The larger the gap, the more vulnerable are the weaker market participants to the harmful unintended consequences generated by the more dominant economic actors.

Finally, numerous empirical studies show that severe inequalities retard economic development. Moreover, the poverty-alleviating impact of growth is diminished by high levels of initial inequality. (This should not be surprising in view of the path dependence we examined in chapter 5.) Those at the bottom of the income distribution are productive and efficient in the use of what little they have and contribute much to the economic life of the larger community, if only they are given the necessary economic means and assets to do so. The success of microcredit provides ample evidence of this. Furthermore, economic inequalities sustain disparities in political power and vice versa. They are two sides of the same coin. The result of this synergy is predictable: deeply entrenched institutions that are geared for accumulating even more power and protecting vested interests rather than promoting the nation's welfare.[40] This is a recipe for a poverty trap, as we indeed see in many stagnating countries of sub-Saharan Africa, Asia, and Latin America.

If these reasons on why relative inequality ought to be kept within limits are valid, then a strategy of need satisfaction is an essential remedy. Need satisfaction ensures that no one is left too far behind and that human and social capital are constantly upgraded in line with the rising entry costs to market participation. Need satisfaction, as we have seen in chapter 6, also provides the necessary resources to recover from particularly damaging adverse pecuniary externalities. A singular focus on allocative efficiency cannot accomplish these goals as it is only concerned with the optimum disposition of scarce resources to their most valued uses.

Nonrivalrous Solution

Broadening the sources of technological creativity via human capital formation is more promising for the knowledge economy than slowing down change or protecting certain sectors. It is admittedly an ambitious and far more expensive response, but the greater outlay of effort, resources, and time in focusing on the individual is warranted because, far from being a threat or a problem, contemporary globalization presents unique opportunities. As already mentioned, in the industrial economy, natural resources and industrial capital were the key sources of wealth and value creation. Unfortunately, as these resources are finite, subject to rival consumption, and highly concentrated, their rents have been restricted to a fairly small number of market participants. The postindustrial economy heralds new possibilities because the source of wealth creation has shifted to knowledge and, of course, to the underlying human capital in which it is embodied. While it is also relatively unequally divided across the global population, knowledge enjoys clear advantages over natural resources and industrial capital as a source of value creation. Knowledge and human capital are not subject to rival consumption; only the resources that are used for gaining knowledge and developing human capital are subject to such kind of competition.[41] People can benefit from knowledge and develop their human capital without precluding others from doing the same.

Compared to tangible material resources, knowledge is relatively easier to diffuse; it is not as finite. Knowledge may even be subject to increasing, rather than diminishing, returns as it is shared. Put in another way, there are enormous spillover effects for knowledge and human capital formation. Furthermore, individual economic actors have relatively better control over how they acquire knowledge and to what extent they develop their own human capital compared with the ownership of natural resources or industrial capital that are realistically well out of reach for the vast majority of people. Knowledge acquisition and human capital formation are more open to personal striving and effort, and their complementary inputs, such as formal schooling or technical training, are more accessible to the common person than industrial capital. Moreover, failures in governance, lack of support, or the incompetence of the leadership at the international, national, local, or even family level do not automatically preclude the individual from excelling on his or her own initiative.

Indeed, the shift in the principal source of value creation to knowledge and human capital in the postindustrial economy enhances the market's ability to engender widespread socioeconomic participation. It is much easier and less controversial to develop human capital and knowledge than it is to redistribute industrial capital and natural resources. A reallocation of future streams of income is less contentious compared with reshuffling existing wealth or current earnings. The emergence of Bangalore as a hub for high-tech work in less than a decade speaks eloquently of this dynamic. The added advantage to such a strategy of building human capital is that it pays for itself. In theory, it becomes self-sustaining after the first generation of beneficiaries.

In its *World Development Report 2006: Equity and Development*, the World Bank notes that equity is a precondition for long-term development. After all, our emerging knowledge economy is heavily reliant on the quality and distribution of available human capital.

Summary and Conclusions

To conclude part III, recall that Konow's (2003) descriptive study of the theories of distributive justice reveals three principal criteria: efficiency, need, and entitlement. Unfortunately, he did not rank order these three competing standards. These two chapters examined need in relation to efficiency.

Most people would agree that in life-and-death situations, need trumps the two other criteria. The preservation of human life and the requirements of basic health take precedence over other claims. Most people embrace an intrinsic justification to need as a criterion of distributive justice on the basis of human life and dignity. This is a proposition many would readily accept. What is more controversial, however, is the extent to which need trumps the other two criteria in non-life-threatening situations, if at all. Beyond emergencies, should societal resources be distributed according to need, efficiency, or entitlement?

These two chapters have presented an instrumental justification for need as a norm of distributive justice. Over and above its intrinsic value (e.g., preserving human life and basic health), need satisfaction is useful as it facilitates the attainment of long-term efficiency in the knowledge economy. Need satisfaction has functional value for a variety of reasons: it builds the human capital that is critical for tacit knowledge; it provides safeguards against the negative pecuniary externalities of globalization; it enhances efficiency by improving factor mobility in a learning economy; it preempts more costly ex-post ameliorative action; it strengthens the market's praiseworthy quality of nurturing and unleashing private initiative and technological creativity; it keeps severe relative inequalities at bay; it provides a less rivalrous means to a more equitable redistribution of resources. These beneficial effects of need satisfaction mutually reinforce each other.

This instrumental justification to need satisfaction is founded on the observation that knowledge has become the wellspring of value creation in the learning economy. Thus, the vitality of future growth in the digital age is dependent on the quality of human capital, which in turn requires need satisfaction in the earlier periods of economic activity. One could call this strategy the pursuit of "instrumental" equity because need satisfaction in the earlier rounds of economic life is useful for attaining efficiency in later periods.[42] It could also be considered a roundabout investment. The broad-based growth of the East Asian economy is an example of how nations become much more stable, dynamic, and competitive if their economic infrastructure is undergirded by a well-honed social and human capital. "Growth with equity" is a proven winning strategy.[43]

There are at least four implications to such an instrumental (in contrast to intrinsic) justification of need satisfaction. First, there is a confluence of the distributive and the allocative dimensions of price in the knowledge economy. After all, human capital formation (and need satisfaction, by extension) holds the key to reaching long-term efficiency in the knowledge economy. This means that we should no longer view need and efficiency as competing norms of distributive justice because they have become necessary conditions for each other. On the one hand, human capital formation lays the groundwork for subsequent economic efficiency. On the other hand, efficiency ensures that there will be sufficient resources to pay for and sustain a strategy of need satisfaction. Recall that a policy of need satisfaction requires substantial amounts of societal inputs, and a continued supply of such resources is possible only if the market keeps providing the necessary incentives for private initiative to produce and innovate. Thus, economic efficiency is a necessary condition for long-term human capital formation. Need satisfaction and efficiency, while distinct from each other, have become inseparable. One can make this statement even stronger by claiming that need satisfaction and efficiency meld into a complementary pair of distributive criteria in the digital age. We cannot have one without the other. Discourse should no longer be about "equity versus efficiency" but "equity *and* efficiency."

Second, the convergence of equity and efficiency in the information economy narrows the gap between critics and advocates of globalization. Skeptics point to the plight of those who have been marginalized by the market; they have championed need satisfaction as the primary criterion of distributive justice.[44] Unfortunately, they have focused exclusively on the urgent need to redistribute societal resources without paying heed to how these are to be produced in the first place. As a result, their proposed measures often end up causing more harm than good by destroying the incentives that are critical for ensuring the continued production and supply of vital goods and services. The shortages of the egalitarian political economies of the former

Soviet Union and pre-1979 China provide empirical proof of how an uncritical, unbalanced egalitarianism is ultimately counterproductive. On the other hand, laissez-faire proponents acclaim the market's ability to produce value and wealth without considering its adverse distributive ramifications.[45]

The knowledge economy narrows the gap between these two camps because future output is now even more dependent on equity in the distribution of resources in the earlier periods of economic life. In the learning economy, the requirements of equity and efficiency converge because both revolve around the central importance of human capital. The major changes in the market's core efficiency occasioned by ICTs (described in chapter 2) require corresponding alterations in the pursuit of allocative efficiency that make it more sensitive to how human needs are satisfied in the course of market operations. In effect, in the digital age, *the market's allocative efficiency requires an inclusive efficiency.* This is a welcome development that should narrow the divide between proponents and critics of globalization.

Third, most discourse on need as a criterion of distributive justice limit it only to the necessities of human survival, such as food, clothing, shelter, and medical care. My instrumental justification requires a much broader reach. Bringing about efficiency in the knowledge economy has many more requirements than simply assuring physical survival and basic health. Thus, one would expect a much larger basket of goods and services to be included as part of need satisfaction. Specifying the precise content of such a basket of needs is beyond the scope of this project. Moreover, it is an exercise that cannot be done separately from the actual context in which it is to be implemented. Nonetheless, we can say that it must, at a minimum, include the goods and services that are critical for human capital formation and a meaningful participation in the marketplace. Education, job-skills training, and work experience immediately come to mind.

Finally, on its own, an unfettered marketplace will not necessarily develop the human capital that is so essential for allocative efficiency in the knowledge economy because of market failures. For example, we have the case of missing markets in chapter 6 in which impoverished families are unable to borrow from their children's future streams of income in order to invest in the education and better health that will bring about such future income. Or, we may have a collective-action problem in which individuals with the wherewithal do not have the incentive to advance the "intellectual commons" of the community. Their appropriable private benefits are far less than the social benefits of such an improvement. Or, people may simply have a short time horizon and not invest in themselves or in their children. In all these, a case can be made for a strategy of need satisfaction. Such action need not necessarily be shouldered exclusively by the state but may also come from private voluntary (nonprofit) organizations or the new breed of social entrepreneurs. Of course, it could also take the form of economic rights.

Part IV

Entitlement as a Criterion of Distributive Justice

P art IV considers entitlement as a suitable principle of distributive justice. Chapter 8 describes ownership externalities in the marketplace in which many factor inputs are left unpaid for their real social contribution. These ownership externalities are inescapable by the nature of the market as a public good in which anyone with the requisite purchasing power can avail of its services. Furthermore, the market acts like a network externality as it confers ever-greater benefits on its participants as it expands its geographic reach and scale, just as technologies, currencies, and languages become even more valuable to early adopters as more people use them. Unfortunately, the resulting gains are difficult, if not impossible, to assign to their rightful owners, thereby exacerbating the gap between private and social costs or benefits. Thus, by its nature, the market rarely pays factor inputs according to their true social contribution because of its manifold unintended consequences (externalities). This means that market outcomes and processes do not meet Nozick's two conditions of justice in acquisition and justice in transfer. Extra-market correctives are needed if we are to satisfy these twin provisos and employ entitlement as a norm of distributive justice.

Chapter 8

Ownership Externalities and the Market as a Public Good

Nozick's Entitlement Theory

Distribution according to entitlement is the third criterion examined by Konow (2003). The best exponent of this approach is Robert Nozick (1974, 150–53) who argues that justice in both the acquisition and transfer of properties entitles their proprietors to receive whatever is their due from ownership of such holdings. Societal output ought to be divided according to what people bring to the marketplace and what they contribute.

Nozick's position finds resonance in neoclassical economic analysis. For example, consider an economy with two factors of production, labor and capital. How should output be divided between these two inputs and on what basis? In the marginal productivity theory of factor payments, inputs are paid according to the value of their marginal product. Thus, the wage of a worker is determined by the marginal product of labor multiplied by the market price of the output produced. Likewise, capital is paid at a rate equal to its marginal product multiplied by the market price of the output. There is great appeal in such a distributive criterion because factors are paid only according to what they produce and contribute to the economy. Most people find this intuitively fair. Even more important, however, this method of factor payment simplifies the problem of rank ordering the three criteria of distributive justice we are weighing because in a perfectly competitive economy with no externalities or market failures, paying factors of production according to their marginal productivity is a necessary condition of allocative efficiency. Thus, the criterion of entitlement is subsumed under that of efficiency.

The criticisms of both Nozick's entitlement theory of justice and the marginal productivity theory of factor payments are extensive, and we do not have the space to examine them in this chapter. Instead, I will demonstrate that by using Nozick's own two preconditions of justice, entitlement as a norm and the marginal productivity theory of factor payments cannot be applied without extensive corrective work. Justice in acquisition and justice in the transfer of private properties are violated because market participants do not pay much of the social costs that are incurred in market operations, just as they are probably unpaid for many of their unseen or unmeasured social contributions. There is a gap between the private and the social costs or benefits of participating in the marketplace. Unless these social costs (benefits) are paid, entitlement as a measure of distributive justice fails because some people are getting more than their due, at the expense of others who bear more than their share of the cost of sustaining market operations. Extra-market remedies ensure that people shoulder the true social cost of the benefits they reap from the marketplace. It is only after we have rectified such a market failure that we can truly say that people get what is rightfully theirs. Recall that the marginal productivity theory of factor payments works only in the absence of externalities.

Ownership Externalities

In his example of apple orchards and apiaries, Meade (1952) provides an excellent exposition on two types of ownership externalities. Beekeepers reap benefits from nearby apple orchards as their bees feed on the nectar of apple blossoms and produce honey in the process. Thus, an increase in the apple harvest produces a collateral increment in honey production without the beekeepers having to do anything. Orchard owners, however, are unable to share in the extra revenues from beekeepers' augmented honey production because they (the apple growers) are unable to exclude the bees of nonpaying apiaries from their orchards. Hence, the social benefit of the apple orchards exceeds the private gains of their owners. It would have been optimum for the entire community to increase apple production given the latter's positive externality. Likewise, the private cost of beekeeping is less than its true social cost because this sector does not have to internalize part of the cost of running apple orchards. Beekeepers are, in effect, getting a free ride at the expense of the apple growers. Put in another way, there is an underproduction of apple blossoms and an overproduction of honey compared to what is called for under allocative efficiency in which private costs and benefits truly reflect social costs and benefits. Beekeepers get to keep the windfall from the additional honey while not having to expend anything for the upkeep of the apple orchards. Meade calls this a case of unpaid factors.

In a second example, "the creation of atmosphere," Meade presents the case of timber growers and wheat farmers. Trees affect atmospheric conditions positively by inducing more rainfall. This is a boon for wheat growers. Thus, the planting of more trees provides beneficial spillover effects for the wheat farms. Farmers do not have to pay the timber industry for such gains. As a result, just as in the case of the beekeepers and the apple growers, there is an overproduction of wheat and an underproduction of timber because the true social costs and benefits are not included in the private cost-and-benefit calculations of farmers and timber growers.

Meade's "creation of atmosphere" is similar to Marshall's external economies in which individual firms benefit from the "general development of the industry."[1] For example, industry growth may lead to a decline in the cost of inputs, a better exchange of ideas through trade journals and professional associations, an increase in the number and quality of ancillary firms providing auxiliary services to the entire industry, a larger pool of workers with industry-specific skills, and an improvement in the physical infrastructure, such as roads, railways, power generation, and port facilities. These are all offshoots of an advancing industry that provide real benefits to individual firms at no cost to the latter. These are external economies, improvements in the general conditions of the industry enjoyed by the firms.

The main difference between Meade's two examples is that in the case of the "unpaid factors," there is only a fixed amount of beneficial spillover effects (apple nectar) to go around. Thus, an increase in the number of beekeepers leads to a decline in the gains enjoyed by every apiary in the area. In other words, the benefits are subject to rival consumption. In contrast, the increase in rainfall precipitated by the grove of trees is enjoyed equally by all the farmers. The propitious atmosphere created is not subject to rival consumption.

More important, however, are the similarities between the two cases presented by Meade. Bator (1958, 364) refers to the case of unpaid apple nectar as an ownership externality in which "[n]onappropriation, divorce of scarcity from effective ownership, is *the* binding consideration" (emphasis original). It is fundamentally a problem of enforcement because there is simply no feasible technical means of excluding bees from apiaries that do not pay the orchards or of distinguishing which bees are from which apiaries.[2] The limitation here is the inability to keep a proper accounting of the spillover effects.

Hence, Bator calls it an "ownership externality." To my mind, Meade's second case of the "creation of atmosphere" is also a similar instance of unpaid factors because timber growers are not compensated by farmers for the latter's increased wheat output. Both examples are rightly cases of unpaid factors and ownership externalities. The key point in Meade's and Marshall's discussions is that there is a market failure because of the market's inability to internalize the true social benefit or cost and, as a result, the economy is not at its optimum product mix. I will use Marshall's, Meade's, and Bator's insights to make my case for the rest of the chapter.

By its nature, the market is fraught with ownership externalities stemming from the market both (1) as a network externality and (2) as a public good. Each of these is akin to Meade's "creation of atmosphere" or to Marshall's external economies whose benefits are appropriated by market participants without having to pay the factors responsible for such gains. Each is a case of manifold unpaid factors.

Network Externality

Increasing Returns

The term "network externality" is most often associated with technology adoption. Take the case of the placement of the letters and characters on the keyboard, conveniently referred to as "QWERTY," after the first few letters of the second top row. It has long been known that there are superior alternative ways of rearranging the keyboard that would have provided greater efficiency, speed, and accuracy in typing. However, typewriter and computer manufacturers have not dared to change QWERTY because they would have shut themselves out of the market.[3] People are willing to put up with QWERTY because of the tremendous time and effort it would take to be proficient with a totally new keyboard. Equally important is the ubiquity of QWERTY keyboards; people want the convenience and assurance that they will always have access to the same keyboard wherever they go and whenever they need one. The outlay in terms of time and resources in retraining people and then replacing every keyboard is simply too prohibitive and may even outweigh the gains in speed and efficiency from such a new keyboard configuration. In other words, network externality is the phenomenon in which a particular technology or convention becomes *the* standard simply by virtue of its widespread use and adoption. As a result, there is the case of a lock-in, a path dependence in which new entrants to the market are forced to adopt the same convention or technology, thereby strengthening that technology and convention even further as the standard for everybody else.

Another example of a network externality is the use of the U.S. dollar by most nations for their international economic transactions and for holding their international reserves. Even with the availability of other currencies like the euro and the yen that are also strong and stable, most participants in the global marketplace, even those at odds with the United States on its foreign policy, are compelled to buy or sell their goods and services in U.S. dollars because everybody else does. Both convenience and necessity demand that they follow suit. As a currency gains universal acceptance, more and more people are encouraged or driven to use it because of the ready liquidity and safety it affords; one will always and easily find people who are willing to accept it. Whether they like it or not, nations are forced to adopt the currency because it has become the de facto medium of international exchange. And, note that it is convention, rather than a formal global treaty, that made the U.S. dollar the primary international currency of exchange among nations.

A third example of a network externality is the use of English as the de facto language of the Internet and global media. By the sheer weight of its broad usage, many countries now require their schools to teach English as a second language. Learning English has become a matter of necessity, perhaps even of survival, in the knowledge economy. If one wants to communicate with others overseas or have ready access to materials on the Internet, English is extremely helpful, if not essential.[4] There is every incentive to learn and speak the language as more people use it; the gains from learning English rise as more people adopt it. Again, note that there is no international treaty that has designated English as the language of the Internet. It emerged spontaneously as the medium of communications by virtue of its pervasive use.

In sum, whether in the use of technologies, currencies, or languages, a network externality describes the phenomenon in which a particular convention or practice gets "locked in" through mass appeal and becomes the standard. Moreover, early adopters benefit as more people subsequently follow suit in embracing the same convention or practice for it widens their circle of exchange and communication. There are mutual and increasing returns to having more people adopt the same standard. According to Metcalfe's Law, the value of a network grows in direct proportion to the square of the number of users.[5]

Nature of the Market

The market, by its nature, is a network externality. Take the case of the Dutch markets at the end of the feudal era of isolated communities and animal husbandry.[6] Commercial activity was limited prior to the modern economy; people produced primarily for their own consumption. Such self-sufficiency was partly forced on them because of a rudimentary transportation and communications infrastructure. Moreover, it was also a problem of how to bring together buyers and sellers. Recall that market exchange is fundamentally an information problem, that is, knowing who wants to buy or sell what, at what price and quality, in what quantities, where, and when. It is a task of matching people with coincident needs and wants. The Dutch took advantage of their central geographic location and organized market fairs in which people looking to buy or sell their goods and wares could get together. This solved the information problem because people knew where and when to go to sell or procure goods. And, of course, these markets took on even greater importance as more people came to use them, which, in turn, became an incentive for many others to come to these fairs during the next rounds of economic activity. In other words, the Dutch markets took on a life of their own in which large-scale use bred even more subsequent acceptance and adoption. There is a self-feeding mechanism at work here.

The recent success of eBay can be attributed to a similar dynamic of a network externality. The success of eBay is a result of its filling a genuine need. It solves the information problem of getting buyers and sellers together. The larger the pool of eBay's buyers and sellers, the better is the overall selection of goods and services available.[7] Anecdotal accounts attest to this. Most people are happy with eBay because they are able to locate supplies of particular goods or services they could not find elsewhere.[8] In addition, these economic agents benefit from the ease and convenience provided by eBay. They reap huge savings in time and effort. There are gains from time and place utility as a result of eBay's service. Furthermore, there are the intangible gains of getting new ideas from the demonstration effect of seeing what others do or place on the market. The more people use eBay to buy or sell merchandise, the more people are encouraged to use the website because of the greater probability of finding a matching buyer or seller.

Both the Dutch market fairs and eBay provide excellent illustrations of how and why it is that the market is a network externality.[9] In being part of a large and ever growing pool of buyers and sellers, market participants reap substantial benefits, to wit: access to a greater variety of goods and services, contact with a wider circle of potential buyers or sellers, comparison shopping that alerts one to the best price and the best quality available, and great ease in consummating mutually beneficial and timely exchanges. In getting buyers and sellers together in one place, whether physically or virtually, a market saves people time and effort, even while giving them the best possible deal available by precluding monopoly power. These advantages are similar to the theoretical benefits afforded by a perfectly competitive market in which there is ease of entry and exit, resulting in the ready availability of a large pool of people with whom one can transact.

Of course, too many choices can become a burden. Just as instrumental rationality can overwhelm the computational capabilities of *homo oeconomicus*, [10] a superfluity of choices can put market participants in the same well-known dilemma as Buridan's ass. Moreover, there is also the risk of market congestion beyond a certain point of expansion. These are legitimate concerns. However, ICTs mitigate these potential problems because of the powerful tools they provide in assisting people sift through immense amounts of data with minimal effort. Google, eBay, and the search-engine industry are very good examples of how microelectronics has kept the transaction costs (searching, bargaining, enforcement, etc.) low despite the deluge of choices occasioned by market widening and deepening. ICTs have pushed back that point of diminishing returns when further market expansion would be more of a hindrance.

In sum, the market, by its nature, has properties of a network externality; it becomes even more valuable as an institution and more effective in its service the more it is shared and used; it has a self-augmenting dynamic in that a growing market size attracts even more participants, thereby expanding its scope even further in the next rounds of economic exchange.

Gains from Trade

The property of the market as a network externality is also illustrated in the well-known theoretical gains from trade. Basic international trade theory lists at least four benefits from cross-border exchange, namely: the venting of surplus, consumption gains, production gains, and dynamic gains. First, trade augments the demand for goods and services produced within a nation. In the case in which there is insufficient local demand to fully employ a nation's resources, trade is beneficial since idle domestic factor inputs are put to use in supplying overseas markets. This is a gain from trade that was discussed as early as Adam Smith's *Wealth of Nations*. One could, thus, aptly call trade a "vent for surplus."[11] If the overseas demand is sizable, trade may even bring the economy to full employment.[12]

A second gain from trade comes from an increase in the consumption opportunity set of economic actors. With international trade, they are able to buy imports at a much cheaper price than would have been the case had these goods been produced domestically. At the same time, their exports are sold at a relatively higher price abroad than would have been the case had they been sold only in the home market. In both instances, there is an increase in the real incomes of consumers. Trade changes the relative price of goods within the domestic economy to that prevailing in the international market, and the cost of people's basket of goods and services consumed is changed accordingly. There is an increase in real incomes because consumers now have access to cheaper goods and services compared to their pre-trade position. This revaluation is called a consumption gain.[13] Observe, too, that the nation enjoys a consumption basket different from its production bundle. Moreover, unlike autarky in which consumption is limited to what it can produce given the state of its technology and resources, the nation is able to consume beyond its production possibilities frontier as a result of trade.

A third benefit from trade is the production gain that stems from the nation changing its product mix and moving toward its comparative advantage.[14] This leads to an increase in real incomes because the nation can shift its resources away from the manufacture of goods (that can be imported cheaply) to the production of goods that it can sell abroad at a higher price.

A fourth source of gain comes from the outward shift of the production possibilities frontier in the next rounds of economic exchange. This gain results from the expected technological changes and innovations that flow from the nation's specialization in what it does best (its comparative advantage), from possible economies of scale, and from its access to overseas technology through trade links. These benefits can also be called Schumpeterian gains to underscore the role of trade in nurturing the "gales of creative destruction" that are distinctive of the capitalist economy.

Achieving these four types of gains require, at a minimum, collaboration between nations willing to trade with each other. Consumers and producers in these trading nations enjoy the aforesaid benefits both in the short run and in the long term. The key question that should then be asked is how these gains ought to be distributed among market participants. Who should appropriate the additional consumer and producer surplus in moving from autarky to international trade? Should we simply allow exporters and consumers to keep these for themselves? And, if so, why?

The four gains from trade discussed above would not have come about without the efforts of previous economic agents responsible for setting up the necessary infrastructure for successful cross-border exchange. Participating in the global marketplace is a straightforward exercise only when taught in a classroom setting. In actual practice and as we have seen in chapter 5, there are many preconditions that must be satisfied for the market to function smoothly. This preparatory work requires the expenditure of real resources over a long period of time. Moreover, perfect mobility is an assumption that is true only in the textbook model of a perfectly competitive market. In practice, we incur frictional and transaction costs in moving goods and factor inputs across the economy. These economic changes inflict costs on certain segments of the population who find their welfare relatively (or even absolutely) diminished as a result of the shift from autarkic to international prices.[15] Thus, gains from trade also come at the expense of people who have to bear the cost of the ensuing relative price adjustments.

These two groups of market participants (those who did the spade work to make trade possible and those who bear the adverse pecuniary externalities of trade) can be aptly described as having been directly or indirectly responsible for what Meade calls the "creation of atmosphere" or Marshall's external economies that paved the way for others' gains, especially exporters and consumers. Thus, we have to examine seriously whether or not these beneficiaries rightly deserve to appropriate the entire windfall for themselves. These gains from trade would not have been possible in the first place without the efforts of the economic agents who had been responsible for the necessary "creation of atmosphere" conducive to international trade. These correspond to Meade's "unpaid factors" because in actual markets there is no practical way to keep tabs on who is contributing what to the creation of the necessary infrastructure for cross-border exchange. Moreover, actual markets are not designed to enforce the Hicks-Kaldor compensation scheme in which winners indemnify losers.[16] Thus, when it comes to distributive justice in international trade, Nozick's notion of justice based on entitlement from property ownership cannot be applied without first ensuring that these unseen and "unpaid factors" responsible for making trade possible are remunerated according to their contribution. We would be violating Nozick's two preconditions of justice in acquisition and transfer if we did not attend to these ownership externalities.

A final note before we leave this section. This discussion on gains from trade is standard in any course in international trade. However, this analytical framework is not limited to depicting the state of nations. In fact, it could even be used to describe the economic position of individual market participants. Just like entire nations, individual economic actors also have their personal production possibilities frontier; they have endowments that may be unemployed or underemployed; and they can generate additional consumer-producer surplus for themselves by trading with others. Becker's (1965) and Lancaster's (1966) household production model (described in chapter 5) is particularly apt for this framework. Thus, this section's exposition on the gains from international trade can be generalized as the gains from any market exchange, be it domestic or international, large-scale or small-scale.

The Market as a Public Good

A quick way of understanding and appreciating the nature of the market as a public good is to describe market operations as part of the collective tacit knowledge. The market does not arise spontaneously on its own nor does it emerge out of a vacuum. There is a communal "entrepreneurial" effort that spans several generations responsible for making the market what it is today. It is an integral part of a community's social capital; it is part of the "economic commons" inherited from generations past. As seen in chapter 5, market participants use bounded, rather than instrumental, rationality in their daily economic decisions. Recall that instrumental rationality entails a maximization exercise using available information to calculate the optimum means to reach given ends. This is an unrealistic and tedious process, beyond the computational capacities of *homo oeconomicus*. Thus, Simon (1976) proposes that economic agents do not run a maximization exercise for every decision they make, but simply follow rules of thumb whose outcomes will rarely be optimal. These conventions define what is permissible and what is not within the marketplace. They save time and communicate what market participants may or may not expect of each other. In other words, people "satisfice" rather than maximize. This is bounded rationality. The formal and informal rules constituting bounded rationality are built up over time from custom, law, and usage. These are refined and strengthened further as people subscribe to them in the self-reinforcing dynamic of both path dependence and network externalities. Thus, market operations produce and accumulate a considerable wealth of collective tacit knowledge over time in a communal process of learning by doing. Such collective knowledge is the outcome of a very costly process of mistakes made and lessons learned and remembered.

This collective tacit knowledge is also aptly called "embedded knowledge." After all, just like tacit knowledge for individuals, collective tacit knowledge also deals with intangibles. It is not codifiable in its entirety and, therefore, is not completely transferable. And, just as personal tacit knowledge is embodied in and inseparable from the individual, collective tacit knowledge is also embodied in a society's institutions, in its culture, in its informal rules of thumb, and in its customs, law, and usage.

> Embedded knowledge is the collective form of tacit knowledge residing in organizational routines and shared norms. It is . . . based on shared beliefs and understanding within an organization which makes effective communication possible. It is rooted in an organization's "communities of practice," . . . [denoting] the socially constructed and interactive nature of learning. Embedded knowledge is relation-specific, contextual and dispersed. It is organic and dynamic: an emergent form of knowledge capable of supporting complex patterns of interaction in the absence of written rules.[17]

Since tacit knowledge is not codifiable and can only be acquired through a process of learning by doing, economic agents wanting to access it have to be part of the collective that embodies such communal tacit knowledge. The only way to use and benefit from the community's store of intangible economic know-how is to be part of the marketplace.

The market cannot charge a nominal user's fee for access to this accumulated wealth of collective tacit knowledge. It cannot exclude people from the "economic commons" painstakingly built up over time. For example, anyone coming off the street to purchase a cup of coffee is in effect availing of and benefiting from the infrastructure that makes it possible to complete such a simple transaction that enables one to enjoy, with minimal effort and at a modest cost, coffee beans grown halfway across the world. There was no need to meet and bargain with an entire range of people, from the small-scale farmers who planted and harvested the beans; to the middlemen who consolidated the coffee beans from remote and widely dispersed farms; to the processors who roasted the beans; to the wholesalers who repackaged, warehoused, transported, and distributed the coffee beans for commercial use; and finally, to the local store that ground the coffee beans and brewed them. Consumers simply walk to the local coffee shop, enjoy a cup of freshly brewed coffee, and, most importantly, are spared from having to perform all the aforesaid tasks by themselves, thanks to the market and its division of labor. Indeed, behind such a simple economic exchange as buying a cup of coffee is hidden a multitude of antecedent transactions with attendant legal, commercial, and financial paperwork.

The market takes care of all these requisite protocols and enables consumers to satisfy their preferences with ease and convenience. We often take the market's services for granted and have come to expect them as a normal part of everyday living because the marketplace has been so successful in providing them unobtrusively and seamlessly, so much so that the entire process is practically invisible to all but the most avid student of economics. And, to top it all, the marketplace produces and widely dispenses the enormous gains reaped from the division of labor and the economies of scale it facilitates. For example, despite the long aforesaid chain of transactions to produce a freshly brewed cup of coffee, even the ordinary person off the street can purchase it at minimal cost.

Or, take Nozick's (1974, 160–74) argument against unwarranted interference in market exchanges. If people are willing to pay to watch Wilt Chamberlain play basketball, and in the process make him a very wealthy person, Nozick contends that it would be wrong for society to take part of Chamberlain's earnings and redistribute it to the poor. To do so would be no different than forced labor in which those who are capable and productive in the community are, in effect, compelled to work on behalf of others. I dispute Nozick's claim on the basis of ownership externalities. No matter how private the transactions between Wilt Chamberlain and his fans may appear, it is nonetheless still the market's existing infrastructure and established conventions, not to mention a stable social order, that facilitate the consummation of such economic exchanges. Thus, taxing Wilt Chamberlain's earnings can be viewed as a "user's fee" to cover the costs incurred in meeting the preconditions that make private economic transactions possible to begin with, including the maintenance of a stable political economy.

The market's utility goes beyond its most widely recognized function of allocating scarce resources to their most valued uses. It plays many other roles: as a route to full employment; as an engine of growth; as an information processor; as a necessary complement to alternative forms of transactions.[18] To appreciate the significance of the market, let us examine the counterfactual. Without the market, consumers and producers are left on their own to look for buyers and sellers of the goods and services they need, through a barter that requires a coincidence of needs. The hungry cobbler has to look for that unshod farmer willing and needing to exchange food for a pair of shoes. The market spares people the inconvenience and limitations of a pure barter economy; and it does not charge a user's fee for the service. It is akin to eBay not charging any commissions at all for its services.

This is the nature of the market as a public good. No one who has purchasing power or a valued asset can be barred from availing of the market's services. No one can be charged a nominal fee before being able to buy or sell. There is ease of entry and exit in the marketplace. Market participants do not have to pay for the consumer surplus, producer surplus, and dynamic gains that flow from market operations. For example, firms in industrialized countries are able to borrow at much better terms from international financial markets than their counterparts in emerging nations whose political economies are unstable, at best. Not having to pay an extra risk premium is a boon to firms in stable countries, a benefit that comes with the market as a public good. Economic agents do not have to pay for the gains they enjoy from network externalities and capitalism's "gales of creative destruction." They do not have to pay in order to access the wisdom and convenience afforded by rules of thumb patiently accumulated and honed over time. They do not have to pay whenever they learn better ways of conducting or organizing their economic affairs through the demonstration effect of others' best practices gleaned from the marketplace. Most of all, market participants do not have to pay for the information derived from market price adjustments that enable them to make better and timely decisions and perhaps even reap rents in the process.[19]

Like any public good, the market does not get paid for the utility it provides unless there are extra-market mechanisms put in place. The irony here is that even the market itself requires extra-market redress in order to raise the revenues to cover the cost of maintaining the requisite institutions that make it (the market) work smoothly.

Windfall Rents, Unpaid Factors, and Uncompensated Burdens

If the market does not get paid for the valuable services it provides, then who pays for the cost of sustaining the formal and informal institutions and the preconditions that permit the market to operate? The state uses tax revenues to maintain the necessary legal infrastructure of the marketplace (e.g., rule of law, property rights, mechanisms for enforcement, and courts). The increasing returns from the market as a network externality and the four gains from trade are public ownership externalities.[20] Nonetheless, both the marketplace and these four gains are undergirded by microeconomic foundations that are fraught with private ownership externalities. I have already briefly alluded to two such private ownership externalities, but I would like to highlight them further.

First are the people who are adversely affected by pecuniary externalities. The adjustment in economic agents' decisions in response to price signals is a necessary cost incurred in sustaining market operations. This is paid for by the people who have to bear the market's adverse unintended consequences but are left unrecompensed according to the Hicks-Kaldor compensation criterion.[21] Recall, for example, the displaced manufacturing workers who have to retrain or move to another geographic location. These are unshared market burdens.

Second, we also have all those responsible for setting up the dynamic and institutional preconditions of the marketplace described in chapter 4. Because of the public-good nature of the market, these economic actors are in all likelihood inadequately remunerated, if at all, for all their contributions to making the market work the way it does. These are the people from earlier rounds of economic exchange responsible for handing down the custom, law, and usage that now form the bounded rationality and the informal rules of thumb running the marketplace. Another more recent example of such unpaid or insufficiently paid factors are the individuals responsible for coming up with the idea and then setting up the basic infrastructure and technologies for the Internet as we know it today.

In both cases, it is impossible to keep track of the social value of people's contributions. Market operations are permeated with ownership externalities. There are manifold unpaid factors and uncompensated market burdens, and since the economy constitutes a single whole of interrelated parts, there will be other factors that are correspondingly remunerated more than their actual social contribution.

So, who should pay for the costs of the market's adverse pecuniary externalities and who should appropriate the rents from its network externalities? In leaving the market to allocate these gains and costs by itself, we are in effect letting these economic benefits and burdens be held or borne privately, based on chance and contingency, sociohistorical location, or personal contribution and striving, or all of these.

Consumers enjoy an increase in their real incomes because of cheaper imports. Exporters benefit from the better prices they secure from the international marketplace. Besides being in their sociohistorical location at the time when the nation opened its borders to international trade, these consumers and exporters did not do anything to merit the *entirety* of the resulting additional consumer or producer surplus. It was the change in relative prices that brought them such windfall. These are appropriable rents that they will reap for themselves in the absence of extra-market intervention—rents that could and should have partially gone to pay the factors that had been instrumental in setting up and maintaining the necessary infrastructure undergirding the nation's successful participation in the global marketplace.[22] Part of these rents must first be redistributed to the unpaid factors before we are able to claim that market outcomes are just because they remunerate factors of production according to their actual contribution.

Unfortunately, such precise measures and distributions are easier said than done, for at least three reasons. First, even if we wanted to pay factors of production according to their contribution as per the marginal productivity theory of factor payments, we still have to correct the ownership externalities that leave some inputs under- or uncompensated for their contribution. But rectifying ownership externalities is the major problem to begin with. By their nature, these externalities arise precisely because of the technical difficulties of accounting for who contributes what. In Meade's example of the beekeepers and the apple growers, it is impossible for apple growers to distinguish which bees are from which apiaries. In addition, we have the even more difficult problem of compelling beekeepers to pay up because there is no practical way of excluding the bees of nonpaying apiaries from drawing nectar from the apple blossoms or, for that matter, of shutting out all bees from the orchards altogether.[23] Similarly in the case of the market, ownership externalities entail a dual problem of measurement and enforcement. These unmeasured or unmeasurable ownership externalities are likely to be considerable because of the properties of the market as a public good and as a network externality.[24]

Second, the difficulty of our problem is compounded because the market operates in an extremely fluid environment. As it is, we are already faced with numerous measurement problems associated with evaluating static costs and benefits. Identifying and filtering out these gains and losses in a dynamic setting makes the task all the more arduous, if not impossible. The economy is not a laboratory that lends itself to controlled and repeated experiments while we figure out its mechanics. Moreover, proper remuneration requires being able to match costs or benefits to economic actors who are constantly on the move within the marketplace, not a simple exercise. In addition, the marketplace generates a steady stream of new data, thereby requiring a constant recalculation of market participants' gains and losses. Furthermore, there is also need to keep track of the market's manifold unintended consequences (externalities). On top of all these, how do we remunerate earlier generations for all their contributions still producing positive externalities today?[25] Indeed, accurate accounting is extremely difficult in a setting of constant economic change.[26]

Even if we were able to get around ownership externalities and measurement problems, we still have to contend with a third technological impediment: the proper disposition of surplus in an economy of diminishing returns. In a world of constant returns to scale, paying factors according to their marginal productivity fully exhausts the product, as per Euler's theorem, and people get their due. Unfortunately, the economy is in fact not characterized by constant returns to scale. The market as a network externality is a phenomenon of increasing returns. In addition, technological change may, in fact, be endogenous rather than exogenous.[27] This means that the knowledge economy is also characterized by increasing returns. This would be consistent with the earlier discussion on the autocorrelated nature of tacit knowledge. If knowledge truly builds on itself, then we would indeed have a situation in which those who have, will have even more, while those who have little, will end up having less or nothing at all. Nevertheless, even if we were to make allowances for increasing returns in a knowledge-based economy, it is very likely that such increasing returns are limited to pockets within an entire economy, and that the economy as a whole exhibits diminishing returns. Such an assumption of an operative diminishing returns is not entirely unreasonable because even knowledge creation itself requires complementary inputs that are finite in supply. Moreover, not all economic agents will be able to keep up with the exacting demands of a knowledge economy; many will in fact fall by the wayside. Thus, even in the most optimistic scenario, the phenomenon of increasing returns will be limited to segments of a much larger economy that will still be governed, on the whole, by diminishing returns. In a world of diminishing returns, paying factors of production according to their marginal productivity (and by extension, Nozick's entitlement as a criterion of distributive justice) will leave some leftover output still to be distributed. The problem then becomes how to disburse this surplus among the factors of production and on what basis? Who gets to keep the residuals?[28]

Toward a Solution

Nozick's entitlement as a principle of distributive justice cannot be implemented for as long as we are unable to measure or at least reasonably approximate the productivity and contributions of various factor inputs in the economy. We run the risk of falling into the same problem that Simon (1976) observed in his critique of instrumental rationality. The computational requirements may simply be beyond human abilities. Moreover, the community will be left with little time for anything else. A less precise, but more practical, alternative solution is needed.

We have to address the two aforementioned problems of unearned rents and uncompensated burdens, whose solutions happily coincide. On the one hand, we have a public-good problem in which the market is unable to levy a user's fee to sustain the institutions responsible for facilitating exchange among economic agents. This causes a problem of the commons in that no one ends up paying for the maintenance of the marketplace. People get more than they should and there is an unpaid social mortgage. Like other public goods, the ideal solution is to charge a user's fee proportional to the gains reaped by market participants (cf. price discrimination). Most people would likely argue for "pay for what you get." On the other hand, we also have the problem of uncompensated private losses due to adverse pecuniary externalities (e.g., displaced workers, lower pay for unskilled workers). This flaw is often left unaddressed because it is hidden and often does not have the urgency of highly visible, immediate, dire consequences (e.g., pollution). Moreover, these burdens are often imposed on those who are least influential or unable to assert their claims. Such a situation goes against most people's sense of fairness; few would want chance and contingency to be the final arbiters of outcomes in their lives. The ideal solution here is a Hicks-Kaldor compensation scheme in which winners reimburse losers. Thus, we have a two-edged problem of an unpaid social mortgage and uncompensated market burdens. The gains from the market as a network externality are public goods even while the attendant costs of operating the market are often privately borne. This is a dilemma familiar to most students of international trade: The gains reaped are widespread and enjoyed by many, while the adjustment costs are imposed only on a few.

A possible solution to both problems is a tax-subsidy strategy. Since we are unable to keep tabs on market participants' real marginal social contribution relative to the private gains they actually reap, a progressive income-wealth tax would at least reduce the unpaid social mortgage. It seems reasonable to assume that wealth and income are good proxies for gauging the extent to which economic agents benefit from the market's services. A negative progressive income-wealth tax is then able to address part of the corollary problem of uncompensated market burdens. Such a scheme is, in effect, an attempt to implement the Hicks-Kaldor compensation scheme in which winners share their gains with losers.

The aforesaid solution is nonetheless still flawed and will require a significant amount of practical fine-tuning based on further empirical work. There are many remaining concerns that require attention. First, if we were to rank order economic agents from the wealthiest to the poorest, a progressive income-wealth tax-subsidy strategy will most likely produce ambiguities for people in the middle segment of such a ranking. The gains reaped or the costs borne as a result of market operations are fairly clear for the two opposite ends of the spectrum—the very rich and the poor. However, the middle segment will produce severe measurement problems because these are the people who simultaneously benefit and suffer from the market's pecuniary externalities. After all, market participation occurs across time, place, and different sectors of the economy, and outcomes of market transactions will vary accordingly. Ascertaining the balance of gains versus losses in an unambiguous manner will be difficult. Take the case of innovators. It has been observed that innovators get a "free ride" in having to pay only a fraction of the total cost to society's having paved the way for such innovations.[29] At the same, however, these innovators are not able to appropriate the full gains from their own innovations (due to the same market failures and externalities). At the end of the day, do they get more or less than their actual social contribution? Do their unearned private gains from drawing from the intellectual commons merely cancel out their uncompensated contributions to the same intellectual commons? One cannot be sure unless we are able to make the requisite measurements, which, unfortunately, is what gives rise to our quandary of ownership externalities to begin with.

Second, as we have seen, people cannot be excluded from availing of a public good. Moreover, it can be enjoyed simultaneously by many; it is nonrival in consumption. Despite these two features, people draw widely different benefits from public goods. Nature lovers benefit more from public parks, the poor reap larger gains from a public transport system, and disciplined students profit more than their indolent peers from the pubic provision of education. The market as a public good is no different. As we have seen in chapter 5, economic agents draw varying degrees of benefits from the marketplace depending on their human capital and sociohistorical location. In fact, in certain cases, the market can even be regressive in the distribution of its benefits and burdens across market participants. Policymakers must take this into account as they design a tax-subsidy scheme to rectify ownership externalities.

Third, in talking of an unpaid social mortgage or of unearned economic rents, one must be very careful not to ignore the importance and the role of individual effort and striving. The distribution of the market's output is not a simple matter of pure chance, contingency, or sociohistorical location, nor is it purely a matter of distribution according to contribution; it is a combination of both. And, that is what makes the task much more difficult. In addition to their sociohistorical location, economic agents reap benefits from the marketplace based on their work ethic, their past investments in their human capital, and their virtue. These are positive contributions to the market's stability and strength and must be rewarded accordingly. But providing such proper recompense is difficult to accomplish. For example, take the well-known dilemma in dispensing aid in higher education. A family that has been frugal in saving earnestly for the college education of its children may not be eligible for grants, or may get less aid compared to a family with very little savings because of an indulgent and indolent lifestyle. We still face a severe information problem even as we try to solve the market's ownership externalities with a second-best strategy of progressive income-wealth taxes and subsidies. Effort, virtue, initiative, and risk-taking are some of the intangible private contributions to making the market what it is, and these are not subject to easy measurement. Nonetheless, they must still be rewarded accordingly.

Finally, a negative income tax must have sufficient safeguards to prevent the problem of free-ridership and dependency. This proposed solution may end up causing an even bigger disincentive predicament if we are not careful in striking a delicate balance as we design an ameliorative program for ownership externalities.[30] Personal responsibility matters enormously.

Summary and Conclusions

This chapter has examined two properties of the market—its network and ownership externalities. First, the marketplace delivers substantial collective gains to its participants because of its property as a network externality. Second, the market, by its nature, is fraught with many ownership externalities that leave factors inaccurately or incompletely paid, if at all, for their actual social contribution to the common productive effort. Contemporary globalization's market widening and deepening magnify the impact of both of these features of the marketplace. In the absence of extra-market remedial measures, there is an intrinsic unpaid social mortgage to market operations. This means that many of the beneficiaries of market exchange are appropriating more than their share of the collective gains at the expense of other market participants, especially those adversely affected by pecuniary externalities. The distribution of these gains is based neither on the marginal productivity theory of factor payments nor on Nozick's entitlement approach as a norm of distributive justice. The disposition of these rents is most likely determined by a combination of market participants' efforts and sociohistorical location, in addition to chance and contingency. The most successful economic agents are getting a "freebie" from not having to pay the full cost of setting up and maintaining the market from which they have derived so much. There is need to correct for ownership externalities by making marginal social costs and benefits equal to marginal private costs and benefits. Not only is this fair by Nozick's entitlement criterion, but it is also a necessary condition of allocative efficiency.[31]

Equating marginal social and private costs (benefits) is not a simple, straightforward exercise of taxing winners and subsidizing losers. Ownership externalities do not lend themselves to such an approach because these arise precisely because of the difficulty of keeping track of who benefits from what and by how much. In being unable to measure precisely who owes what to which unpaid factors, it is necessary to come up with an alternative solution that at least narrows the gap between social and private costs (benefits). Using the proceeds from a progressive income-wealth tax to fund the strategy of need satisfaction described in chapters 6 and 7 is a possible second-best solution. In this proposal, (1) we are able to retrieve some of the unearned rents, and (2) these are then used to lay the groundwork for efficiency in the next rounds of economic activity.[32]

Chapter 9

Summary and Conclusions: Distributive Justice in the Knowledge Economy

The liveliest debates and the most contentious disputes in political economy revolve around the question of how we ought to divide societal output. What is the appropriate criterion to use for distributive justice? Is it efficiency, need, contribution, entitlement, equality, effort, or ability? Globalization has only compounded the complexity of these unresolved questions. Discourse on globalization and distributive justice can be particularly frustrating because of two extremes. On the one hand we have a highly abstract and formalistic body of literature that is too far removed from what people actually experience in the marketplace. This type of scholarship suffers such a disconnect from reality on the ground that it is often either irrelevant or useless for policy or ethical guidance. On the other hand we have literature that makes sweeping pronouncements on globalization based on selected anecdotal evidence without the benefit of a sustained critical examination of the larger picture of its outcomes and processes. Personal narratives are important, but they cannot fully replace hard evidence and objective analysis. This approach generally fails to take into account the nature of both the market and the knowledge economy seriously.

I have tried to avoid both pitfalls by using the intrinsic properties of the market and the knowledge economy as the larger overarching framework within which to examine distributive justice in contemporary globalization. Thus, in this book, we have examined the market as an effective vehicle for discovery and information processing, as an effective price discriminator, as fraught with both beneficial and adverse unintended consequences and ownership externalities, as dependent on institutional preconditions and bounded rationality, as path-dependent and autocorrelated in its dynamics, and as a network externality. The preceding chapters have used these characteristic features of the market to shed light on the questions of whether need, efficiency, or entitlement ought to be the basis for distributive justice and whether globalization has been a blessing or a curse. This has been a descriptive, analytic, and normative study.

Distributive Justice

There is no consensus on the appropriate principle to use for distributive justice, much less a rank ordering of the different approaches proposed. However, the most widely used and accepted criteria in analytical or comparative works are egalitarianism, need, efficiency, and entitlement.[1] We have already examined three of these—efficiency, need, and entitlement—in parts II, III, and IV respectively. It now remains for us to deal briefly with egalitarianism as a possible norm of distributive justice in the knowledge economy.

Embedded Egalitarianism

In part III, I argued that a strategy of need satisfaction is a necessary condition for long-term economic efficiency in the knowledge economy. Moreover, we also saw that a key unanswered issue with such a strategy is the specification of the precise content of the basket of needs to be satisfied. While acknowledging this to be a highly contextual exercise, we are nonetheless able to outline a priori some of the most essential human needs. In particular, in order to form the requisite human capital for a knowledge economy, the basket of needs must, at a minimum, include basic civil and political rights-liberties and the opportunity and resources needed to participate in socioeconomic life. After all, the all-important tacit knowledge (know-how and know-who) in the learning economy can only be gained and accumulated through a process of "learning by doing." Thus, the strategy of need satisfaction proposed in part III, in effect, also includes simple egalitarianism (equality of basic civil and political rights-liberties) and welfare egalitarianism (equality of opportunity). I would not go so far as to claim the need for a socialist egalitarianism because a mandated equality of outcomes is counterproductive, indeed impossible to attain, when dealing with human knowledge as the basis for wealth and value creation. Human capital is person-specific and to force an artificial, arbitrary parity in its outcomes for the sake of an egalitarian ideal is to level down human creativity to the lowest common denominator. This is self-defeating. In other words, the need-satisfaction strategy I propose is one that incorporates egalitarianism, albeit one that is not as intrusive as its radical or socialist variant.

Complementary Criteria

Far from being in competition with each other, the commonly accepted principal criteria of distributive justice are, in fact, necessary complements, especially in the knowledge economy. In particular, need satisfaction and efficiency are indispensable conditions for each other. As tacit knowledge is the key factor in the learning economy, long-term efficiency is ultimately determined by the quality of the available pool of human capital. A strategy of need satisfaction (and its aforesaid implicit egalitarianism) is a proactive approach to ensuring that the community's most valuable resource—human capital—is truly put to optimum use, thereby laying the groundwork for sustained economic growth in the knowledge economy.

In its own turn, long-term economic efficiency is a necessary condition for a strategy of need satisfaction. Recall the basic-needs approach to development pursued in the late 1970s and the 1980s. In a turnaround in its thinking, the World Bank shifted to a policy of directly alleviating poverty through the provision of basic needs as it was taking a long time for the benefits of large-scale infrastructure lending (building roads, bridges, ports, etc.) to trickle down to the poor, if at all. Unfortunately, this was an approach to economic development that could not be sustained for long. Without directly and quickly increasing production, a basic-needs strategy ends up as a redistribution program—a reapportionment in the slices of the proverbial economic pie. Economic growth is a necessary condition if the provision of basic needs is to be sustained into the long term. Only a growing economic pie can supply the necessary surplus for a nation to continue investing in its "human capital." In other words, it is long-term economic efficiency that guarantees the viability of need satisfaction as a norm of distributive justice.

As need satisfaction and long-term efficiency are necessary conditions for each other, especially in the knowledge economy, these two standards of distributive justice converge into a complementary pair. Recall, too, that within a strategy of need satisfaction is an embedded egalitarianism. Thus, we have all three approaches to distributive justice (need, efficiency, and equality) intersecting and mutually reinforcing each other. What about Nozick's entitlement? Where does it fit in? Does it even have a role to play?

As we have seen in the preceding chapter, Nozick's entitlement as a principle of distributive justice requires extensive extra-market adjustments and revaluations if it is to satisfy its own conditions of justice in acquisition and justice in transfers. Extensive ownership externalities, by the nature of the market, leave many factors of production unpaid or underpaid for their genuine social contribution, just as other factors get more than their share based on their actual productivity. Thus, there is need to close the gap between private and social costs (benefits), to whatever extent possible, before we can pursue a distributive justice based on Nozick's entitlement. Unfortunately, this extra-market adjustment is neither a simple nor an easy exercise. After all, ownership externalities arise precisely because of their inherent measurement and enforcement difficulties. The most that can be accomplished are second-best tax-subsidy schemes that bring private and social costs (benefits) closer to each other. Nonetheless, one must not forget that these are very blunt instruments that may even spawn further distortions and collateral problems of their own. These are matters that require extensive empirical work. Should we then simply drop entitlement as a yardstick of distributive justice in the knowledge economy given the enormous additional and complex work required? We cannot.

Human capital formation (and need satisfaction by extension) is a necessary condition of long-term efficiency, but it is not a sufficient condition. The preservation of economic incentives is another necessary condition if allocative efficiency is to be attained at all. Any market-based activity, including the knowledge economy, is founded on private initiative. Schumpeter's much-needed "creative destruction" is dependent on the entrepreneurial vitality of economic agents in the marketplace. Market participants must have incentives to apply themselves in technological innovation, production, and exchange. They must be able to appropriate and keep for themselves both the economic rents and the pertinent returns that accrue to these activities. Entitlement, as a norm of distributive justice, preserves and provides just such incentives. It ensures that economic agents will be able to reap and keep for themselves the fruits of their labor and their properties. The preceding chapter was about making sure that we keep a more accurate accounting of these gains across market participants so that prices truly provide the right incentives that ultimately bring the economy to its optimum efficiency, to whatever extent possible. Having a well-developed human capital is not sufficient to bring us to long-term allocative efficiency in the learning economy because people must also have the necessary pecuniary inducements to make the right economic decisions and to act on these. In other words, without entitlement as a criterion of distributive justice in the knowledge economy, we may end up with a pool of well-developed human capital that is either idle or underutilized. Thus, just like need satisfaction, entitlement is also a necessary condition for long-term economic efficiency.

The vast literature on distributive justice generally presents egalitarianism, efficiency, need, and entitlement as four clashing visions of how we ought to divide scarce societal resources. This book has argued that far from being mutually exclusive, these four criteria of distributive justice are, in fact, complementary. Simple and welfare egalitarianism are embedded within a strategy of need satisfaction. Economic efficiency and need satisfaction, while distinct from each other, are inseparable in the knowledge economy given the pivotal role of human capital for economic growth. For its part, entitlement as a criterion preserves and transmits economic incentives that are critical in moving the economy toward allocative efficiency. The putative rivalry between these four principles of distributive justice is more apparent than real, at least in the knowledge economy. They address different facets of the economy: need satisfaction and egalitarianism deal with human capital, economic efficiency with long-term viability, and entitlement with pecuniary inducements. These four norms mutually reinforce each other and furnish us with a much richer and broader set of conceptual tools with which to weigh the inevitable competing claims that arise in the marketplace. To date, the literature has focused heavily on the trade-offs between these criteria. Note, for example, the classic equity-efficiency tension in economic literature, such as Okun's (1975) famous lecture and Kuznet's (1955; 1963) inverted-U-curve hypothesis. Our emerging knowledge economy presents us with an opportunity to examine their interdependence instead. Fei et al. (1979) and Fields (1995) illustrate just such an approach.

This complementarity should be viewed as an integrated theory rather than a mere composite of various norms lumped together into a single whole. This phenomenon is described by Konow well as he describes his own positive theory of distributive justice.

> [T]he general framework . . . is an *integrated theory*, but not a *composite theory*: justice is more than the sum of its parts. . . . [E]ach category captures an element that is important to crafting a positive theory of justice but that no single family or theory within a family suffices to this end. Instead, fairness views are best explained by an integrated approach that acknowledges the influence of three principles of justice [need, efficiency, and entitlement] whereby the weight of each is determined by the context.[2]

We have been using the nature of the market and the knowledge economy as the context for weighing these standards of distributive justice relative to each other. The integrated, rather than mere composite, nature of my fourfold proposal is based on the self-reinforcing synergy of efficiency, need-egalitarianism, and entitlement in the knowledge economy.

Typology

Pluralist Rather than Hegemonic or Skeptical

Recall from chapter 1 that there are three competing meta-approaches to thinking about social justice, namely: hegemonic, skeptical, and pluralist.[3] The hegemonic school of thought asserts that there is a single, objective, substantive standard for what constitutes social justice that is universally applicable across cultures and across generations (e.g., Marx's distribution according to need and Rawls's difference principle). Skeptics take the opposite argument and claim that there is no such thing as an objective standard because what passes as "social justice" is, in fact, the outcome of a bargaining process in which people promote their own preferences (e.g., utilitarianism). Thus, there is an infinite set of possible rules of "social justice" corresponding to the myriad interests that people have. Pluralists, on the other hand, occupy the middle ground and stick to a small set of criteria.[4] Unlike the hegemonic approach, the pluralist school does not settle for a single, cure-all, standard that can deal effectively and fairly with all the issues that pertain to dividing up scarce societal resources. The socioeconomic terrain is simply too complex to be handled by a solitary rule. However, unlike the amorphous "social justice" of skeptics, the pluralistic stance limits the number of criteria to a handful of clearly superior and well-argued standards.

This book's fourfold approach to distributive justice in the knowledge economy clearly falls in the camp of pluralists. Unlike the hegemonic school, I do not believe that there is a single substantive standard that can deal with all the conflicting claims in the marketplace. In fact, need (with its embedded egalitarianism), efficiency, and entitlement serve particular dimensions of the knowledge economy that the other criteria are unable to address. And, unlike the skeptical outlook, I believe that there is an objective basis for what constitutes social justice. Thus, this study's proposed distributive justice for the knowledge economy is neither hegemonic nor skeptical in its approach to social justice; it is pluralist.

Context Dependent, Not Context Specific

In concluding his positive theory that examines people's views of justice, Konow (2003, 1235) observes that the "most significant challenge" to evaluating theories of justice is arguably the assessment of how the incorporation of context affects the interpretation, rank ordering, and application of disparate principles of justice. This entire book has been about the evaluation of three criteria of distributive justice (need, efficiency, and entitlement) in the context of (1) the nature of markets and (2) an ICT-driven, globalizing knowledge economy. Moreover, my conclusion that these distinct standards of distributive justice turn out to be complementary in our contemporary digital age dovetails Konow's findings that most people subscribe to a multidimensional notion of distributive justice, the precise mix of which largely depends on the particular context in which these rules are to be applied.

Given the central importance of context in assessing theories of justice and their respective claims, we need to ask: Are the skeptics right after all in contending that there is no such thing as an objective social justice but only an array of competing private interests? Konow's (2003, 1231–32, 1215) distinction between "context dependent" and "context specific" is helpful in dispelling the mistaken view that justice is a purely subjective exercise. He argues that justice is a context-dependent rather than a context-specific phenomenon because its principles do not change with context, only their application. At the very least, context sheds light on the reference group, the content and strength of the competing claims to be resolved, the sociohistorical location of claimants, and the nature of the good(s) at risk. In other words, it is context that provides a clear and precise articulation of the resulting trade-offs that any application of justice occasions. Context does not change the fundamental axioms and criteria of distributive justice, only their particular use.

Globalization and Avoiding the Fallacies of Division and Composition

Is globalization a welcome boon or an unmitigated woe? It is very likely that there is an element of truth on both sides of the debate. As we have seen in chapter 4, the market's ability to allocate scarce resources to their most valued uses in the most timely and cost-effective manner is no small accomplishment. The improvement in the lives of hundreds of millions just in the past twenty-five years on account of global economic integration cannot be ignored.[5] Consider, too, the many anecdotal accounts of enriched lives in the NICs and the transformation of Bangalore, India. For all its well-known and acknowledged ills, the market has had an established track record of empowering people and of nurturing and unleashing private initiative since the Industrial Revolution.

No other social institution, thus far, has been able to replicate the market's unique ability to bring about allocative efficiency and to generate continuous "gales of creative destruction." And, by all indications (theoretical and empirical), the market will get to be even more efficient at being efficient. As I have claimed in chapter 2, this is the deeper and more significant impact of microelectronics and cheap information, the "carrier inputs" of our contemporary (fifth) Kondratieff. As we have seen in chapter 4, the technological and organizational changes occasioned by ICTs are self-feeding and have taken a life of their own. Not only has there been an accelerated pace in technological change, but the market itself has become self-sustaining in creating a beneficial cycle of competitive innovations that in turn spawn even further improvements in the core processes and operations of the marketplace. In other words, the market has internalized within itself a self-generating dynamic of constantly improving its efficiency. It is the core process of the market itself that has been the object of radical transformation as part of the fifth long-wave cycle. The consequence of this, of course, is that given the market's ever greater capacity to create value, the opportunity cost of not participating in the marketplace or of impeding its operations will get even higher.

Critics must be careful not to readily dismiss contemporary globalization as an unmitigated failure. To do so is to commit the familiar mistake of "throwing the baby out with the bath water." One should not fall for the fallacy of composition in economic reasoning in which what is observed of a part is immediately said to be true of the whole. There are undoubtedly many anecdotal accounts of economic hardships brought about by globalization. The millions of manufacturing workers who have been displaced as part of the process of deindustrialization in developed countries should indeed be cause for great concern. Neither should we blithely accept the demise of small- and medium-scale firms and farms in emerging nations on account of stiff global competition in the wake of market liberalization. Nor should we ignore the immense damage wrought by speculators on the currencies of developing nations who can ill afford wild swings in their foreign exchange rates. As we have seen in chapter 5, there are matching adverse ripple effects to the beneficial pecuniary externalities generated by the market's price adjustments. International trade, or any market exchange for that matter, is a de facto redistribution of burdens and benefits through its concomitant price and quantity adjustments. Even in the most optimistic, but unlikely, scenario of an absolute increase in incomes for all trading partners, there will nonetheless still be changes in the relative standing of market participants. Neoclassical economic theory itself, the Stolper-Samuelson theorem in particular, shows that there will be relative winners and losers in cross-border exchanges. Nevertheless, despite all these ills, the market easily balances, indeed outweighs, these harmful collateral effects with salutary consequences.

Efficiency matters, but it is not sufficient. As we have seen in chapter 5, the market can be regressive in its redistribution of burdens and benefits across market participants. Moreover, it can easily create a permanent underclass that cannot participate meaningfully in socio-economic life. The market can be said to be autocorrelated as subsequent rounds of economic activity build on the outcomes of earlier periods. In other words, the marketplace is a setting in which economic power can be parlayed into even more power. Furthermore, as we have seen in chapter 3, the "entry cost" of participating effectively in the knowledge economy keeps getting higher. The upshot in all this is that market participants who are unable to keep up with the ever-ratcheting demands of an increasingly competitive and technological marketplace will simply fall by the wayside and find it that much more difficult to be reintegrated back into mainstream economic life. This self-destructive feature of the market cannot be left unattended, especially not in a knowledge economy. After all, the learning economy's long-term efficiency is largely dependent on the quality of its human capital. Thus, in the short run, it is not sufficient to pay attention to allocative efficiency alone. We must also ensure that market outcomes are distributed in such a manner as to afford market participants with the necessary resources and incentives to invest further and continuously in their human capital formation. As people's high discount rate (short time horizons) and collective-action problems (e.g., prisoners' dilemma and problem of the commons) may prevent market participants from investing in their own or in each other's human capital, extra-market action will be needed to ensure that the economy as a whole constantly upgrades its stock of human capital. To fail to do so in the knowledge economy is to put its long-term efficiency in question.

Consequently, critics of globalization should not be dismissed so readily either. In fact, they may even provide a real service by alerting the community to market failures that call for ameliorative work.

Proponents of globalization must recognize that, notwithstanding all the real and substantial benefits it generates, the market still has flaws that need to be remedied. They must have a better appreciation that the market price's allocative and distributive dimensions, while distinct from each other, are inseparable. There will always be distributive ramifications to the requisite price adjustments that bring the economy to its optimum point of allocative efficiency. Many of these negative ripple effects may fall on those who are least able to bear them. Moreover, these collateral distributive results, if left unaddressed, may be detrimental for continued long-term economic efficiency. Just as critics ought to acknowledge the manifold blessings that come with economic exchange, proponents of globalization must in their own turn be balanced in their views. They should recognize the limitations of neoclassical models and analyses and accept the need for a more active extra-market oversight of economic processes and outcomes. Equity in the distribution of market outcomes turns out to be a necessary supplement to efficiency in the knowledge economy. Proponents of globalization must avoid the opposite flaw in economic reasoning, the fallacy of division, in which the good of the whole cannot be assumed to apply uniformly to every part of that whole.

The prescriptions offered on efficiency and need satisfaction as criteria of distributive justice (parts II and III) and the need to correct ownership externalities (chapter 8) strike a balance between the competing schools of thought on the benefits and ills of globalization. My proposal calls for an equitable efficiency. "Equitable" means many things to many people, but for this book, I use this term to refer to (1) the rational strategy of making sure that market participants are provided the means and the inducements to constantly improve their human capital and (2) the extra-market interventions needed to correct the gap between social and private costs (benefits). The appealing feature to both sets of policies is that they improve equity within the economy even as they enhance efficiency. Using our earlier typology, we can say that both advocates and critics of globalization run the danger of being "hegemonic" in their claims if they fail to appreciate the complementary value of some of their opponents' contentions and if they fail to recognize the limitations of their own arguments. Trade must neither be dismissed so readily nor should it be embraced uncritically. The global marketplace can produce sizable gains for many if allowed to operate with minimal interference, but only if it has the necessary underlying institutional foundations that provide timely and effective corrections for some its deleterious outcomes. Such redress usually comes only through extra-market mediation, whether through the state or NGOs, and lately even through the emerging field of "social entrepreneurship." Of course, a consequence of having to rely on multiple criteria for distributive justice is that it becomes even more important for us to have a clear-eyed method in shifting our emphasis seamlessly from one norm to another depending on context and timing.

This book has focused exclusively on the instrumental value of human capital in promoting and sustaining efficiency in the knowledge economy. However, we should not forget that human capital formation and need satisfaction have intrinsic value on their own because of the dignity of the human person. This book does not provide a substitute for the intrinsic justification of need satisfaction based on the inherent worth of human beings. Instead, it merely advances an additional explanation—an instrumental warrant—for need as a criterion of distributive justice, and with the tools of neoclassical economics itself. The intrinsic and instrumental accounts of need satisfaction and human capital formation are not mutually exclusive.

People deserve to have food, clothing, shelter, education, basic health, meaningful opportunities for employment, and participation in the larger socioeconomic life not because human capital formation is profitable in the knowledge economy, but because every person deserves the chance to flourish in life. People are entitled to the satisfaction of their basic needs because of their humanity regardless of how well or how much they contribute to the common productive effort, if at all. And despite significant free-rider abuses and dependency problems such a policy may engender, most societies nevertheless take it upon themselves to furnish a minimum basket of goods to those unable to secure it for themselves. Such a "morality of the depths,"[6] a benchmark below which no one will be allowed to sink, is a measure of the quality of a community's character. After all, we really need to take responsibility for each other's well-being, especially for those who are unable to fend for themselves in a marketplace that can be impersonal and unsparing. The need for mutual solicitude and intelligent planning is greater than ever, especially in a rapidly evolving and increasingly exacting knowledge economy.

Notes

1 Overlapping Questions

1. See Epstein et al. (1996).
2. For example, see Hirst and Thompson (1999).
3. Trade openness is generally measured in terms of exports plus imports as a percentage of GDP. Capital liberalization is often evaluated in terms of cross-border financial flows as a percentage of GDP.
4. Baldwin and Martin (1999); Irwin (2005); Krugman (1995).
5. O'Rourke and Williamson (1999).
6. Barro (1991; 1997). For an exposition on growth convergence, see Barro and Sala-i-Martin (1992; 1995).
7. Lankes (2002). The OECD is the Organisation for Economic Co-operation and Development and includes Australia, Austria, Belgium, Canada, Czech Republic, Denmark, Finland, France, Germany, Greece, Hungary, Iceland, Ireland, Italy, Japan, South Korea, Luxembourg, Mexico, the Netherlands, New Zealand, Norway, Poland, Portugal, Slovak Republic, Spain, Sweden, Switzerland, Turkey, United Kingdom, and the United States. Not all of these nations provide extensive subsidies to their agricultural sectors. The EU, Japan, Switzerland, and the United States are among the most important agricultural protectionists.
8. Romer (1990).
9. Barro (1991; 1997).
10. The Washington Consensus refers to the policy advice of Washington-based financial institutions, such as the IMF and the World Bank, to the Latin American countries in the 1980s that included, at a minimum,

> fiscal discipline; a redirection of public expenditure priorities toward fields offering both high economic returns and the potential to improve income distribution, such as primary health care, primary education, and infrastructure; tax reform (to lower marginal rates and broaden the tax base); interest rate liberalization; a competitive exchange rate; trade liberalization; liberalization of inflows of foreign direct investment; privatization; deregulation (to

abolish barriers to entry and exit); and secure property rights. (Williamson 2000, 252–53)

The term was initially coined by Williamson (1990) and has come to be widely used by antiglobalizers as synonymous with neoliberalism and everything that is wrong with global economic integration. See Williamson (1990; 2000).

11. See, for example, Peters (2004, 139–70); Buckman (2004); and Alternatives Task Force of the International Forum on Globalization (2002) for a sampling of this fourth school of thought.
12. Blair (2005). See Cameron et al. (2006) for a recent exposition on the problems posed by globalization on nation states.
13. Rodrik (1997, 11–27).
14. Samuelson (2004).
15. Peters (2004).
16. Buckman (2004).
17. Hamlin (1995).
18. For example, does the simplifying assumption of a utility-maximizing, self-interested *homo oeconomicus* make students of economics more selfish? See Carter and Irons (1991); Frank et al. (1993); and Marwell and Ames (1981).
19. Aristotle (1941, 1130b30–34, 1131a10–29, 1131b18–19).
20. Marx (1875 [1993], 162).
21. Ryan (1942, 180–88).
22. Rescher (1966, 73–83).
23. Fleischaker (2004, 19–27).
24. See Raphael (2001) for a nonexhaustive survey of the key concepts of justice in the history of thought.
25. Rawls (1971, 302).
26. Nozick (1974, 160–74).
27. Sen (1984a).
28. There are at least three problems in using utility as a measure of the community's welfare. In the first place, interpersonal comparisons of personal utilities are not possible because there is no objective, common metric or scale by which such utilities can be evaluated across individuals (Robbins 1932 [1952]). Second, one cannot aggregate individual utilities into a single, all-encompassing social welfare function without violating the simplest and the most reasonable constraints one would have to impose on such a community utility function (Arrow 1951). Third, it is not possible to subscribe to rights and still come up with an aggregated social utility function at the same time (Sen 1970). For a brief discussion of these problems, see Schokkaert (1992).
29. Aquinas (1947/48, II–II, Q. 66, a.7).
30. See Braybrooke (1987) for other schools of thought on what comprises human needs.
31. Rawls (1971, 90–95, 440–46).
32. For example, see John XXIII (1963).

33. Konow (2003, 1232–34).
34. Hellsten (1998, 818–19); Pojman and Westmoreland (1997).
35. Nonetheless, there are still many debates about globalization that cannot be reduced simply to questions of distributive justice. For example, the loss of a community's cultural heritage, environmental degradation, and the diminution of national sovereignty are more than just about the division of societal resources.
36. Ravallion (2004).
37. Ibid., Figure 3, 32.
38. See, for example, the bibliography in Buckman (2004). See also Sobrino and Wilfred (2001).
39. Chen and Ravallion (2004).
40. Ravallion (2004, 6–7)
41. Population figures are taken from the *Economist* (2003).
42. For a more extensive exposition on the results and the differences in using a population-weighted versus a country-weighted measure of inequality, see Bourguignon et al. (2004) and Firebaugh (2003). Note that the choice between these two methods of weighting is not always merely a matter of taste or political inclination. It also depends on the question that one seeks to address. For example, a comparative analysis of economic policies across nations requires the use of a country-weighted measure.
43. Chen and Ravallion (2004, Table 3, 29).
44. Ibid., Table 2, 28.
45. See Finn (1996) for an alternative, theological assessment of international trade.
46. I draw the following differentiation from Spragens (1993).
47. Spragens (1993, 194).
48. Hellsten (1998, 826–27).

2   Microelectronics and Market Efficiency

1. See, for example, Bairoch and Kozul-Wright (1998). Hirst and Thompson (1999:1–18) go so far as to question the use of the term "globalization" since only a limited number of countries are truly partaking and benefiting from this phenomenon. They suggest that "internationalization" is a more accurate description.
2. For purposes of comparison, it is best to distinguish three periods of globalization: (1) the four decades preceding World War I (1870–1914); (2) the post–World War II era (1950–80); and (3) the current information-driven globalization (1980s and beyond).
3. Krugman (1995).
4. Baldwin and Martin (1999).
5. Ibid. For an account of the triumph of markets in late-twentieth-century economic history, see Kuttner (1997); McMillan (2002); and Yergin and Stanislaw (1998).

6. Jones (1981, 59); Mokyr (1990, 31–38).
7. This taxonomy comes from Freeman and Perez (1988, 45–47).
8. Freeman and Perez (1988, 47–58). Of course, these three features are not independent of each other; in fact, they mutually reinforce one another. For example, the availability of supplies to the point of superfluity accounts for the precipitous drop in their relative cost which, in turn, leads to their widespread use across society.
9. IMF (2001, 105–44).
10. Castells (1996, 30, 60–61).
11. Kondratieff (1935); Schumpeter (1939).
12. See also Freeman (2001, Figure 8.2, 151).
13. Freeman (2001, Table 8.1, 152).
14. Freeman and Perez (1988, 47–58).
15. Castells (1996, 38–39).
16. The preceding figures are taken from Woodall (2000, 8).
17. Castells (1996, 42).
18. Woodall (1996, 7–9).
19. Castells (1996, 42).
20. IMF (2001, 108).
21. Woodall (2000, 8).
22. Ibid.
23. Ibid.
24. Cairncross (2001, Figures 2–3, 37).
25. IMF (2001, Table 3.8, 134).
26. Woodall (2000, 40).
27. For example, we have wireless-digital phones versus the pre-1980s' electromechanical switching systems.
28. Beniger (1986).
29. Examples of organizational innovations include large-scale formal bureaucracies with multiple departments, process control systems, line-and-staff control, accounting firms, Dow Jones reporting, and bonding companies. Examples of new equipment include the telegraph, typewriter, telephone, punch-card tabulators, mimeograph, photostat, and electronic calculators. See Beniger (1986, 430–31) and Hepworth (1989, 2–4) for a list of these "control innovations" between 1830 and 1939.
30. Recall Freeman and Perez's (1988, 45–47) fourfold typology.
31. The Soviet-style economies failed in the past century partly because they substituted central planning for market operations.
32. Woodall (2000, 6) citing Brad DeLong.
33. The theory of second best (Lipsey and Lancaster 1956) warns us that removing one distortion in the presence of other unaddressed distortions does not automatically bring us closer to Pareto efficiency.
34. This section draws from Mayer-Schönberger et al.'s (2000) description of the four components of the ICT revolution. See Freeman and Louca (2001, Chapter 9) for a detailed account of the history behind

these technological developments. Soete and Weel (2005, 2–5) propose a different list of six key characteristics of the ICT revolution: semiconductors, miniaturization, telecommunications, mobile communications, supporting technologies (software and Internet), and the open source movement.

35. This is defined as "Transmission Control Protocol/Internet Protocol, the suite of communications protocols used to connect hosts on the Internet" (www.webopedia.com).

36. This larger pool of users also leads to network externalities, a phenomenon we will examine in chapter 8. A downside to standardization is the risk of a technological "lock-in" just as the case of QWERTY for keyboards. For a further examination of QWERTY, see David (1985).

37. Held et al. (1999, 167–69) observe an increasing intensity and extensity of trade in the twentieth century.

38. Data source: UNCTAD Handbook of Statistics 2005, Tables 1.2 and 7.2 (http://stats.unctad. org/ Handbook, last accessed July 26, 2007).

39. World Bank (2007, 46).

40. Held et al. (1999, 17) refer to this as growth in the "extensity of global networks."

41. Sachs and Warner (1995) classify an economy as closed if it has at least one of these characteristics: nontariff barriers covering more than 40 percent of its total trade, average tariffs of 40 percent or more, a black market exchange rate that is at least 20 percent less than the official rate, a socialist political economy, or if the state has a monopoly over major exports.

42. Data source: UNCTAD Handbook of Statistics 2005, Table 1.1.

43. World Bank (2007, Figure 4.1, 108).

44. IMF (1997, 73).

45. Held et al. (1999, 17) refer to this as growth in the "intensity of global interconnections."

46. Data source: UNCTAD Handbook of Statistics 2005, Table 7.3.

47. World Bank (2007, Figure 2.1, 31).

48. In presenting empirical evidence of an expanding global marketplace, I have limited myself only to merchandise trade in order to keep this presentation to a reasonable length. Global capital market integration is also an impressive indicator of market widening.

49. Kikeri and Kolo (2005).

50. Blair (2005).

51. Dicken (2003, 148–49) provides a concise listing of these efforts dating as far back as the European Common Market in 1957 to the recent agreements in the Americas. See also Appleyard et al. (2006, Table 1, 378) and UNCTAD (2004, 55).

52. IMF (1997, 45–71).

53. Reitman (1994).

54. Michaels and Lunsford (2004).
55. Dean and Tam (2005); Jones et al. (2005).
56. This adds to the growth in the extensity and intensity of global networks and interconnections described by Held et al. (1999, 17).
57. E-medicine is still in its infancy. It includes Web-based physician consultations via e-mail and teleradiology in which diagnostic tests can be read and interpreted from remote sites. A most promising possibility of e-care is the ability to access highly specialized medical centers whose staff could provide advice based on patient's test results and real-time images that can now be easily shared and transmitted electronically (Danzon and Furukawa 2001, 223–25). In an article on outsourcing written for the *New York Times*, Richtel (2005) recounts how a Dallas consultant to firms using offshore labor even received a request from a psychologist who wanted to hire counselors from India to make follow-up calls to his patients on his behalf. See also Maher (2004).
58. Bellman and Koppel (2005). For example, many firms are believed to have outsourced to India the paperwork needed for compliance with Sarbanes-Oxley (Bellman 2005). Recall that this legislation was enacted to ensure better transparency and accountability on the part of corporate officers and directors in the wake of the major corporate scandals at the turn of the millennium.
59. Bellman (2005).
60. Edwards (2004, 7).
61. World Bank (2007, Table 2.1, 34).
62. UNCTAD (2004, 61, 49).
63. World Bank (2007, Figure 4.5, 121).
64. One can even outsource online gaming! Wealthy online gamers who do not have the time and patience (and perhaps the skills?) to work their way up to the higher and more challenging levels of online games simply outsource the earlier rounds overseas to China. Such offshore gamers can earn $250 a month working 12-hour days, 7-days-a-week, playing online games (Barboza 2005).
65. Of course, there are still the difficulties of language and cultural barriers to such offshoring (Richtel 2005).
66. Muller and Fahey (2005).
67. Quote is taken from Richtel (2005).
68. My notions of market widening and market deepening are not identical to Held et al.'s (1999, 17, 150–51) use of "extensity of global networks" (interconnection of countries) and "intensity of global interconnectedness" (trade as a proportion of output). My notion of "market widening" incorporates both the expansion in the geographic scope of trade (extensity) and the increase in the volume of trade (intensity). However, my notion of "market deepening" pertains specifically to the emergence of entire new classes of previously nontraded services that are now routinely exchanged across borders.

Dicken (2003, 12–13) has a different typology. He makes a distinction between "internationalizing processes" and "globalizing processes." The former pertains to the simple extension of economic activity across national borders, as in the case of more countries trading with each other. In contrast, "globalizing processes" entail more than just a geographical expansion of economic activity but the functional integration of disparate economies, as we have seen in international vertical specialization. It is a contrast between what he calls "shallow" versus "deep" integration (20). Note that my notion of market widening encompasses both of Dicken's "internationalizing" and "globalizing" processes.

69. Credit reporting is nothing new. The Mercantile Agency collated information on the creditworthiness of business firms in the United States in the nineteenth century. This agency eventually became Dun & Bradstreet. What is new is the emergence of a market for information on creditworthiness down to the level of the individual. Today, Equifax, TransUnion, and Experian are firms that keep track of personal credit histories. Note, too, the considerable effort expended in gathering data on consumer habits in an effort to hone production and marketing decisions (e.g., gleaning data through credit card purchases, coupon use, surveys, electronic footprints–cookies on the Web). ICTs have made it easier for firms to collect information on their customers in an effort to serve them better and anticipate their needs. Such "customer relationship management" reflects the stiffer competition inaugurated by the digital age (Siegele 2002).

70. Baldwin and Martin (1999).

71. Rosenstein-Rodan (1943).

72. Barboza (2004).

73. Houben and Kakes (2002); IMF (2001, 128–32).

74. Houben and Kakes (2002, 557–58) also find that financial markets enhance the positive impact of ICTs on the real economy. In the best-case scenario, this may be indicative of the complementarity of the real and the financial markets. However, it may also be the case that a stable and well-developed financial market may actually be serving as a proxy for a stable sociopolitical environment, such as legal structures and property rights. Even if this was the case, the correlation is nonetheless still reflective of the importance of the complementarity of smoothly functioning markets.

75. Lash (1994, 119).

76. These are luxury goods.

77. Stevens (1996).

78. Woodall (1996, 43).

79. Granstrand (2000, Table 1.4, 10–12). This is measured in terms of the ratio of market value to book value. By Granstrand's account, even a traditional firm like Coca-Cola is more reliant on its intellectual property than Microsoft.

80. *Economist* (1996).
81. Kash et al. (2002, Table 1, 167). Among the complex technologies are motor vehicles, airplanes, plastics, chemicals, machinery, telecommunications, data processing, and transistors. Among the simple technologies are basic metals, footwear, toys, furniture, and knitwear.
82. Data source: U.S. Census Bureau, Statistical Abstract of the United States 2001 (http://www.census.gov/prod/2002pubs/01statab/labor.pdf, last accessed July 26, 2007).
83. Nakamura (2000, 16–17).
84. Carnoy (2000, Table 2.10, 42).
85. Cline (1997).
86. Richardson (1995) finds that trade is only a moderate contributing factor behind increasing income inequality.
87. Carnoy (2000, Table 2.8, 40, 43). If anything at all, it seems that globalization and the knowledge economy may have arrested the decline of the mid-level jobs. Between 1960 and 1980, the proportion of mid-level jobs declined from 44.7 percent (1960) to 34.4 percent (1980). Low-wage jobs increased from 31.6 percent (1960) to 37.4 percent (1980).
88. Data are from Woodall (2000, 1).
89. Litan and Rivlin (2001, 5–7).
90. Ibid., 19–20. See Qiang and Pitt (2004) for a review of the literature on the impact of ICT on economic growth. Jorgenson et al. (2005) examines at length the impact of ICT and higher education on the total factor productivity of different U.S. industries. See also OECD (2004) for the impact of ICT on the major developed nations.
91. IMF (1997, 45).
92. I have lost track of where I got this term and am thus unable to provide a bibliographic entry.
93. Woodall (2000, 19).
94. IMF (2001, Figure 3.4, 108).
95. Schiller (2000).
96. Kuznets (1966).
97. Recall the Luddites during the early phase of the Industrial Revolution in Great Britain.
98. Each of these will be examined in greater depth in the following chapters.
99. Meier (1995, 456–58).
100. IMF (1997, 51–52).
101. Davis (2004).
102. Men experienced a progressively larger decline in job tenure as they got older. The age groups with their respective change in median job tenure between 1983 and 1998 are 20–24 age group = −0.3 years; 25–34 age group = −0.4 years; 35–44 age group = −1.8 years; 45–54 age group = −3.4 years; 55–64 age group = −4.1 years; 65 and older = −1.2 years. (Source: U.S. Labor Statistics, Monthly Labor Review, The Editor's Desk, October 6, 1998).

103. Data are from *Economist* (2005c).
104. See England (2004); Cantacuze (2003); and Morrison (2003).
105. World Bank (2007, Figure 2.14c, 53).
106. Ravallion and Lokshin (2005).
107. IMF (2001, Table 1.12, 54; Figure 1.18, 55).
108. See Dicken (2003, 437–70) for a succinct description of the micro-electronics industry. See Bayoumi and Haacker (2002) for an examination of the benefits reaped by the different ICT-producing nations.
109. IMF (2001, 127).
110. Ibid., 132.
111. Ibid., Table 3.10, 129.
112. As we will see in chapter 5, knowledge builds on earlier knowledge. Those who have more to begin with are in a much better position (than those who have little) to create and possess even more knowledge in the subsequent rounds of economic activity. Furthermore, disparate fragments of knowledge are often combined to produce a synergy—a whole that is greater than the sum of its parts. In other words, by its nature, knowledge is characterized by IRS.
113. Chichilnisky and Gorbachev (2004, 533).
114. The IRS industries examined are as follows: credit agencies, electronic equipment and instruments, machinery (except electrical), retail trade, security and commodity brokers, telephone and telegraph, and wholesale trade (Chichilnisky and Gorbachev 2004, 540).
115. It is also interesting to note that in dividing the data into two time periods, 1977–86 and 1987–2001, they find that the volatility of the IRS industries became even more pronounced in the second period relative to traditional industries or to the earlier period. See Table 1 and Figures 1 and 2 of Chichilnisky and Gorbachev (2004, 545–46). The significance of this increased volatility over time is worth a closer empirical examination because it was not until the 1990s that we witnessed extensive market penetration by ICTs. One could try to establish a direct causation from ICTs to greater volatility.

3 Requisite Agility

1. For example, the simulations and modeling conducted through ever-more powerful computers lead to faster and better informed decision-making.
2. See Cairncross (2001) for a description of this phenomenon.
3. Litan and Rivlin (2001, 12–15).
4. Siegele (2002).
5. Litan and Rivlin (2001, 13).
6. IMF (2001, 122).
7. Ibid., 125.
8. Richtel (2005).
9. Fry (2001).
10. Litan and Rivlin (2001, 8–12).

11. Ibid., 10–11.
12. Ibid., 11.
13. Markillie (2004).
14. Long (2000).
15. Nocera (2004).
16. Readers are reminded of the difference between accounting and economic profits. Accounting profits are the normal returns accruing to capital. Economic profits are those that are over and above these normal returns to capital.
17. Litan and Rivlin (2001, 16).
18. Parmar (2004); Waldman (2004).
19. Meier (1995, 456–58).
20. Bayoumi et al. (1996); Coe et al. (1997).
21. Nakamura (2000).
22. Lundvall and Archibugi (2001, 1).
23. Klein et al. (2001).
24. IMF (2001, 133).
25. Woodall (1996, 10).
26. Bayoumi and Haacker (2002); IMF (2001, 108).
27. See also Davis and Meyer (1998).
28. This jump in the long-run growth rate of U.S. GDP per capita is, in fact, even more impressive on two counts. First, these high growth rates are calculated over a much larger population base, which began to expand dramatically in the 1950s. Second, we are also talking of growth from a much larger GDP base compared to the nineteenth century.
29. Woodall (2000, 19). There has also been a long-run acceleration in the growth rate of world GDP per capita. For most of human history, global output grew at 0.1 percent per year. This has risen to 1.2 percent per year since 1780, the dawn of the Industrial Revolution (Woodall 2000, 7).
30. James (1998, 61).
31. From 5 billion freight-tons miles in 1980, air carriers as a mode of transportation grew to 15 billion freight-tons miles by 2000 (Source: Bureau of Transportation Statistics, http://www.bts.gov/press_releases/2003/bts001_03.html, last accessed July 26, 2007).
32. From an average daily volume of 4,200 packages in 1974, the express service provided by FedEx grew to 3,167,000 packages by 2004 (http://fedex.com/us/investorrelations/downloads/history/expressfinancialhistory, last accessed July 26, 2007).
33. Bayoumi and Haacker (2002, Table 8, 22).
34. Cairncross (2001, Figures 2–3, 37).
35. David (1990). The dynamo was essential to the commercialization of electricity.
36. Litan and Rivlin (2001, 19–20).
37. Lundvall (1998, 46).

38. Ibid., 46–47.
39. See Green (2006, 44–93).
40. Hirsch (1976).
41. Cowan et al. (2000, 223). We will examine tacit knowledge in greater depth later in the chapter.
42. This means that new knowledge is created by expanding on earlier knowledge; knowledge builds on itself.
43. Path dependence means that present outcomes are heavily shaped by the past. We will examine this phenomenon at length in chapter 5.
44. Leibenstein (1966, 412).
45. Gross (2005).
46. Litan and Rivlin (2001, 15–17, 26).
47. Of course, the downside to the Internet is its network disexternality in which a proliferation of sellers in the market makes it more difficult to get noticed. Thus, many are often driven back to expensive, traditional forms of advertising. For example, some dotcom companies take out multimillion-dollar Super Bowl ads in order to gain name recognition.
48. Nakamura (2000, 21).
49. These hedonic prices are nominal prices adjusted for improvements in the product quality. They are especially important corrections in calculating the decline in the real cost of microelectronics and computers because nominal prices do not reflect the enhanced features of each new model (IMF 2001, 110–11).
50. One must be cautious in dealing with these quality-adjusted prices. In practice, the additional technological capabilities of these new generations of products or services are often left unused or underutilized because of the time and effort it takes to learn how to use them, or because consumers are simply not interested and use the product or service for the most basic, no-frills functions. If this is the case, the new "bells and whistles" do not add as much value to the economy as hedonic prices suggest. They should be acknowledged as potentially unused or underutilized capacities if we are to employ hedonic prices as a way of measuring the contribution of technological innovations to improving the economy and our material well-being.
51. Thus, in the earlier anecdote of Japanese automakers slowing down change (Lundvall 1998, 46–47), they were, in effect, trying to lengthen the payback period to recoup the enormous expense of developing new car models and then retooling their assembly lines.
52. *Economist* (2000a, 33).
53. Best (1990, 14, 144).
54. Schienstock (2001, 164).
55. Nyholm et al. (2001, 255). Nyholm et al. go much further and suggest that success also requires the ability to communicate their core values to internal and external stakeholders and to take responsibility for their obligations to the local and the wider global community.

Given the backlash against globalization in the light of its ill effects, there is much to be said about this point on social responsibility. In fact, I would even claim that the requisite "flexibility and continuous innovation" include the ability to think outside the box and to go beyond the economic goals of profit- and utility-maximization.

56. James (2002, 2, original emphasis).
57. Best (1990, 144)
58. Miles and Boden (2000, Table 10.2, 167).
59. James (2002, 23–40).
60. Ibid., Table 2.1, 36.
61. Lohr (2006).
62. This is not to say that R&D is no longer skewed in its distribution. Helpman (1999, 17) notes that industrialized nations account for 96 percent of global R&D. Moreover, only 15 nations are responsible for the remaining 4 percent attributed to LDCs. Even the strategic R&D alliances are mostly between developed countries (Freeman and Hagedorn 1995, 44). Sachs (2000) argues that it is no longer ideology that divides the world today, but technology. There is an increasing disparity in the economic performance of technological innovators and adopters compared to the technologically excluded.
63. Myers et al. (2000).
64. James (1998, 61–62).
65. Levy and Grewal (2000).
66. James (1998, 61–62).
67. James (1998, 62) notes that car and fashion apparel suppliers serving the U.S. market are concentrated in Mexico, Canada, and the Caribbean.
68. This is exactly the same phenomenon documented by Bayoumi and Haacker's (2002) study in which ICT users, and not their producers, enjoy the biggest gains from the digital age.
69. Litan and Rivlin (2001, 22).
70. Nyholm et al. (2001, 254).
71. *Economist* (2000b, 22).
72. *Economist* (2005b, 81).
73. In this case, I am referring to both accounting and economic profits.
74. The share of labor has been on the decline from around 56 percent in 2001 to 54 percent in 2006.
75. Walker (2007); author's calculations using data from the Bureau of Labor Statistics.
76. Arthur (1996); *Economist* (1996, 35).
77. James (1998, 60).
78. Frank and Cook (1996).
79. Nakamura (2000, 21).
80. Dicken (2003, 140–44); Lundvall (1998, 44).
81. Alster (1988).
82. Rossant (2004).

83. We see this in the beleaguered U.S. airline industry in the post-911 era of anemic earnings, high oil prices, and pesky discount start-up carriers. While the unexpected surge in oil prices for 2004–6 pushed the major airlines deeper into insolvency, relatively younger budget carriers used this economic shock as an occasion to expand their market share and even add new routes. High-volume and profitable routes were fiercely contested with different promotional entice-ments, and traditional stalwarts in the airline industry were forced to imitate each other's drastic measures, such as Chapter-11 bankruptcy relief, union contract givebacks, downsizing, pension cutbacks, con-solidation, and the outsourcing of services that were traditionally performed in-house.

84. *Economist* (2005a, 9, emphasis added).

85. The following distinctions are from Roberts (2000, 430).

86. The following distinctions are drawn from Lam (2000, 490).

87. See Cowan et al. (2000, 214–24) for a history of the emergence and use of tacit knowledge in economics.

88. Lam (2000, 490).

89. Of course, some tacit knowledge requires formal schooling and the extensive use of codifiable knowledge.

90. Arora et al. (2002, 11); Cowan et al. (2002, 222–23); Johnson et al. (2002, 249–54); von Hippel (1994). Cohendet and Joly (2001, 66) propose a different taxonomy for knowledge, to wit: scientific knowl-edge and knowledge from applied research. Within applied research are technological and engineering knowledge. Technological knowl-edge pertains to the accumulated stock of learning that is shared by everyone in the industry, such as the technical parameters and proper-ties of materials, products, and processes. This generic industry-wide knowledge is codified in professional journals and textbooks, just like scientific knowledge. Engineering knowledge, however, is proprietary in nature and is firm- or person-specific. It is knowledge gleaned from the constant effort to improve current practices through a process of experimentation and trial and error. This is tacit knowledge.

91. Lam (2000, 490).

92. Lundvall (1998, 35–36, 274–76); Johnson et al. (2002, 249–54). See Johnson et al. (2002, 250, n. 5) for a comparison of these four cate-gories with Aristotle's distinctions on the different kinds of knowledge.

93. Lundvall (1998, 36).

94. Cowan et al. (2000, 224–34) are skeptical of the distinction between codification and tacitness because reading the "codebook" after codi-fication requires a particular vocabulary and an antecedent reference point. In other words, codifiable knowledge, just like tacit knowledge, has an unavoidable embedded "context—temporal, spatial, cultural, and social" (225). Thus, one cannot separate tacitness from codified knowledge. Roberts (2000, 431) agrees that codified knowledge is also contextual. Cowan et al. propose an alternative taxonomy,

namely: articulated (and thus codified), unarticulated, and unarticulable. Johnson et al. (2002) disagree with such a classification. Which taxonomy is more appropriate and accurate is not important for my thesis. At the end of the day, both approaches unequivocally point to the central importance of human capital formation.

95. Nyholm et al. (2001, 257–67).
96. Freeman and Louca (2001, 309).
97. Castells (1996, 193); Freeman and Louca (2001, 309).
98. Johnson et al. (2002, 250).
99. Cohendet and Joly (2001, 64).
100. Lam (2000, 490–93).
101. For example, Microsoft and Yahoo have formed an alliance to take on Google (Guth and Delaney 2006).
102. Castells (1996); Johnson et al. (2002, 250); Lundvall (1998, 36). This phenomenon is also true at a macroeconomic level because nations' differential economic performance and technological dynamism in globalization have been a function of their respective social capital (Dosi et al. 1990).
103. Anderson et al. (2002, Figures 2, 4, and 5, 53–55).
104. Freeman and Louca (2001, 327). See Archibugi and Michie (1997) for a description of the globalization of technology in the 1980s.
105. Anderson et al. (2002, Table 2, 54).
106. Moris and Jankowski (2002, Figure 2, 124).
107. Turnipseed et al. (1999).
108. Castells (1996, 162–64).
109. Leo and Stock (2005).
110. Freeman (1994, 471).
111. Anderson et al. (2002, Table 5, Figure 3, 59–60).
112. Ricadela (2005); Clark et al. (2005).
113. Anderson et al. (2002, Figure 1, 53).
114. See Shapiro and Varian (1999, 227–59) for numerous other examples of strategic cooperation and alliances, even among competitors, out of expediency or self-interest.
115. Radosevic (1999).
116. IMF (2002, 129).
117. Studies identify trust and strategic behavior as important reasons for why firms network with each other. Freeman (1994, 471) suggests that fear and power are also proximate causes of networking that should be seriously considered.
118. See Dicken (2003, 355–508) for a concise survey of developments in these sectors as a result of globalization.
119. Shirouzu (2004).
120. Dunning (2000, 10–11; 30, n.11).
121. Schienstock (2001, 164).
122. Short segments of this subsection on *Higher Requisite Human Capital* and chapter 6's subsections on *Need Satisfaction and Coping*

with Disruptive Pecuniary Externalities and on *Need Satisfaction and Preemptive Action* are drawn from my essay "Economic Rights in the Knowledge Economy: An Instrumental Justification" (Barrera, 2007). Copyright by Cambridge University Press. Reprinted with permission.

123. Shapiro and Varian (1999, 8–9). I agree with the second claim but not with the first. After all, one must remember that with our enhanced capacity to manipulate information for our own ends, we are, in effect, producing new data. Thus, an improvement in our ability to handle and analyze information brings in its wake an increase in the volume of new data as we are constantly adding the results of our analysis to the existing body of knowledge. Thus, there is a self-feeding dynamic in which more data and better information-handling technologies lead to even more analyses and even more information produced for the next rounds of economic activity. I cite the overnight emergence of the blogosphere as evidence of this point.

124. Readers are cautioned that rents do not arise merely from the process of creative destruction. In fact, we find so many troubling examples of noncompetitive or "unearned" rents reaped from nonproductive activities (e.g., lobbying for government protection or subsidies) or worse, from unethical or illegal behavior.

125. Green (2006, 24–43). The impact of ICTs on the labor market is disputed. See Borghans and Weel (2005) for alternative findings on the extent to which ICTs require highly skilled workers.

126. This is the phenomenon of network externalities which will be examined in greater depth in chapter 8.

127. Cowan et al. (2000, 224–25, 227) claim that codified and tacit knowledge are complementary. Tacit knowledge is needed to make sense of and use codified knowledge. On the other hand, codified knowledge facilitates the acquisition of tacit knowledge by speeding up the process of learning. One can build on others' experiences and avoid their mistakes to the extent that these have been recorded and analyzed as part of codified knowledge.

128. Lundvall (2001, 276).

129. Nakamura (2000, 21).

130. Schultz (1975). We will examine this phenomenon in greater depth in chapter 6.

131. Lundvall (1998, 43; 2001, 273).

132. White (2006).

133. Lundvall and Archibugi (2001, 1).

134. Schienstock (2001, 164).

135. Lundvall and Archibugi (2001, 1).

136. Lash (1994, 119–35).

137. Carter (1997, 24–25).

138. See the subsection on *Knowledge as the New Source of Value Creation*.

139. Freeman and Perez (1988).

4 Efficiency Matters Even More in the Information Age

1. Smith (1776).
2. O'Rourke and Williamson (1999).
3. See UNCTAD (2004, 55) for a listing of these regional trade groupings and their respective years of formation.
4. See, for example, the National Bureau of Economic Research (NBER) special conference series on *Foreign Trade Regimes and Economic Development* from 1974 to 1978. In particular, see Krueger (1978).
5. Read, for example, the anecdotal accounts of the improvements in Calcutta in the wake of the influx of high-tech, high-paying jobs (Slater 2004).
6. Being on the highest possible indifference curve presupposes that the budget line is tangent to the production possibilities frontier. Thus, Keynesian efficiency is a necessary condition of microeconomic efficiency. The reverse is not true. One may be on the production possibilities frontier but with the wrong production bundle that does not provide the largest consumption possibilities frontier. Thus, we have a Keynesian but not a microeconomic efficiency.
7. Each of these efficiencies is discussed by Shipman (1999) in his Chapters 2, 3, 4, 9, and 10 respectively.
8. In this I follow Shipman (1999, 32).
9. Shipman (1999).
10. The market is merely a necessary but not a sufficient condition for economic efficiency because as we will see in the next chapters, extra-market interventions and institutional preconditions are needed for smoothly functioning markets. For example, moral norms are necessary to ensure the proper operation of markets (Finn 2006; Schultz 2001; Sen 1995). In other words, unfettered markets alone will not bring us economic efficiency.
11. Robbins (1932 [1952]).
12. Efficiency is, of course, not the only end, nor perhaps even the most important end for which the market exists. Other possible ends include the satisfaction of people's basic needs and the provision of venues for interpersonal and international collaboration and cooperation.
13. This is a nonexhaustive list.
14. Lundvall (1998).
15. Nelson and Winter (1982, 276).
16. Buchanan and Vanberg (1991); Hayek (1978 [1998]); Kirzner (1997).
17. See Shipman (1999; 2002) for a detailed exposition on the nature of the market.
18. Hamlin (1995, 141).
19. Recall that relative prices are at the heart of the three equimarginal conditions of welfare maximization. See Bator (1957).
20. Hayek (1944; 1978 [1998]); Buchanan and Vanberg (1991).

21. Rosenberg and Birdzell (1986).
22. Unfettered market operations are, in fact, not value-free. For example, they promote efficiency as the appropriate criterion to use for distributive justice.
23. Observe that I am careful to note that the freedom of entry or exit applies only to particular transactions. The contemporary economic actor cannot completely exit from all market transactions and exist in a state of pure autarky. Thus, the wide-ranging freedoms ascribed to *homo oeconomicus* should not be exaggerated. Autonomy is dependent on the degree to which the person's choices are not driven by unmet basic needs (Raz 1982: 112). See Barrera (2005, 3–42) and references therein for an exposition on how the market may occasionally compel people to make choices they would normally not undertake under ordinary conditions.
24. Hamlin (1995, 140–41). His two other moral bases for the market are its efficient outcomes and its invaluable input in resolving the economic problem. These three moral bases for the market are not mutually exclusive but, in fact, reinforce each other. In particular, the market's efficient outcomes and deft decision making are due to the wide-ranging freedoms it accords economic actors.
25. Berggren (2003) and Paldam (2003). Correlation does not automatically mean causation. All I am claiming is that private initiative and societal material welfare seem to go hand in hand. Establishing causation requires further empirical work.
26. Of course, one must also acknowledge that rents often arise from monopoly power, corruption, nonproductive rent-seeking activities (e.g., lobbying), and government largesse.
27. Marxists and other heterodox schools of economic thought would, of course, dispute this claim. As we will see in the next chapter, market distribution is often partly determined by one's sociohistorical location rather than by merit or contribution alone.
28. Meier (1995, 7–9).
29. Nelson and Winter (1982, 276).
30. Bayoumi and Haacker (2002).
31. Woodall (2000, 19).
32. Dosi et al. (1990, 247).
33. McMillan (2002); Yergin and Stanislaw (1998); Kuttner (1997).
34. Thus, we see an international trend toward the privatization of state-owned enterprises, even in the erstwhile communist states. See, for example, Kikeri and Kolo (2005).
35. Moreover, the market economy supplies useful entrepreneurial skills for the other, noneconomic realms of society. For example, we have seen the transfer of business practices to the nonprofit sector in addressing some of our societal problems. This emerging field has been called social entrepreneurship (Frumkin 2002, 129–62).
36. Bell and Pavitt (1997, 98–99).

37. The following description is taken from Rosenberg (1996, 340–53).
38. Rosenberg (1996, 344–45).
39. Freeman and Perez (1988, 45–47).
40. Rosenberg (1996, 345–47).
41. Ibid., 347.
42. More will be said about this when we briefly examine research networks toward the end of the chapter. Recall, too, the history of how maritime insurance emerged.
43. Castells (1996, 51).
44. Rosenberg (1996, 353).
45. Shipman (1998, 178–85).
46. Rosenberg (1996, 353).
47. This, of course, is in addition to the ability of the marketplace to spread the risks inherent in developing new technologies.
48. Castells (1996, 63–64).
49. Ibid., 37; Mokyr (1990).
50. Dosi et al. (1990, 9).
51. Castells (1996, 37).
52. Arora et al. (2002).
53. Bayoumi et al. (1996); Helpman (1999).
54. Klein et al. (2001).
55. Granstrand (2000, 57).
56. Dosi et al. (1990, 247–48).
57. Dicken (2003, 86, emphasis added).
58. Castells (1996, 191); Ernst (1994, 5–6).
59. Take the laptop computer as an example. The hard disk drives are made in Japan, China, Singapore, and the United States; the power supplies and magnesium casings come from China; the memory chips are produced in South Korea, Taiwan, the United States, and Germany; the liquid crystal displays (LCDs) are manufactured in South Korea, Taiwan, Japan, and China; and the microprocessors come from the Unites States. The graphics processors are designed in the United States and Canada, but made in Taiwan. This list does not even include the other components that constitute these major systems of the laptop (Dean and Tam 2005).
60. Shapiro and Varian (1999, 227–96) describe the intricacies of such standards "warfare."
61. Castells (1996, 171). The two most predominant forms of organization are the market and hierarchical (Fordist) arrangements. Freeman (1994, 471) notes that neo-Schumpeterian studies suggest that networks may in fact provide a third, intermediate, form of economic organization.
62. For example, we have seen the collaboration of erstwhile rivals: Microsoft and RealNetworks in the area of home entertainment technologies (Ricadela 2005), and Sony and Samsung in the field of flat-panel technology (Dvorak and Ramstad 2006). Or, recall the strategic

partnership forged between AOL and Google at the expense of Microsoft (Angwin and Delaney 2005).

63. James (1998, 58).

64. Krugman (1995).

65. Castells (1996, 171, original emphasis).

66. This is exactly the same function exercised by the market in matching the coincidence of needs (that is, bringing together the seller and buyer for a specific good) that would have been extremely difficult in a barter economy.

67. Deardorff (2001, 25, n.7) lists the different names used by scholars to describe this phenomenon, namely: "disintegration" (Feenstra), "internationalization" (Grossman and Helpman), "intra-product specialization" (Arndt), "multistage production" (Dixit and Grossman), "vertical specialization" (Hummels et al.), and "fragmentation" (Jones and Kierzkowski). Feenstra (1998, 31–32, 39) lists other names, to wit: "kaleidescope comparative advantage" (Bhagwati and Dehejia), "slicing the value chain" (Krugman), "delocalization" (Leaner), "intra-mediate trade" (Antweiler and Trefler), and "intraproduct specialization" (Arndt). In the case of services, the World Bank (2007, 120) suggests "global sourcing of services."

68. Brynjolfsson and Hitt (2000, 26, 36) find a statistical correlation between investments in ICTs and smaller or less vertically integrated firms.

69. Jones et al. (2005).

70. IMF (2001, 133) cites Portes and Rey's (1999) empirical work in which adding variables on information flows reduces the negative impact of distance in models of international trade.

71. Freeman (1994, 483).

72. Brynjolfsson and Hitt (2000, 25–26).

73. IMF (2001, 107–8).

74. Castells (1996).

75. Brynjolfsson and Hitt (2000, 25–26, 36). For some scholars, partial organizational changes are not good enough. In fact, Hammer (1990) proposes an all-or-nothing strategy of radical organizational reengineering. What is needed is not merely upgrading but "obliterating" existing structures. The creation of appropriate institutional infrastructure is a key determinant of whether investments in ICTs fail or produce windfall rents (Brynjolfsson and Hitt 2000, 25–26). A good example of such a radical reengineering in the wake of ICTs is international vertical specialization.

76. Schienstock (2001, 164).

77. IMF (2001, 133).

78. Michaels and Lunsford (2004).

79. Nyholm et al.'s (2001) Figures 14.2 and 14.3 and Tables 14.2 and 14.3 are particularly informative in comparing the difference between vertical and horizontal integration.

80. Andreasen et al. (1995).
81. Kahn (2004).
82. Nyholm et al. (2001, 263, emphasis added).
83. Brynjolfsson and Hitt (2000, 24).
84. Castells (1996; 1997; 1998).
85. Freeman and Louca (2001, 327) would even go so far as to suggest that Castells's theory of the network firm may in fact be a viable alternative to the methodological individualism of orthodox economic theory.
86. Richtel (2005).
87. Freeman and Perez (1988).
88. Muller and Fahey (2005).
89. Sutcliffe and Glyn (2003, 73) are skeptical of claims of an increasingly globally integrated production because very little hard evidence has been presented. Moreover, they contend that the recorded increases in intra-industry trade are very likely due to the marketing activities of subsidiaries, especially in consumer electronics, computers, and vehicles.
90. This includes Australia, Hong Kong SAR, South Korea, Malaysia, Philippines, Singapore, Taiwan, and Thailand.
91. Data are from Figure 3.8 of IMF (2001, 123).
92. It averages to around 10 percent of the entire region's output but could go as high as 25 percent, as in the case of Malaysia, and 20 percent in the case of Singapore (IMF 2001, 123).
93. IMF (2001, 123–28). Given the high proportion of ICT exports in Asia compared to the rest of the world, it should not come as a surprise to see its much higher ratio of merchandise trade to merchandise value-added. For the year 2000, the average for the major industrialized countries was 76.3 percent compared to Asia at 168.5 percent and for the NICs (including Hong Kong SAR, South Korea, Singapore, and Taiwan) at a stunning 365.5 percent! In other words, countries that are heavily into ICT production and exports exhibit a correspondingly high degree of intra-industry trade (IMF 2002, 128).
94. IMF (2002, 126, Table 3.8).
95. Barboza (2006).
96. Yeats (2001, 130).
97. Dollar and Kraay (2001b).
98. Coe et al. (1997); Helpman (1999).
99. There is also a self-reinforcing dynamic at a microeconomic level. As we have seen in the preceding sections, ICTs have been responsible for the organizational changes supporting a globally integrated production structure for electronic goods. These globally integrated production networks have, in their own turn, expanded global markets through the cross-border trade of their parts and components. The importance of market widening and deepening for the ICT sector is reflected in the ratio of international sales to total sales for ICT versus non-ICT firms. Between 1990 and 2000, this ratio declined from

around 33 to 31 percent for non-ICT firms, but increased from 32 percent to 42 percent for ICT firms. The bulk of this rise in international sales occurred between 1998 and 2000. Thus, there is a mutually reinforcing interaction between ICTs, on the one hand, and market deepening and widening, on the other hand. Data are taken from Figure 3.9 (IMF 2001, 211, 128).

100. Bayoumi and Haacker (2002).
101. Yergin and Stanislaw (1998).
102. See Castells (1996, 36, n.30) for the origins and development of the use of this term.
103. Lundvall (2001, 283). See also Chandler (1998). Van den Ende and Dolfsma (2005) provide an excellent study on the role of supply and demand factors in the development of computing technology.
104. Schumpeter (1942, 81–86).

5 Preconditions and Limitations of Efficiency

1. Recall, for example, how the first-order conditions in the theories of consumption and production are expressed in terms of relative prices. See Bator (1957).
2. Barrera (2005, 43–74).
3. Note the high returns recorded in the human capital literature and the increasing disparity in the incomes of skilled or college-educated workers versus those who are unskilled or with less than twelve years of schooling. We will examine such returns in chapter 6.
4. Barrera (1990).
5. In the case of nations, one may even include geography as part of its sociohistorical location. After all, distance from markets, resource endowments, and vulnerability to pests and tropical diseases are important determinants of economic performance. See IMF (2003, 99) and references therein.
6. I am measuring the "full" price not in terms of the opportunity cost of time, but in terms of the time and effort expended. Poor human capital leads to a low wage, and therefore a reduced opportunity cost of time. Consequently, if we were to use the opportunity cost of time as a measure of the "full" price that I am proposing, we may get the perverse result in which the "full" cost to a person with a poor human capital is minimal. For example, take the many women and children in developing countries who spend so much time gathering water and firewood. Because they could only earn minimal wages, if any wages at all, the use of the opportunity cost of time would suggest that the "full cost" of gathering firewood and water is minimal. In actuality, the "full" cost is enormous because the time and effort expended by these women and children could have been better employed in more productive activities, especially in skills development. Another illustration of the problem of using the opportunity cost of time in such analyses

is the Larry Summers memo (Hausman and McPherson 1996, 9). Recall that this note argued that from a purely economic view, it made rational sense to export dirtier industries from industrialized countries to developing nations. One explanation was that the cost of the resulting morbidity and mortality (from the dirty industries) would be lower in the latter than in the former given their minimal wages and, therefore, their lower opportunity loss. Indeed, one has to be careful in the use of lost wages in calculating the opportunity cost of time. Thus, in using "full" price or cost, I am referring to the human time and effort expended, rather than the market value of such time and effort in terms of the lost (low) wages.

7. Freeman and Perez (1988).
8. There are surely many other causes, but I am highlighting only these three as they are relevant for my thesis.
9. Rosenberg and Birdzell (1986). See Dunning (2003) for an exposition on key constituent institutions (markets, governments, multilateral agencies, and civil society) undergirding global capitalism.
10. North (1990).
11. IMF (2003, 96–97).
12. IMF (2003, 97).
13. Finn (2006) is a good recent exposition on the moral ecology of the marketplace.
14. Landes (1998).
15. Dunning (2003); Fukuyama (1995); Schultz (2001); Sen (1995).
16. IMF (2003); World Bank (2001).
17. Shipman (2002).
18. Of course, in the textbook model of the perfectly competitive market, the economic actor will be able to do these calculations instantaneously because of the assumption of perfect knowledge.
19. See Heap (1989, 116–47) for a more in-depth exposition of bounded rationality.
20. The Coase theorem notes that any initial distribution of property rights would lead to a Pareto efficient condition for as long as people are free to contract exchanges with each other, the transaction costs are minimal, and only a small group of parties is involved in such bargaining.
21. Cooter (1987: 457).
22. Hausman (1992: 103, fn 21).
23. More open economies in nineteenth-century globalization also did much better than those that were isolated from the market (Dowrick and DeLong 2003).
24. The following findings are taken from Bourguignon et al. (2004).
25. Data are drawn from the World Bank's *World Development Indicators 2004*. As noted in chapter 1, there is controversy on how to weight measures of inequality. In this study, Bourguignon et al. weight each country by its population instead of assigning equal weights to all

countries regardless of their demographic size. In other words, they are giving people, rather than countries, equal weights in the calculation of poverty and inequality.

26. Bouirguignon et al. (2004, 19, Table 1). GNI per capita figures are in constant terms and PPP-adjusted.

27. These countries were: Malawi, Guinea-Bissau, Mozambique, Congo, Chad, and Burundi.

28. Bouirguignon et al.'s (2004, 21, Table 2) "mobility matrix" is an excellent succinct presentation of these changes in income patterns.

29. Castells (1998, 71) defines polarization as the phenomenon of a shrinking middle class because of the increasing size of the opposite ends of the income spectrum—the wealthiest and the poorest classes.

30. Borjas and Ramey (1994); Kim (1997); Pritchett (1997); Williamson (1997); Wood (1994, 1995, 1997).

31. Milanovic (2005, Table 6.2, 55). Note that these deciles are formed according to GDP per capita. Decile means are unweighted.

32. Figures are taken from IMF (2003, Table 3.1, 96). These are in 1995 U.S. dollars.

33. IMF, (2003, 95–96).

34. World Bank (2005, 66). Figure 3.11 is a good diagrammatic overview of this shift across countries and regions. See also http://iresearch. worldbank.org/PovcalNet/jsp/index.jsp, last accessed July 26, 2007.

35. Chen and Ravallion (2004).

36. Global real GDP growth rate declined by a third from 4.5 percent (1960–80) to 3 percent (1980–2000).

37. In 2000, 60 percent of its population was in the lowest three deciles of global income. By 2030, this is expected to increase to 80 percent (4 out every 5). In 2000, 30 percent of people in the bottom decile of world income came from the region. By 2030, it is projected that more than half will be from sub-Saharan Africa.

38. Data are drawn from World Bank (2007, Figures 3.3, 3.4, and 3.8; Table 1.1).

39. Data source: UNCTAD Handbook of Statistics 2005, Table 1.1 (http://stats.unctad.org/ Handbook, last accessed July 26, 2007).

40. Castells (1998, 70–165).

41. Mulligan (1999, S186–87) does a literature survey of 45 household-level empirical studies done on different countries, including two on the United States.

42. These are all expressed in log.

43. These results are drawn from Bourguignon et al. (2003).

44. It would be interesting to study the causation between Brazil's long-standing income inequality and these findings of an unusually strong intergenerational transmission of inequality.

45. The fourth quintile moved from 15.2 to 14.8 percent, the third quintile from 9.7 to 8 percent, and the second quintile from 7.5 to 5.5 percent. Figures are from McClain (2005) and U.S. Census.

46. This includes government benefits received.
47. Data are taken from Bernanke (2007).
48. In his description of the rise of the fourth world, Castells (1998, 128–49) does not just cite sub-Saharan Africa but also devotes an extended section on what he calls "Dual America" in which many of its citizens have been excluded from the benefits of the information age.
49. Figure 2.1 of World Bank (2005, 30) provides a good diagrammatic summary of these patterns.
50. For example, see Barrera (1990).
51. See Figures 2.2 and 2.3 of World Bank (2005, 30–31).
52. See World Bank (2006, Figure 3.5, 85).
53. Komives et al. (2006); UNDP-World Bank (1999); World Bank (2005, 32; Figure 5.1, 90; Figure 8.4, 173).
54. *New York Times* (2005). See also George (2006).
55. Note that we have not even examined the literature on how castes and ethnicity account for variations in people's socioeconomic opportunities and accomplishments.
56. Chapter 5 of the World Bank's *World Development Report 2006: Equity and Development* provides more examples of the regressive distribution of burdens and benefits in economic life. See World Bank (2005, 89–104).
57. Milanovic (2002).
58. This is a policy proposal made by Bannister and Thugge (2001).
59. Wood (1994).
60. Adelman and Fuwa (1994).
61. Fields (1995).
62. Dollar and Kraay (2001a).
63. Bannister and Thugge (2001).
64. Recall the Stolper-Samuelson theorem that states that trade leads to an increase in the relative income of the more abundant factor compared to the scarce factor input.
65. For example, interminable war and corrupt governments in sub-Saharan Africa have only compounded the region's hostile tropical environment and the health emergency caused by HIV/AIDS.
66. Temple and Johnson (1998).
67. IMF (2003, 98).
68. De la Torre et al. (2002); Prasad et al. (2003).
69. Obstfeld and Taylor (2004, 259–300).
70. Diwan and Revenga (1995a). One gets an idea of the potency of path dependence by noting that even if these reforms were implemented under the most optimistic conditions, inequality will drop only slightly from a ratio 60 to 1 in 1992 to a ratio of 50 to 1 in 2010. In the worst-case scenario, this study projects that such inequality can worsen to a ratio of 70 to 1 between a skilled OECD worker and an African farmer.
71. Freeman and Hagedorn (1995, 44).

72. Bayoumi and Haacker (2002).
73. For example, see Stiglitz (2002).

6   Need Satisfaction as a Necessary
Condition of Efficiency

1. Note that I am not arguing that these are the only goods or services that must be part of this indispensable basket. As I have already stated in my preface and later in the concluding chapter, need satisfaction as a criterion of distributive justice can also be justified based on its intrinsic worth, that is, on the dignity of the human person. Such an intrinsic justification would in all likelihood also require its own additional basket of needs to be satisfied.

2. Even this, however, is still not completely satisfactory because it is impossible in practice to compartmentalize the spheres of life from each other. Economics, politics, religion, and culture necessarily overflow and shape each other.

3. The Asian Tigers are South Korea, Taiwan, and Singapore. Prior to its handover in 1997, Hong Kong was also part of this group. The cubs include Malaysia and Thailand.

4. See, for example, Yergin and Stanislaw (1998).

5. Fei et al. (1979).

6. See Bator (1957) for a review of these conditions.

7. Recall the two welfare theorems that highlight only the ability of the market to bring the economy to an equilibrium on the contract curve from any initial point in the Edgeworth box diagram. The theory does not delve into the question of where the economy ought to be on the contract curve (i.e., the distribution of relative welfare).

8. Please note that we are talking of relative income shares as it is possible for absolute returns for both factors to increase simultaneously.

9. One pattern that is readily observable in the literature on technological change is the importance of both social and human capital across all phases of technological innovation—from development, to use, to further improvement. Since it is technical change that provides the knowledge economy with its potency and vibrancy, human capital is essentially the building block of a learning economy.

10. Haveman and Wolfe (1984, 378–90) provide a succinct and excellent review of the literature that identifies not only the various channels but also the corresponding research that examines them. I summarize their findings in the next two paragraphs.

11. Keeping personnel turnover rates low and getting the best talent are a must in the knowledge economy. Thus, such nonwage compensation has taken on even greater importance in contemporary economic life. Take the case of executive pay. The bulk of most CEOs' compensation is in the generous fringe benefits from stock options, bonus-performance pay, severance pay, club memberships, housing, and travel among others. This has also been the primary source of the rising gap

between executive and rank-and-file compensation. Note that generous nonwage compensation is also standard practice in many of the most competitive IT firms and *Fortune* magazine's annual list of the best 100 companies to work for. Fringe benefits include gourmet cafeteria, health club memberships, day care, car wash and oil change facilities on site, sabbaticals, family vacations, subsidized housing and transportation, flexible hours, maternity leave, and time for personal creativity and projects.

12. Recall that most leisure goods are luxury goods. Furthermore, in the aforesaid examples of nonwage compensation, the time savings from having car wash and oil change facilities on company premises provides even more free time after work or during the weekends when such chores are generally done.

13. One word of caution to avoid any misinterpretation. What is brought up here is the efficiency with which people use their available time and information to make choices and not whether they make wise or good choices. For most neoclassical economists, the latter is beyond the scope of economics as a discipline.

14. See Psachararopoulos and Patrinos (2002, Tables 3, 4; 14). In this survey of the literature, the authors review the most updated statistics and studies on returns to education from different countries. See their Appendix Table A1 for a listing of these countries and the studies cited.

15. Low-income countries are defined as those with a per capita income less than $755. See Psachararopoulos and Patrinos (2002, Tables 2, 3; 14).

16. World Bank (2007, Table 3.2, 3.3, 88).

17. See World Bank (2006, Figure 4.4, 102).

18. Besides, there may also be an operative diminishing returns to work experience.

19. World Bank (2007, Figure 9, xviii).

20. The gap is measured between the ninetieth and the tenth percentile earners. See World Bank (2007, Figure 4.2, 106).

21. Data are from Bernanke (2007). Between 1979 and 1987, average wages for men with only a high-school education fell by 20 percent even as the earnings of college graduates rose by 11 percent in real terms (Diwan and Revenga 1995b, 8).

22. Wood (1994; 1995).

23. Rodrik (1997, 11–27).

24. Diwan and Revenga (1995b, 8).

25. Borjas and Ramey (1994).

26. Wood (1997). He accounts for the disparity in the East Asian and Latin American experience by pointing to the different global conditions at the time they respectively embarked on trade expansion. I would argue, however, that at the time they entered the global stage, the East Asian countries were coming out of an export-promotion strategy to development in which great effort was expended in making sure

that their firms were market-hardened and disciplined. In contrast, one must recall the lingering damage inflicted by the import-substitution strategy to development pursued by the Latin American countries. Such a strategy bred not only inefficiencies within their economies but also entrenched powerful vested interests that lobbied heavily against the lifting of the market-distorting protections they had long enjoyed. In other words, besides entering a different global marketplace compared to the East Asian nations, the Latin American countries did not have comparable institutions that would have enabled them to reap the full benefits of trade. Included in this contrast is the much higher level of human capital available to the East Asian nations as they liberalized their markets. Fields (1995) calls it a broad-based growth, while Fei et al. (1979) describe it as "growth with equity." Institutional preconditions account for much of the disparities in the East Asian and Latin American experience with respect to trade.

27. Rodrik (1997, 49–67; 1998).
28. Diwan and Revenga (1995b, 8).
29. Cline (1997).
30. World Bank (2007, Table 2.14b and c, 53).
31. World Bank 2007 (2007, Table 3.6, 84) Not surprisingly, many of these are in sub-Saharan Africa.
32. Welch (1970, 36).
33. Psachararopoulos and Patrinos (2002).
34. High-income countries are those with a per capita income greater than $9266; low-income countries have a per capita income of less than $755; middle-income countries have a per capita income between $755–$9265. See Psachararopoulos and Patrinos (2002, Figure 3, 14).
35. Psachararopoulos and Patrinos (2002, 2, Table A4, 25–28). Compare this decline with world average private returns to investment in education at 26.6 percent for primary school, 17 percent for high school, and 19 percent for higher education.
36. Psachararopoulos and Patrinos (2002, 3).
37. Welch (1970, 37–38).
38. Nelson and Phelps (1966, 69). The following example from U.S. agriculture is also drawn from this study.
39. Welch (1970).
40. Griliches (1969).
41. Schultz (1975, 828).
42. Psachararopoulos and Patrinos (2002, 1).
43. I preface this claim with the qualifier "everything else equal" because of Lipsey and Lancaster's (1956) theory of second best.
44. This is not even to mention the ever-advancing levels of expertise required by an increasingly technological and specialized economy.
45. See, for example, the *New York Times* series "The Downsizing of America," from March 3–9, 1996. For a more comprehensive treatment of downsizing in the United States, see Baumol et al. (2003).

46. Carnoy (2000, 39).
47. The rate of families returning to agriculture from the nonfarming sector was higher among the low-income families.
48. Out of the U.S. South and from rural to urban areas.
49. Schultz (1975, 836–39).
50. Rodrik (1998, 120).
51. Matusz and Tarr (1999, 18).
52. World Bank (2006, Figure 4.6, 104–5).
53. Lundvall and Archibugi (2001, 1).
54. See Paxson and Shady (2005, Figure 2, 26) and World Bank (2005, Figure 2, 6).
55. In the comparison using wealth disparity, the median score of the privileged children rose by only about 10 points between three and five years of age. The increase was even smaller (4 points) in the comparison using mother's education. See Paxson and Shady (2005, Figure 2, 26) and World Bank (2005, Figure 2, 6).
56. In the comparison using wealth disparity, the median score of the disadvantaged children fell drastically by over 20 points (a 25 percent drop) between three and five years of age. The fall is even slightly bigger in the comparison using mother's education. See Paxson and Shady (2005, Figure 2, 26) and World Bank (2005, Figure 2, 6).
57. It is hobbled by many instances of market failures. In this particular example, the market does not properly value the future contribution of the children who are at risk. In other words, private and social benefits do not match up. The social benefit to the community of developing the intellectual capacities of the disadvantaged children greatly exceeds the private benefits of economic agents who are able to do something about the problem. For example, the wealthiest 25 percent of the population will not find it in their interest to expend the resources to assist in the cognitive development of children from the bottom 25 percent because they (the wealthy 25 percent) will not be able to internalize or capture the subsequent benefits from such an investment. And even if we were to assume conditions of slavery or indentured labor, for the sake of argument, there is still an agency problem in recouping these investments because the wealthy cannot be assured of the quality of the subsequent service rendered in repayment of their earlier expenditures. There is a monitoring problem.
58. The strongest argument against child labor and child malnutrition is the intrinsic dignity of the human person. Readers are reminded, however, that I am limiting myself to the instrumental reasons in showing how neoclassical economics itself can be used to argue for need satisfaction as a necessary condition in bringing about the knowledge economy's long-term allocative efficiency.
59. Basic education is particularly effective and exhibits IRS (Trostel 2004).
60. The preceding observations are from Lundvall (1998, 45–46, 283).
61. Blair (2005).

62. Lundvall and Archibugi (2001, 150; original emphasis).

63. Of course, this assumes that there are functioning markets that permit society to borrow from its future stream of earnings to develop its human and social capital today.

64. The following description and statistics on CCT programs are taken from Rawlings and Rubio (2003).

65. This was called PROGRESA until March of 2002.

66. World Bank (2006, Figure 10, 12).

67. World Bank (2006, Figure 4.4, 102).

68. World Bank (2006, Box 5, 23).

69. These are calculated using the present value of future benefits.

70. See Sachs (2005) for a discussion of the concrete steps that can be taken to put an end to poverty.

7 Broader Base for Market Initiative, Creativity, and Stability

1. See, for example, the appendices of the annual *World Development Report* of the World Bank and the annual *Human Development Report* of the UNDP.

2. Cairncross (2001).

3. Castells (1996).

4. James (1999, 17–21).

5. Parmar (2004).

6. Lundvall (1998, 47).

7. Ibid., 46.

8. Ibid., 45.

9. Dicken (2003, 105).

10. For example, in the 1980s, the United States, EU, and Japan cornered 92 to 96 percent of strategic alliances in IT, such as computers, industrial automation, microelectronics, software, telecommunications, and heavy electronics (Freeman and Hagedorn 1995, 44; James 1998, Table 2.5, 61).

11. Rossant (2004). Recall the Japanese and European subsidies to develop high-definition television (Alster 1988).

12. One could call these "administered transactions" because government has a very visible hand in directing economic agents on what ought to be done. See Shipman (1999, 239–62).

13. Lundvall (1998, 44–47).

14. Rosenberg and Birdzell (1986).

15. Landes (1969).

16. This has come to be known as the Solow productivity paradox, after Robert Solow's (1987) quip that "You can see the computer age everywhere but in the productivity statistics" (Triplett 1999). Gordon (2000, 62, 72) even believes that computer technologies may have hit diminishing returns because of limitations in available time and human capital.

17. Qiang and Pitt (2004, 10, 17–18).
18. This is not completely alien to Lundvall's (1998) thinking as he also acknowledges the value of mass education.
19. Lundvall (1998).
20. Recall the pivotal importance of human capital in the Becker-Lancaster household production model discussed in chapter 5.
21. Castells (1996).
22. Recall that such entry costs are largely person-specific if we are to view each market participant not merely as a consuming economic actor but as a micro-firm "producing" various commodities for himself or herself. Consequently, the prices faced by the economic actor consist of both the nominal prices of goods and services used and the amount of personal time and effort needed to "produce" these commodities. In the Beckerian-Lancasterian household production model, human capital is the key factor in determining such requisite personal time and effort. In other words, the cost of participating in the market is person-specific, that is, dependent on the human capital of the economic agent.
23. Cline (1997, 1–34).
24. This dynamic is replicated in product development as well. Cell phones, computers, and many consumer electronic products have such a fast rate of obsolescence to the point where competitors are driven to imitate or outdo each other's new product features and innovations.
25. Barboza (2004).
26. This may be one explanation to the finding that inequality reduces the efficacy of economic growth in reducing poverty. The poverty elasticity of growth is diminished as inequality rises (World Bank 2007, Figure 3.7, 84).
27. McGregor (1988–89). Bartlett (1989) emphasizes the unavoidable role of power in economics.
28. See, for example, Schultz (2001) and Sen (1995).
29. Ravallion (2004, 17) quotes Pigou (1949, 50) as observing that relative inequalities created, "a sense of being unfairly treated . . . [and is] in itself an evil."
30. Cairncross (2001).
31. James (2000, 85–102).
32. See Chapter 5 of James (2000) entitled "Do Consumers in Developing Countries Gain or Lose from Globalization?"
33. Elster (1982). See George (2001) for a more recent exposition on the malleability of consumer preferences.
34. Chua (2003) and Ravallion (2004, 19). We find empirical evidence of this in the many ultimatum-game experiments in the literature. See, for example, Falk et al. (2003). In the ultimatum game, player A is given windfall resources (e.g., money) that he/she then shares with player B. Player A shares as much as or as little as he/she decides with player B. However, if player B rejects what A offers, then neither

player A nor B get to keep such a windfall. Thus, it is contingent on player A to convince B of the fairness and mutual advantage in the division of the windfall.

35. IMF (2003, 113, 95–128).

36. Malkin (2007).

37. See, for example, the series of *New York Times* editorials (*Harvesting Poverty*) published in 2003. Go to www.nytimes.com/harvesting-poverty. See also Barrera (2005, 178–212).

38. Another historical example is the debt crisis of LDCs in the 1980s. This was partly caused by the sudden jump in U.S. interest rates given the Federal Reserve's efforts to contain inflation.

39. Recall from trade theory how we have to make a distinction between a small and a large country (in terms of market share or dominance). A large country is not a price-taker and its buying and selling behavior affects final prices. In fact, it can even improve its economic welfare at the expense of the smaller nations by imposing trade barriers. Smaller economies, on the other hand, have no choice but to be price-takers and to accept even a deterioration in their terms of trade caused by the economic policies of their larger trading partners.

40. Part II of the World Bank's (2005, 73–126) *World Development Report 2006* develops these points in greater depth.

41. Of course, the exceptions here are the positional goods (Hirsch 1976). For example, the desire to be the smartest may preclude some from sharing knowledge or from assisting others in their human capital formation.

42. It is akin to an intertemporal smoothing of consumption for the entire community.

43. Fei et al. (1979) and Fields (1995). The World Bank (2005) accentuates the critical link between equity and development; the former is a necessary condition for the latter.

44. Recall Ravallion's (2004) description of the normative commitments undergirding the various measures of inequality most commonly employed by people to support their arguments (chapter 1). Antiglobalizers choose what is called "horizontal" measures of inequality in which the focus is on select groups of people (the marginalized). How these at-risk populations fare over time becomes the standard with which to gauge the performance of the market. There is also a preference for absolute measures, such as the number of people living below $1 or $2 a day.

45. Recall from Ravallion's (2004) typology that pro-globalizers have a preference for "vertical" measures in which aggregated, macroeconomic variables are used to track the overall improvement of entire economies over time. See, for example, studies by Dollar and Kraay (2001a and b) that show the beneficial effects of globalization. There is a greater reliance on relative measures of inequality, such as using the proportion of the population living under $1 or $2 a day instead

of the number of people living below these thresholds. The selection of absolute or relative measures makes a big difference in the conclusions one can draw about globalization.

8 Ownership Externalities and the Market as a Public Good

1. Marshall (1890 [1961] I, 284, 314, 320).
2. Bator (1958, 353–54) enumerates five different modes of market failures: failure of existence, failure by signal, failure by incentive, failure by structure, and failure by enforcement.
3. QWERTY is a configuration from the 1870s (Hepworth 1989, 3).
4. As of 1999, 78.3 percent of all Web sites were in English (Cairncross 2001, 281).
5. Woodall (2000, 1).
6. North and Thomas (1973, 134–38).
7. Of course, we must also take into account fraudulent economic agents who take advantage of such a market expansion. Hence, recall the importance of moral norms and trust as preconditions for the smooth functioning of the market (Schultz 2001; Sen 1995).
8. Fry (2001).
9. Other examples include commodity markets such as the Chicago Board of Trade, the stock exchanges, and the foreign currency markets.
10. Simon (1976).
11. Myint (1958).
12. Graphically, this is represented as a movement from a point inside the production possibilities frontier to a point on the production possibilities frontier itself.
13. One exception, of course, is if domestic consumers have a highly income-elastic demand for the export good or if the latter constitutes a large proportion of the household budget. In these cases, the higher price for the export good may lead to a drop in real incomes.
14. This is graphically presented as a movement along the production possibilities frontier.
15. Recall, for example, the Stolper-Samuelson theorem in which trade leads to an increase in the returns of the more abundant factor relative to the scarce factor input.
16. Hicks (1940); Kaldor (1939); Samuelson (1950); Scitovsky (1941).
17. Lam (2000, 493).
18. Shipman (1999). Alternatives to market exchange include relational, informed, and administered transactions. Strictly speaking, these are not truly alternatives in the proper sense of the term because they can produce benefits only when they work alongside the market. In other words, they are limited to a particular range of exchanges and cannot completely replace the market. Moreover, despite Coase's (1937) "Nature of the Firm," which argues that firms can do a much better

job than the market for certain transactions, these firms nevertheless still have to work with and through the market if they are to produce any gains at all. For a more in-depth discussion of these "alternatives" to market exchange, see Shipman (1999, 196–312).

19. It is important to make a distinction between my earlier claim in chapter 4 that there are unavoidable person-specific "entry costs" to participating in the marketplace versus this section's claim that the market is unable to charge a user's fee for the services it provides. The public-good nature of the market means that anyone can simply walk into the marketplace and consummate transactions without having to pay a nominal user's fee. On the other hand, the "entry cost" to market participation refers to the degree of ease or difficulty with which people are able to reap benefits from the marketplace. Everyone can participate in the marketplace, but not everyone will secure the same gains or be required to exert the same amount of effort or time. My notion of "entry cost" to market participation refers to the differing degrees of personal striving needed to procure welfare gains. Those with poor human capital will have to expend much more effort compared to those who are well endowed and who would most likely reap advantages for themselves from the marketplace with ease.

20. Bator (1958, 364) notes that an ownership externality is not dependent on whether the unpaid factors are in the private or public domain. The kind of ownership is irrelevant. What is critical is the inability to get factors paid properly and in full. Nonetheless, for purposes of analysis, one could still make a distinction between a public ownership externality (in which the unpaid factors are in the public domain) and a private ownership externality (in which the unpaid factors are in the private realm).

21. Hicks (1940); Kaldor (1939); Samuelson (1950); Scitovsky (1941).

22. In the earlier example of the micro-outsourcers, these small-scale entrepreneurs are not paying any fees to the countless earlier market participants who were responsible for putting together the current global market infrastructure that has been instrumental in facilitating their current ability to run "virtual" businesses with ease. They are literally standing on the shoulders of economic agents who laid the groundwork for an ICT-run marketplace that confers so many benefits we have come to expect and take for granted.

23. Of course, this is not an intractable problem because all beekeepers could simply be charged a fee based on the number of bees on their farms. Such a prorated fee could be calculated on the basis of the total cost beekeepers owe to apple growers in a particular area. The revenues raised could then be distributed to the different orchards in proportion to the number of apple blossoms they produce. The problem is principally one of enforcement.

24. Take the case of investments in ICTs. Brynjolfsson and Hitt (2000, 31) list empirical studies that show an average annual return of over

60 percent for investments in computers compared with an expected rate of return of 42 percent. Such an unusually high rate of return may be due to other unmeasured inputs. Long-term returns to investments in IT are two to eight times that of short-term returns, suggestive of the importance of complementary factors and investments that accumulate in the general background over time, such as intangible assets in the form of new software, organizational changes, and better skilled workers (33–34). We might also consider improvements in general market conditions that enhance the productivity of these factors. These are positive spillover effects from factors whose owners are unpaid.

25. In this case, one could treat this as a bequest for society as a whole, thus strengthening the case for the community's right to tax or subsidize economic outcomes as it sees fit.
26. Carter (1997, 33).
27. Romer (1990).
28. In a world of increasing returns, the problem is reversed. The output will be exhausted and there will be need to bring in external resources in order to compensate factors according to their marginal productivity.
29. Carter (1997, 33).
30. The conditional cash transfer programs discussed earlier and the scholarship on basic income guarantee programs should be helpful in this regard.
31. Recall that Pareto efficiency can be easily attained in perfectly competitive markets because neoclassical economic theory assumes the absence of externalities.
32. Of course, this proposed solution must be mindful of Lipsey and Lancaster's (1956) point that second-best solutions need not bring us any closer to the optimum position.

9 Summary and Conclusions

1. For example, see Konow (2003); Frolich, and Oppenheimer (1992, 1994); Scott et al. (2001).
2. Konow (2003, 1190, original emphasis).
3. Spragens (1993).
4. Examples include Aristotle (1941); Miller (1976); Nussbaum (1992); and Sen (1984b, 1993).
5. See, for example, Chen and Ravallion (2004).
6. Shue (1980, 18).

References

Adelman, Irma and Nobuhiko Fuwa. 1994. "Income Inequality and Development: The 1970s and 1980s Compared," *Economie Applique* 46: 7–29.

Alster, Norm. 1988. "TV's High-Stakes, High-Tech Battle," *Fortune* October 24: 161–65.

Alternatives Task Force of the International Forum on Globalization. 2002. *Alternatives to Economic Globalization: A Better World Is Possible.* San Francisco, CA: Berrett-Koehler.

Anderson, Frances, Chuck McNiven, and Antoine Rose. 2002. "An Analysis of Patterns of Collaboration in Canadian Manufacturing and Biotechnology Firms," In *Networks, Alliances and Partnerships in the Innovation Process.* Edited by John de la Mothe and Albert Link. Dordrecht, Holland: Kluwer.

Andreasen, Lars Erik, Benjamin Coriat, Friso den Hertog, and Raphael Kaplinsky. 1995. "Flexible Organisation: European Industry and Services in Transition," In *Europe's Next Step: Organisational Innovation, Competition and Employment.* Edited by Lars Erik Andreasen, Benjamin Coriat, Friso den Hertog, and Raphael Kaplinsky. Ilford, UK and Portland, OR: Frank Cass.

Angwin, Julia and Kevin Delaney. 2005. "AOL, Google Expand Partnership, with a Key Ad-Sales Provision," *Wall Street Journal.* December 21.

Appleyard, Dennis, Alfred Field, and Steven Cobb. 2006. *International Economics.* Fifth edition. New York: McGraw-Hill.

Aquinas, Thomas. 1947/48. *Summa Theologica.* Translated by the Fathers of the English Dominican Province. 3 volumes. New York: Benzinger Brothers.

Archibugi, Daniele and Bengt-Åke Lundvall, eds. 2001. *The Globalizing Learning Economy.* New York: Oxford University Press.

Archibugi, Daniele and Jonathan Michie. 1997. "The Globalisation of Technology: A New Taxonomy," In *Technology, Globalisation and Economic Performance.* Edited by Daniele Archibugi and Jonathan Michie. Cambridge: Cambridge University Press.

Aristotle. 1941. "Nicomachean Ethics," In *The Basic Works of Aristotle.* Edited by Richard McKeon. New York: Random House.

Arora, Ashish, Andrea Fosfuri, and Alfonso Gambardella. 2002. *Markets for Technology: The Economics of Innovation and Corporate Strategy.* Cambridge, MA: MIT Press.

Arrow, Kenneth. 1951. *Social Choice and Individual Values.* New York: Wiley.

Arthur, Brian. 1996. "Increasing Returns and the New World of Business," *Harvard Business Review* 75: 4 (July): 100–109.

Bairoch, Paul and Richard Kozul-Wright. 1998. "Globalization Myths: Some Historical Reflections on Integration, Industrialization and Growth in the World Economy," In *Transnational Corporations and the Global Economy.* Edited by Richard Kozul-Wright and Robert Rowthorn. World Institute for Development Economics Research, The United Nations University. New York: St. Martin's Press.

Baldwin, Richard and Philippe Martin. 1999. "Two Waves of Globalisation: Superficial Similarities, Fundamental Differences," National Bureau of Economic Research (NBER) Working Paper # 6904. Cambridge, MA: NBER.

Bannister, Geoffrey and Kamau Thugge. 2001. "International Trade and Poverty Alleviation," *Finance and Development* 38:4: 48–51. Also published as International Monetary Fund Working Paper # WP/01/54. Washington, DC: IMF.

Barboza, David. 2004. "In Roaring China, Sweaters Are West of Socks City," *New York Times.* December 24.

———. 2005. "Ogre to Slay? Outsource It to Chinese," *New York Times.* December 9.

———. 2006. "Some Assembly Needed: China as Asia Factory," *New York Times* February 9.

Barrera, Albino. 1990. "The Role of Maternal Schooling and Its Interaction with Public Health Programs in Child Health Production," *Journal of Development Economics* 32: 69–91.

———. 2005. *Economic Compulsion and Christian Ethics.* Cambridge and New York: Cambridge University Press.

———. 2007. "Economic Rights in the Knowledge Economy: An Instrumental Justification," In *Economic Rights: Conceptual, Measurement and Policy Issues.* Edited by Shareen Hertel, Lanse Minkler, and Richard Wilson. New York: Cambridge University Press.

Barro, Robert. 1991. "Economic Growth in a Cross Section of Countries," *Quarterly Journal of Economics* 106:2: 407–43.

———. 1997. *Determinants of Economic Growth: A Cross-Country Empirical Study.* Cambridge, MA: MIT Press.

Barro, Robert and Xavier Sala-i-Martin. 1992. "Convergence," *Journal of Political Economy* 100:21: 223–51.

———. 1995. *Economic Growth.* New York: McGraw Hill.

Bartlett, Randall. 1989. *Economics and Power.* Cambridge: Cambridge University Press.

Bator, Francis. 1957. "The Simple Analytics of Welfare Maximization," *American Economic Review* 47: 22–59.

———. 1958. "The Anatomy of Market Failure," *Quarterly Journal of Economics* 72: 351–79.

Baumol, William, Alan Blinder, and Edward Wolff. 2003. *Downsizing in America: Reality, Causes, and Consequences.* New York: Russell Sage Foundation.

Bayoumi, Tamim and Markus Haacker. 2002. "It's Not What You Make, It's How You Use IT: Measuring the Welfare Benefits of the IT Revolution across Countries," International Monetary Fund Working Paper # WP/02/117. Washington, DC: IMF.

Bayoumi, Tamim, David T. Coe, and Elhanan Helpman. 1996. "R&D Spillovers and Global Growth," International Monetary Fund Working Paper # WP/96/47. Washington, DC: IMF.

Becker, Gary. 1965. "A Theory of the Allocation of Time," *Economic Journal* 75: 493–515.

Bell, Martin and Keith Pavitt. 1997. "Technological Accumulation and Industrial Growth: Contrasts between Developed and Developing Countries," In *Technology, Globalisation and Economic Performance.* Edited by Daniele Archibugi and Jonathan Michie. Cambridge: Cambridge University Press.

Bellman, Eric. 2005. "One More Cost of Sarbanes-Oxley: Outsourcing to India," *Wall Street Journal.* July 14.

Bellman, Eric and Nathan Koppel. 2005. "More U.S. Legal Work Moves to India's Low-Cost Lawyers," *Wall Street Journal.* September 28.

Berggren, Niclas. 2003. "The Benefits of Economic Freedom: A Survey," *Independent Review* 8: 193–211.

Bernanke, Ben. 2007. *The Level and Distribution of Economic Well-Being* (Speech before the Greater Omaha Chamber of Commerce). February 6. http://www.federalreserve.gov/Boarddocs/speeches/2007/20070206/, last accessed July 26, 2007.

Best, Michael. 1990. *The New Competition: Institutions of Industrial Restructuring.* Cambridge, MA: Harvard University Press.

Bhagwati, Jagdish. 2004. *In Defense of Globalization.* New York: Oxford University Press.

Blair, Tony. 2005. Speech to the European Parliament, June 23, 2005. Press Association (http://www.pm.gov.uk/output/Page7714.asp, last accessed July 26, 2007).

Borghans, Lex and Bas ter Weel. 2005. "How Computerization Has Changed the Labour Market: A Review of the Evidence and a New Perspective," In *The Economics of the Digital Society.* Edited by Luc Soete and Bas ter Weel. Northampton, MA: Edward Elgar.

Borjas, George and Valerie Ramey. 1994. "The Relationship between Wage Inequality and International Trade," In *The Changing Distribution of Income in an Open U.S. Economy.* Edited by Jeffrey H. Bergstrand, Thomas F. Cosimano, John W. Houck, and Richard G. Sheehan. New York: Elsevier.

Bourguignon, François, Francisco Ferreira, and Marta Menendez. 2003. "Inequality of Outcomes and Inequality of Opportunities in Brazil,"

World Bank Policy Research Working Paper # 3174. Washington, DC: World Bank.

Bourguignon, François, Victoria Levin, and David Rosenblatt. 2004. "Declining Economic Inequality and Economic Divergence: Reviewing the Evidence through Different Lenses," *Economic Internationale* 100: 13–25.

Braybrooke, David. 1987. *Meeting Needs.* Princeton, NJ: Princeton University Press.

Brynjolfsson, Erik and Lorin Hitt. 2000. "Beyond Computation: Information Technology, Organizational Transformation and Business Performance," *Journal of Economic Perspectives* 14: 23–48.

Buchanan, James and Viktor Vanberg. 1991. "The Market as a Creative Process," *Economics and Philosophy* 7: 167–86.

Buckman, Greg. 2004. *Globalization: Tame It or Scrap It?* New York: Zed.

Cairncross, Frances. 2001. *The Death of Distance: How the Communications Revolution Is Changing Our Lives.* Second edition. Boston: Harvard Business School Press.

Cameron, David, Gustav Ranis, and Annalisa Zinn. 2006. *Globalization and Self-determination: Is the Nation-State under Siege?* Routledge Studies in the Modern World Economy. New York: Routledge.

Cantacuze, Serge. 2003. "Depressed Coffee Prices Set to End?" *Financial Times.* April 23.

Carnoy, Martin. 2000. *Sustaining the New Economy: Work, Family, and Community in the Information Age.* New York: Russell Sage and Cambridge, MA: Harvard University Press.

Carter, Anne. 1997. "Change as Economic Activity," In *Prices, Growth and Cycles.* Edited by Andras Simonovits and Albert Steenge. New York: St. Martin's Press.

Carter, John and Michael Irons. 1991. "Are Economists Different, and If So, Why?" *Journal of Economic Perspectives* 5: 171–77.

Castells, Manuel. 1996. *The Rise of the Network Society.* Vol. 1, The Information Age: Economy, Society and Culture series. Cambridge, MA: Blackwell.

———. 1997. The Power of Identity. Vol. 2, The Information Age: Economy, Society and Culture series. Cambridge, MA: Blackwell.

———. 1998. *End of the Millennium.* Vol. 3, The Information Age: Economy, Society and Culture series. Cambridge, MA: Blackwell.

Chandler Jr., Alfred. 1998. "Technological and Organizational Underpinnings of Modern Industrial Multinational Enterprise: The Dynamics of Competitive Advantage," In *Historical Foundations of Globalization.* Edited by James Foreman-Peck. The Globalization of the World Economy series. Northampton, MA: Edward Elgar.

Chen, Shaohua and Martin Ravallion. 2004. "How Have the World's Poorest Fared since the Early 1980s?" World Bank Policy Research Working Paper # 3341. Washington, DC: World Bank.

Chichilnisky, Graciela and Olga Gorbachev. 2004. "Volatility in the Knowledge Economy," *Economic Theory* 24: 531–47.

Chua, Amy. 2003. *World on Fire: How Exporting Free Market Democracy Breeds Ethnic Hatred and Global Instability*. New York: Doubleday.

Clark, Don, Nick Wingfield, and William M. Bulkeley. 2005. "Apple Is Poised to Shift to Intel as Chip Supplier; Move Could Open Door to More-Powerful Macs; Cutting Long Ties to IBM," *Wall Street Journal*. June 6.

Cline, William. 1997. *Trade and Income Distribution*. Washington, DC: Institute for International Economics.

Coase, Ronald. 1937. "The Nature of the Firm," *Economica* 4: 386–405.

———. 1960. "The Problem of Social Cost," *Journal of Law and Economics* 3:1–44.

Coe, David, Elhanan Helpman, and Alexander Hoffmaister. 1997. "North-South R&D Spillovers." *Economic Journal* 107: 134–49.

Cohendet, Patrick and Pierre-Benoit Joly. 2001. "The Production of Technological Knowledge: New Issues in a Learning Economy," In Archibugi and Lundvall (2001).

Cooter, Robert. 1987. "Coase Theorem," *The New Palgrave Dictionary of Economics*. 4 volumes. New York: Macmillan Press.

Cowan, Robin, Paul David, and Dominique Foray. 2000. "The Explicit Economics of Knowledge Codification and Tacitness," *Industrial and Corporate Change* 9: 2: 211–53.

Danzon, Patricia and Michael Furukawa. 2001. "Health Care: Competition and Productivity," In *The Economic Payoff from the Internet Revolution*. Edited by Robert Litan and Alice Rivlin. Washington, DC: Brookings.

David, Paul.1985. "Clio and the Economics of QWERTY," *American Economic Review* 75: 332–37.

———. 1990. "The Dynamo and the Computer: An Historical Perspective on the Modern Productivity Paradox," *American Economic Review* 80: 355–61.

Davis, Bob. 2004. "Migration of Skilled Jobs Abroad Unsettles Global Economy Fans," *Wall Street Journal*. January 26.

Davis, Stanley and Christopher Meyer. 1998. *Blur: The Speed of Change in the Connected Economy*. Reading, MA: Addison-Wesley.

De la Torre, Augusto, Eduardo Levy Yeyati, and Sergio Schmukler. 2002. "Financial Globalization: Unequal Blessings," World Bank Policy Research Working Paper # 2903. Washington, DC: World Bank.

Dean, Jason and Pui-Wing Tam. 2005. "The Laptop Trail," *Wall Street Journal*. June 9.

Deardorff, Alan. 2001. "International Provision of Trade Services, Trade and Fragmentation," World Bank Policy Research Working Paper # 2548. Washington, DC: World Bank.

Dicken, Peter. 2003. Global Shift: Reshaping the Global Economic Map in the 21st Century. Fourth edition. New York: Guilford Press.

Diwan, Ishac and Ana Revenga. 1995a. "The Outlook for Workers in the 21st Century," *Finance and Development* 32: 10–11.

———. 1995b. "Wages, Inequality, and International Integration," *Finance and Development* 32: 7–9.

Dollar, David and Awart Kraay. 2001a. "Growth Is Good for the Poor," World Bank Policy Research Working Paper # 2587. Washington, DC: World Bank.

———. 2001b. "Trade, Growth, and Poverty," World Bank Policy Research Working Paper # 2615. Washington, DC: World Bank.

Dosi, Giovanni, Keith Pavitt, and Luc Soete. 1990. *The Economics of Technical Change and International Trade*. New York: New York University Press.

Dowrick, Steve and J. Bradford DeLong. 2003. "Globalization and Convergence," In *Globalization in Historical Perspective*. Edited by Michael Bordo, Alan Taylor, and Jeffrey Williamson. Chicago and London: University of Chicago Press.

Dunning, John. 2000. "Regions, Globalization, and the Knowledge Economy: The Issues Stated," In *Regions, Globalization, and the Knowledge-Based Economy*. Edited by John Dunning. New York: Oxford University Press.

———, ed. 2003. *Making Globalization Good: The Moral Challenges of Global Capitalism*. New York: Oxford University Press.

Dvorak, Phred and Evan Ramstad. 2006. "TV Marriage: Behind Sony-Samsung Rivalry, An Unlikely Alliance Develops," *Wall Street Journal*. January 3.

Economist. 1996. "Survey: The World Economy" *The Economist*. September 28.

———. 2000a. "Survey: The New Economy" *The Economist*. September 23.

———. 2000b. "The World's View of Multinationals," *The Economist*. January 29.

———. 2003. *World in Figures 2003*. London: The Economist Newspaper Ltd.

———. 2005a. "Anniversary Lessons from eBay," *The Economist*. June 11.

———. 2005b. "A Foreign Affair," *The Economist*. October 22.

———. 2005c. "The Peaks and Troughs," *The Economist*. June 18.

Edwards, Ben. 2004. "A World of Work: A Survey of Outsourcing," Survey series. *The Economist*. November 13.

Elster, Jon. 1982. "Sour Grapes-Utilitarianism and the Genesis of Wants." *Utilitarianism and Beyond*. Edited by A. K. Sen and B. Williams. Cambridge: Cambridge University Press.

England, Andrew. 2004. "Low Coffee Prices Leave Kenyans Feeling Bitter," *Financial Times*. September 17.

Epstein, Gerald, James Crotty, and Patricia Kelly, 1996. "Winners and Losers in the Global Economics Game." *Current History* 95: 604, 377–81.

Ernst, Dieter. 1994. "Inter-firms, Networks and Market Structure: Driving Forces, Barriers and Patterns of Control." BRIE Research Paper. Berkeley, CA: University of California.

Falk, Armin, Ernst Fehr, and Urs Fischbacher. 2003. "On the Nature of Fair Behavior," *Economic Inquiry* 41: 20–26.

Feenstra, Robert. 1998. "Integration of Trade and Disintegration of Production in the Global Economy," *Journal of Economic Perspectives* 12:4: 31–50.

Fei, John, Gustav Ranis, and Shirley Kuo. 1979. *Growth with Equity: The Taiwan Case.* New York: Published for the World Bank by Oxford University Press.

Fields, Gary. 1995. "Income Distribution in Developing Economies: Conceptual, Data, and Policy Issues in Broad-Based Growth," In *Critical Issues in Asian Development.* Edited by M.G. Quibria. Hong Kong and New York: Oxford University Press.

Finn, Daniel. 1996. *Just Trading: On the Ethics and Economics of International Trade.* Nashville, TN: Abingdon Press. Washington, DC: Churches' Center for Theology and Public Policy.

———. 2006. *The Moral Ecology of Markets.* Cambridge and New York: Cambridge University Press.

Firebaugh, Glenn. 2003. *The New Geography of Global Income Inequality.* Cambridge, MA: Harvard University Press.

Fleischaker, Samuel. 2004. *A Short History of Distributive Justice.* Cambridge, MA: Harvard University Press.

Frank, Robert and Philip Cook. 1996. *The Winner-Take-All Society: Why the Few at the Top Get So Much More than the Rest of Us.* New York: Penguin Books.

Frank, Robert, Thomas Gilovich, and Dennis Regan. 1993. "Does Studying Economics Inhibit Cooperation?" *Journal of Economic Perspectives* 7:2: 159–71. Reprinted in *Economics, Ethics, and Public Policy.* Edited by Charles Wilber. 1998. New York: Rowman & Littlefield.

Freeman, Chris. 1994. "The Economics of Technical Change," *Cambridge Journal of Economics* 18: 463–514.

———. 2001. "The Learning Economy and International Inequality," In Archibugi and Lundvall (2001).

Freeman, Chris and John Hagedorn. 1995. "Convergence and Divergence in the Internationalization of Technology," In *Technical Change and the World Economy: Convergence and Divergence in Technology Strategies.* Edited by John Hagedorn. Aldershot, UK and Brookfield, VT: Edward Elgar.

Freeman, Chris and Francisco Louca. 2001. *As Time Goes By: From the Industrial Revolutions to the Information Revolution.* New York: Oxford University Press.

Freeman, Chris and Carlota Perez. 1988. "Structural Crises of Adjustment, Business Cycles and Investment Behaviour," In *Technical Change and Economic Theory.* Edited by Giovanni Dosi, Christopher Freeman, Richard Nelson, Gerald Silverberg, and Luc Soete. London and New York: Pinter Publishers.

Friedman, Thomas. 1999. *The Lexus and the Olive Tree.* New York: Farrar, Straus, Giroux.

Frolich, Norman and Joe Oppenheimer. 1992. *Choosing Justice: An Experimental Approach to Ethical Theory.* Berkley and Los Angeles: University of California Press.

Frolich, Norman and Joe Oppenheimer. 1994. "Preferences for Income Distribution and Distributive Justice: A Window on the Problems of Using Experimental Data in Economics and Ethics," *Eastern Economic Journal* 20: 147–55.

Frumkin, Peter. 2002. *On Being Nonprofit: A Conceptual and Policy Primer.* Cambridge, MA: Harvard University Press.

Fry, Jason. 2001. "E-Commerce (A Special Report)," *Wall Street Journal.* February 12.

Fukuyama, Francis. 1995. *Trust: The Social Virtues and the Creation of Prosperity.* New York: Free Press.

George, David. 2001. *Preference Pollution: How the Market Creates the Desires We Dislike.* Ann Arbor, MI: University of Michigan Press.

———. 2006. "Social Class and Social Identity: The Odd Couple," *Review of Social Economy* 64: 429–45.

Gordon, Robert. 2000. "Does the 'New Economy' Measure up to the Great Inventions of the Past?" *Journal of Economic Perspectives* 14: 49–74.

Granstrand, Ove. 2000. *The Economics and Management of Intellectual Property: Towards Intellectual Capitalism.* Northampton, MA: Edward Elgar.

Green, Francis. 2006. *Demanding Work: The Paradox of Job Quality in the Affluent Economy.* Princeton, NJ: Princeton University Press.

Griliches, Zvi. 1969. "Capital-Skill Complementarity," *Review of Economics and Statistics* 51: 465–68.

Gross, Daniel. 2005. "What Makes a Nation More Productive? It's Not Just Technology," *New York Times.* December 25.

Guth, Robert and Kevin Delaney. 2006. "A Microsoft, Yahoo Tie-Up?; MSN Veterans Want a Pact to Bolster Web-Search Ads and Better Challenge Google," *Wall Street Journal.* May 3.

Hamlin, Alan. 1995. "The Moral of the Market," In *Market Capitalism and Moral Values: Proceedings of Section F (Economics) of the British Association for the Advancement of Science Keele 1993.* Edited by Samuel Brittan and Alan Hamlin. Brookfield, VT: Edward Elgar.

Hammer, M. 1990. "Reengineering Work: Don't Automate, Obliterate," *Harvard Business Review* July–August: 104–12.

Hausman, Daniel. 1992. "When Jack and Jill Make a Deal," In *Economic Rights.* Edited by Ellen Frankel Paul, Fred Miller, Jr., and Jeffrey Paul. New York: Cambridge University Press; Bowling Green, OH: Social Philosophy and Policy Foundation.

Hausman, Daniel and Michael McPherson. 1996. *Economic Analysis and Moral Philosophy.* Cambridge Surveys of Economic Literature. Cambridge and New York: Cambridge University Press.

Haveman, Robert and Barbara Wolfe. 1984. "Schooling and Economic Well-Being: The Role of Nonmarket Effects," *Journal of Human Resources* 19: 377–407.

Hayek, F. A. 1944. *The Road to Serfdom*. Chicago: University of Chicago Press.

———. 1978 [1998] "Competition as a Discovery Process," In *New Studies in Philosophy, Politics, Economics and the History of Ideas*. Chicago: University of Chicago Press. Reprinted in *Market Process Theories, Volume II: Heterodox Approaches*. Edited by Peter Boettke and David Prychitko. Cheltenham, UK and Northampton, MA: Edward Elgar.

Heap, Shaun Hargreaves. 1989. *Rationality in Economics*. Oxford and New York: Basil Blackwell.

Held, David, Anthony McGrew, David Goldblatt and Jonathan Perraton. 1999. *Global Transformations: Politics, Economics and Culture*. Stanford, CA: Stanford University Press.

Hellsten, Sirkku. 1998. "Distributive Justice, Theories of," In *Encyclopedia of Applied Ethics*. Volume 1. Edited by Ruth Chadwick. New York: Academic Press.

Helpman, Elhanan. 1999. "R&D and Productivity: The International Connection," In *The Economics of Globalization: Policy Perspectives from Public Economics*. Edited by Assaf Razin and Efraim Sadka. Cambridge, UK: Cambridge University Press.

Hepworth, Mark. 1989. *Geography of the Information Economy*. London: Belhaven Press.

Hicks, John. 1940. "The Valuation of Social Income," *Economica* 7: 105–24.

Hirsch, Fred. 1976. *Social Limits to Growth*. Cambridge, MA: Harvard University Press.

Hirst, Paul and Grahame Thompson. 1999. *Globalization in Question: The International Economy and the Possibilities of Governance*. Second edition. Cambridge, UK: Polity.

Houben, Arerdt and Jan Kakes. 2002. "ICT Innovation and Economic Performance: The Role of Financial Intermediation," *Kyklos* 55: 543–62.

International Monetary Fund (IMF). 1997. *World Economic Outlook*. Washington, DC: International Monetary Fund. May.

———. 2001. *The Information Technology Revolution*. World Economic Outlook annual series. Washington, DC: International Monetary Fund. October.

———. 2002. *Trade and Finance*. World Economic Outlook annual series. Washington, DC: International Monetary Fund. September.

———. 2003. *Growth and Institutions*. World Economic Outlook annual series. Washington, DC: International Monetary Fund. April.

Irwin, Douglas. 2002. *Free Trade under Fire*. Princeton, NJ: Princeton University Press.

———. 2005. "Trade and Globalization," In *Globalization: What's New?* Edited by Michael Weinstein. New York: Columbia University Press.

James, Jeffrey. 1998. "Information Technology, Globalization and Marginalization," In *Globalization, Growth and Marginalization*. Edited by A. S. Bhalla. New York: St. Martin's Press.

———. 1999. *Globalization, Information Technology and Development*. New York: St. Martin's Press.

James, Jeffrey. 2000. *Consumption, Globalization and Development.* New York: St. Martin's Press.

———. 2002. *Technology, Globalization and Poverty.* Northampton, MA: Edward Elgar.

John XXIII. 1963. *Pacem in Terris.* Boston: Daughters of St. Paul.

Johnson, Bjorn, Edward Lorenz, and Bengt-Åke Lundvall. 2002. "Why All This Fuss about Codified and Tacit Knowledge?" *Industrial and Corporate Change* 11:2:245–62.

Jones, Eric. 1981. *The European Miracle: Environments, Economies and Geopolitics in the History of Europe and Asia.* Cambridge: Cambridge University Press.

Jones, Ronald, Henryk Kierzkowski, and Chen Lurong. 2005. "What Does Evidence Tell Us about Fragmentation and Outsourcing?" *International Review of Economics & Finance* 14: 305–16.

Jorgenson, Dale, Mun Ho, and Kevin Stiroh. 2005. "Growth of U.S. Industries and Investments in Information and Higher Education," In *Measuring Capital in the New Economy.* Edited by Carol Corrado, John Haltiwanger, and Daniel Sichel. Chicago: University of Chicago Press.

Kaldor, Nicholas. 1939. "Welfare Propositions of Economics and Interpersonal Comparisons of Utility," *Economic Journal* 49: 549–61.

Kahn, Gabriel. 2004. "Making Labels for Less," *Wall Street Journal.* August 13.

Kash, Don, Robin Auger, and Ning Li. 2002. "Organizational Requirements for the Innovation of Complex Technologies," In *Networks, Alliances and Partnerships in the Innovation Process.* Edited by John de la Mothe and Albert Link. Dordrecht, Holland: Kluwer.

Kikeri, Sunita and Aishetu Kolo. 2005. "Privatization: Trends and Recent Developments." World Bank Policy Research Working Paper # 3765. Washington, DC: World Bank.

Kim, Kwan. 1997. "Income Distribution and Poverty: An Interregional Comparison," *World Development* 25: 1909–24.

Kirzner, Israel. 1997. "Entrepreneurial Discovery and the Competitive Market Process: An Austrian Approach," *Journal of Economic Literature* 35: 60–85.

Klein, Michael, Cal Aaron, and Bita Hadjimichael. 2001. "Foreign Direct Investment and Poverty Reduction," World Bank Policy Research Working Paper # 2613. Washington, DC: World Bank.

Komives, Kristin, Jonathan Halpern, Vivien Foster, and Quentin Wodon. 2006. "The Distributional Incidence of Residential Water and Electricity Subsidies," World Bank Policy Research Working Paper # 3878. Washington, DC: World Bank.

Kondratieff, N.D. 1935. "The Long Waves in Economic Life," *Review of Economics and Statistics* 17: 105–15.

Konow, James. 2003. "Which Is the Fairest One of All? A Positive Analysis of Justice Theories," *Journal of Economic Literature* 41: 1188–1239.

Krueger, Anne. 1978. *Liberalization Attempts and Consequences.* Foreign Trade Regimes and Economic Development NBER conference series. Cambridge, MA: Ballinger.

Krugman, Paul. 1995. "Growing World Trade: Causes and Consequences," *Brookings Papers on Economic Activity* 1: 327–77.

Kuttner, Robert. 1997. *Everything for Sale: The Virtues and Limits of Markets.* New York: Alfred A. Knopf.

Kuznets, Simon. 1955. "Economic Growth and Income Inequality," *American Economic Review* 45: 1–28.

———. 1963. "Quantitative Aspects of Economic Growth of Nations: VIII. Distribution of Income by Size," *Economic Development and Cultural Change* 11:2: 1–80.

———. 1966. *Modern Economic Growth: Rate, Structure, and Spread.* New Haven, CT: Yale University Press.

Lam, Alice. 2000. "Tacit Knowledge, Organizational Learning and Societal Institutions: An Integrated Framework," *Organization Studies* 21:3: 487–513.

Lancaster, Kelvin. 1966, "A New Approach to Consumer Theory," *Journal of Political Economy* 74: 132–57.

Landes, David. 1969. *Unbound Prometheus: Technical Change and Industrial Development in Western Europe from 1750 to the Present.* London: Cambridge University Press.

———. 1998. *The Wealth and Poverty of Nations.* New York: W. W. Norton.

Lankes, Hans Peter. 2002. "Market Access for Developing Countries," *Finance and Development* 39: 8–13.

Lash, Scott. 1994. "Reflexivity and Its Doubles: Structure, Aesthetics, Community," In *Reflexive Modernization: Politics, Tradition and Aesthetics in the Modern Social Order.* Edited by Ulrich Beck, Anthony Giddens, and Scott Lash. Stanford, CA: Stanford University Press.

Leibenstein, Harvey. 1966. "Allocative Efficiency vs. 'X-Efficiency,'" *American Economic Review* 56: 392–415.

Leo, Luca Di and Jenny Stock. 2005. "Trying to Stay a Cut above Chinese Textiles," *Wall Street Journal.* July 25.

Levy, Michael and Dhruv Grewal. 2000. "Supply Chain Management in a Networked Economy," *Journal of Retailing* 76: 415–29.

Lipsey, R. G. and Kelvin Lancaster. 1956. "The General Theory of Second Best," *Review of Economic Studies* 24: 11–32.

Litan, Robert and Alice Rivlin, eds. 2001. *The Economic Payoff from the Internet Revolution.* Washington, DC: Brookings.

Lohr, Steve. 2006. "Outsourcing Is Climbing Skills Ladder," *New York Times.* February 16.

Long, Simon. 2000. "Online Financing," Survey series. *The Economist.* May 18.

Lundvall, Bengt-Åke. 1998. "The Learning Economy: Challenges to Economic Theory and Policy," In *Institutions and Economic Change: New Perspectives on Markets, Firms and Technology.* Edited by Klaus Nielsen and Bjorn Johnson. Cheltenham, UK and Northampton, MA: Edward Elgar.

———. 2001. "Innovation Policy in the Globalizing Learning Economy," In Archibugi and Lundvall (2001).

Lundvall, Bengt-Åke and Daniele Archibugi. 2001. "Introduction: Europe and the Learning Economy," In Archibugi and Lundvall (2001).

Maher, Kris. 2004. "Next on the Outsourcing List," *Wall Street Journal*. March 23.

Malkin, Elisabeth. 2007. "Thousands in Mexico Protest Rising Food Prices," *New York Times*. February 1.

Markillie, Paul. 2004. "E-Commerce," Survey series. *The Economist*. May 13.

Marshall, Alfred. 1890 [1961]. *Principles of Economics*. Ninth (variorum) edition. 2 volumes. London: Macmillan.

Marwell, Gerald and Ruth Ames.1981. "Economists Free Ride, Does Anyone Else?" *Journal of Public Economics* 15: June: 295–310.

Marx, Karl. 1875 [1993]. "Critique of the Gotha Programme," In *Justice*. Edited by Alan Ryan. Oxford: Oxford University Press.

Matusz, Steven and David Tarr. 1999. "Adjusting to Trade Policy Reform," World Bank Policy Research Working Paper # 2142. Washington, DC: World Bank.

Mayer-Schönberger, Viktor Hurley, and Deborah Hurley. 2000. "Globalization of Communication," In *Governance in a Globalizing World*. Edited by Joseph Nye, Jr. and John Donahue. Washington, DC: Brookings Institution Press.

McClain, Dylan Loeb. 2005. "Richer than Ever, but Watch Out for Missing Costs," *New York Times*. December 5.

McGregor, Joan. 1988–89. "Bargaining Advantages and Coercion in the Market," *Philosophy Research Archives* 14: 23–50.

McMillan, John. 2002. *Reinventing the Bazaar: A Natural History of Markets*. New York: W. W. Norton.

Meade, J. E. 1952. "External Economies and Diseconomies in a Competitive Situation," *Economic Journal* 62: 54–67.

Meier, Gerald. 1995. *Leading Issues in Economic Development*. Sixth edition. New York and Oxford: Oxford University Press.

Michaels, Daniel and J. Lynn Lunsford. 2004. "Globalization Blunts Air Trade Rivalry," *Wall Street Journal*. July 19.

Milanovic, Branko. 2002. "Can We Discern the Effect of Globalization on Income Distribution? Evidence from Household Budget Surveys," World Bank Policy Research Working paper # 2876. Washington, DC: World Bank.

———. 2005. *Worlds Apart: Measuring International and Global Inequality*. Princeton, NJ: Princeton University Press.

Miles, Ian and Mark Boden. 2000. "Services, Knowledge and Intellectual Property," In *Knowledge and Innovation in the New Service Economy*. Edited by Birgitte Andersen, Jeremy Howells, Richard Hull, Ian Miles, and Joanne Roberts. Cheltenham, UK: Edward Elgar.

Miller, David. 1976. *Social Justice*. Oxford: Clarendon Press.

Mokyr, Joel. 1990. *The Lever of Riches: Technological Creativity and Economic Progress*. Oxford and New York: Oxford University Press.

Moris, Francisco and John Jankowski. 2002. "R&D Alliances and Networks: Indicators at the Division of Science Resources Statistics, National Science Foundation," In *Networks, Alliances and Partnerships in the Innovation*

Process. Edited by John de la Mothe and Albert Link. Dordrecht, Holland: Kluwer.

Morrison, Kevin. 2003. "Brazilian Frost Froth Helps Coffee Bubble Briefly," *Financial Times*. May 24.

Muller, Joann and Jonathan Fahey. 2005. "The Fabless Car Company," *Forbes*. November 14.

Mulligan, Casey. 1999. "Galton versus the Human Capital Approach to Inheritance," *Journal of Political Economy* 107:S184–S224.

Myers, Matthew, Patricia Daugherty, and Chad W Autry. 2000. "The Effectiveness of Automatic Inventory Replenishment in Supply Chain Operations: Antecedents and Outcomes," *Journal of Retailing* 76: 455–81.

Myint, H. 1958. "The 'Classical Theory' of International Trade and the Underdeveloped Countries," *Economic Journal* 68: 317–37.

Nakamura, Leonard. 2000. "Economics and the New Economy: The Invisible Hand Meets Creative Destruction," *Federal Reserve Bank of Philadelphia Business Review*: July–August:15–30.

Nelson, Richard and Edmund Phelps. 1966. "Investment in Humans, Technological Diffusion, and Economic Growth," *American Economic Review* 65: 69–75.

Nelson, Richard and Sidney Winter. 1982. *An Evolutionary Theory of Economic Change*. Cambridge, MA: Belknap Press of Harvard University Press.

New York Times. 2005. *Class Matters*. New York: Times Books.

Nocera, Joseph. 2004. "Two Cheers for the Google IPO," *Fortune*. September 6:42.

North, Douglass. 1990. *Institutions, Institutional Change and Economic Performance*. New York: Cambridge University Press.

North, Douglass and Robert Paul Thomas. 1973. *The Rise of the Western World: A New Economic History*. Cambridge: Cambridge University Press.

Nozick, Robert. 1974. *Anarchy, State, and Utopia*. New York: Basic Books.

Nussbaum, Martha 1992. "Human Functioning and Social Justice: In Defense of Aristotelian Essentialism," *Political Theory* 20: 202–46.

Nyholm, Jens, Lars Normann, Claus Frelle-Petersen, Mark Riis, and Peter Torstensen. 2001. "Innovation Policy in the Knowledge-Based Economy—Can Theory Guide Policy Making?" In Archibugi and Lundvall (2001).

Obstfeld, Maurice and Alan Taylor. 2004. *Global Capital Markets: Integration, Crisis, and Growth*. New York: Cambridge University Press.

Okun, Arthur. 1975. *Equality and Efficiency: The Big Tradeoff*. Washington, DC: Brookings Institution.

Organisation for Economic Co-operation and Development (OECD). 2004. *The Economic Impact of ICT: Measurement, Evidence and Implications*. Paris: OECD.

O'Rourke, Kevin and Jeffrey Williamson. 1999. *Globalization and History: The Evolution of a Nineteenth-Century Atlantic Economy*. Cambridge, MA: MIT Press.

Paldam, Martin. 2003. "Economic Freedom and the Success of the Asian Tigers: An Essay on Controversy," *European Journal of Political Economy* 19: 453–77.

Parmar, Arundhati. 2004. "Indian Farmers Reap Web Harvest," *Marketing News.* June 1.

Paxson, Christina and Norbert Schady. 2005. "Cognitive Development among Young Children in Ecuador: The Roles of Wealth, Health and Parenting," World Bank Policy Research Working Paper # 3605. Washington, DC: World Bank.

Peters, Rebecca Todd. 2004. *In Search of the Good Life: The Ethics of Globalization.* New York and London: Continuum.

Pigou, A. C. 1949. *A Study in Public Finance.* Third edition. London: Macmillan.

Pojman, Louis and Robert Westmoreland. 1997. *Equality: Selected Readings.* Oxford, UK and New York: Oxford University Press.

Portes, Richard and Helene Rey. 1999. "The Determinants of Cross-Border Equity Flows," National Bureau of Economic Research (NBER) Working Papers # 7336. Cambridge, MA: NBER.

Prasad, Eswar, Kenneth Rogoff, Shang-Jin Wei, and M. Ayhan Kose. 2003. "Effects of Financial Globalization on Developing Countries: Some Empirical Evidence," International Monetary Fund Occasional Paper # 220. Washington, DC: International Monetary Fund.

Pritchett, Lant. 1997. "Divergence, Big Time," *Journal of Economic Perspectives* 11: 3–17.

Psachararopoulos, Goerge and Harry Anthony Patrinos. 2002. "Returns to Investment in Education: A Further Update," World Bank Policy Research Working Paper # 2881. Washington, DC: World Bank.

Qiang, Christine Zhen-Wei and Alexander Pitt. 2004. "Contribution of Information and Communication Technologies to Growth," World Bank Working Paper # 24. Washington, DC: World Bank.

Radosevic, Slavo. 1999. *International Technology Transfer and Catch-up in Economic Development.* Northampton, MA: Edward Elgar.

Raphael, D. D. 2001. *Concepts of Justice.* Oxford: Clarendon Press.

Ravallion, Martin. 2004. "Competing Concepts of Inequality in the Globalization Debate," World Bank Policy Research Working Paper # 3243. Washington, DC: World Bank.

Ravallion, Martin and Michael Lokshin. 2005. "Lasting Local Impacts of an Economy-wide Crisis," World Bank Policy Research Working Paper # 3503. Washington, DC: World Bank.

Rawlings, Laura and Gloria Rubio. 2003. "Evaluating the Impact of Conditional Cash Transfer Programs: Lessons from Latin America," World Bank Policy Research Working Paper # 3119. Washington, DC: World Bank.

Rawls, John. 1971. *A Theory of Justice.* Cambridge, MA: Belknap Press of Harvard University Press.

Raz, Joseph. 1982. "Liberalism, Autonomy, and the Politics of Neutral Concern," In *Social and Political Philosophy.* Edited by Peter French, Theodore Uehling, Jr. and Howard Wettstein. Midwest Studies in Philosophy. Minneapolis, MN: University of Minnesota Press.

Reitman, Valerie. 1994. "At the Roots of the U.S.-Japan Trade Gap: Detroit's Big Three Gripe about Japan—and Then Import Car Parts Galore," *Wall Street Journal.* October 10.

Rescher, Nicholas. 1966. *Distributive Justice: A Constructive Critique of the Utilitarian Theory of Distribution.* New York: Bobbs-Merrill.

Ricadela, Aaron. 2005. "Microsoft Plays Real's Tune," *Information Week.* October 17.

Ricardo, David. 1817 [1929]. *The Principles of Political Economy and Taxation.* New York: E. P. Dutton.

Richardson, J. David. 1995. "Income Inequality and Trade: How to Think, What to Conclude," *Journal of Economic Perspectives* 9: 33–55.

Richtel, Matt. 2005. "Outsourced All the Way," *New York Times.* June 21.

Robbins, Lionel. 1932 [1952]. *An Essay on the Nature and Significance of Economic Science.* London: Macmillan.

Roberts, Joanne. 2000. "From Know-How to Show-How? Questioning the Role of Information and Communication Technologies in Knowledge Transfer," *Technology Analysis and Strategic Management* 12: 429–43.

Rodrik, Dani. 1997. *Has Globalization Gone Too Far?* Washington, DC: Institute for International Economics.

———. 1998. "Why Do More Open Economies Have Bigger Governments?" *Journal of Political Economy* 106: 997–1032.

Romer, Paul. 1990. "Endogenous Technological Change," *Journal of Political Economy* 98: S71–S102.

Rosenberg, Nathan. 1996. "Uncertainty and Technological Change," In *The Mosaic of Economic Growth.* Edited by Ralph Landau, Timothy Taylor, and Gavin Wright. Stanford, CA: Stanford University Press.

Rosenberg, Nathan and L. E. Birdzell, Jr. 1986. *How the West Grew Rich: The Economic Transformation of the Industrial World.* New York: Basic Books.

Rosenstein-Rodan, P. 1943. "Problems of Industrialization of Eastern and South-Eastern Europe," *Economic Journal* 53: 204–7.

Rossant, John. 2004. "France's Industrial Power Trip," *Business Week.* November 29.

Ryan, John. 1942. *Distributive Justice.* Third edition. New York: Macmillan.

Sachs, Jeffrey. 2000. "A New Map of the World," *The Economist.* June 24.

———. 2005. *End of Poverty: Economic Possibilities for Our Time.* New York: Penguin.

Sachs, Jeffrey and Andrew Warner. 1995. "Economic Convergence and Economic Policies," National Bureau of Economic Research (NBER) Working Paper # 5039. Cambridge, MA: NBER.

Samuelson, Paul. 1950. "Evaluation of Real National Income," *Oxford Economic Papers* 2: 1–29.

Samuelson, Paul. 2004. "Where Ricardo and Mill Rebut and Confirm Arguments of Mainstream Economists Supporting Globalization," *Journal of Economic Perspectives* 18: 135–46.

Schienstock, Gerd. 2001. "Social Exclusion in the Learning Economy," In *The Globalizing Learning Economy*. Edited by Archibugi Daniele and Bengt-Åke Lundvall. New York: Oxford University Press.

Schiller, Robert. 2000. *Irrational Exuberance*. Princeton, NJ: Princeton University Press.

Schokkaert, Erik. 1992. "The Economics of Distributive Justice, Welfare and Freedom," In *Justice: Interdisciplinary Perspectives*. Edited by Klaus Scherer. Cambridge: Cambridge University Press.

Schultz, Theodore W. 1975. "The Value of the Ability to Deal with Disequilibria," *Journal of Economic Literature* 13: 827–46.

Schultz, Walter. 2001. *The Moral Conditions of Economic Efficiency*. Cambridge: Cambridge University Press.

Schumpeter, Joseph. 1939. *Business Cycles: A Theoretical, Historical and Statistical Analysis of the Capitalist Process*. 2 volumes. New York: McGraw Hill.

———. 1942. *Capitalism, Socialism and Democracy*. New York: Harper.

———. 1955. *The Theory of Economic Development*. Cambridge, MA: Harvard University Press.

Scitovsky, Tibor. 1941. "A Note on Welfare Propositions in Economics," *Review of Economic Studies* 9: 77–88.

Scott, John, Richard Matland, Philip Michelbach, and Brian Bornstein. 2001. "Just Deserts: An Experimental Study of Distributive Justice Norms," *American Journal of Political Science* 45: 749–67.

Sen, Amartya. 1970. "The Impossibility of a Paretian Liberal," *Journal of Political Economy* 78:152–57.

———. 1984a. "Ethical Issues in Income Distribution: National and International," In *Resources, Values and Development*. Cambridge, MA: Harvard University Press.

———. 1984b. "Rights and Capabilities," In *Resources, Values and Development*. Cambridge, MA: Harvard University Press.

———. 1993. "Capability and Well-Being," In *The Quality of Life*. Edited by Martha Nussbaum and Amartya Sen. Oxford: Clarendon.

———. 1995. "Moral Codes and Economic Success," In *Market Capitalism and Moral Values: Proceedings of Section F (Economics) of the British Association for the Advancement of Science Keele 1993*. Edited by Samuel Brittan and Alan Hamlin. Brookfield, VT: Edward Elgar.

Shapiro, Carl and Hal Varian. 1999. *Information Rules: A Strategic Guide to the Network Economy*. Boston: Harvard Business School Press.

Shapiro, Thomas. 2004. *The Hidden Cost of Being African American: How Wealth Perpetuates Inequality*. New York: Oxford.

Shipler, David. 2004. *The Working Poor: Invisible in America*. New York: Knopf.

Shipman, Alan. 1999. *The Market Revolution and Its Limits: A Price for Everything.* London and New York: Routledge.

———. 2002. *Transcending Transaction: The Search for Self-generating Markets.* London and New York: Routledge.

Shirouzu, Norihiko. 2004. "Chain Reaction—Big Three's Outsourcing Plan," *Wall Street Journal.* June 10.

Shue, Henry. 1980. *Basic Rights: Subsistence, Affluence, and U.S. Foreign Policy.* Princeton, NJ: Princeton University Press.

Siegele, Ludwig. 2002. "The Real-Time Economy," Survey series. *The Economist.* January 31.

Simon, Herbert. 1976. "From Substantive to Procedural Rationality," In *Method and Appraisal in Economics.* Edited by S. Latsis. Cambridge: Cambridge University Press. Reprinted in *Philosophy and Economic Theory.* Edited by Frank Hahn and Martin Hollis. New York: Oxford University Press, 1979.

Slater, Joanna. 2004. "Influx of Tech Jobs Ushers in Malls, Modernity to Calcutta," *Wall Street Journal.* April 28.

Smith, Adam. 1776 [1937]. *The Wealth of Nations.* Edited by Edwin Canaan. New York: Modern Library.

Sobrino, Jon and Felix Wilfred, eds. 2001. *Globalization and Its Victims.* Concilium 2001/5. London: SCM Press.

Soete, Luc and Bas ter Weel. 2005. "Introduction and Summary," In *The Economics of the Digital Society.* Edited by Luc Soete and Bas ter Weel. Northampton, MA: Edward Elgar.

Solow, Robert. 1987. "We'd Better Watch Out," Book Review. *New York Times.* July 12.

Spragens, Thomas. 1993. "The Antinomies of Social Justice," *Review of Politics* 55: 193–216.

Stevens, Candice. 1996. "The Knowledge-Driven Economy." *OECD Observer* June–July 200: 6–11.

Stiglitz, Joseph. 2002. *Globalization and Its Discontents.* London and New York: W. W. Norton.

Sutcliffe, Bob and Andrew Glyn. 2003. "Measures of Globalisation and Their Misinterpretation," In The *Handbook of Globalisation.* Edited by Jonathan Michie. Northampton, MA: Edward Elgar.

Temple, Jonathan and Paul Johnson. 1998. "Social Capability and Economic Growth," *Quarterly Journal of Economics* 113: 965–90.

Triplett, Jack. 1999. "The Solow Productivity Paradox: What Do Computers Do to Productivity?" *Canadian Journal of Economics* 32: 309–34.

Trostel, Philip. 2004. "Returns to Scale in Producing Human Capital from Schooling," *Oxford Economic Papers* 56: 461–84.

Turnipseed, David, Ali Rassuli, Ron Sardessai, and Carol Park. 1999. "A History and Evaluation of Boeing's Coalition Strategy with Japan in Aircraft Development and Production," *International Journal of Commerce & Management* 9: 59–84.

United Nations Conference on Trade and Development (UNCTAD). 2004. *Development and Globalization: Facts and Figures.* New York and Geneva: United Nations.

United Nations Development Programme (UNDP)—World Bank. 1999. *Water for India's Poor: Who Pays the Price for Broken Promises?* Water and Sanitation Program. Report # 23721. Washington, DC: World Bank.

Van den Ende, Jan and Wilfred Dolfsma. 2005. "Technology-push, Demand-pull and the Shaping of Technological Paradigms—Patterns in the Development of Computing Technology," *Journal of Evolutionary Economics* 15: 83–99.

Von Hippel, Eric. 1994. "'Sticky Information' and the Locus of Problem Solving: Implications for Innovation," *Management Science* 40: 429–39.

Waldman, Amy. 2004. "Indian Soybean Farmers Join the Global Village," *New York Times.* January 1.

Walker, Marcus. 2007. "Just How Good Is Globalization?" *Wall Street Journal.* January 25.

Walzer, Michael. 1983. *Spheres of Justice: A Defense of Pluralism and Equality.* New York: Basic Books.

Welch, Finis. 1970. "Education in Production," *Journal of Political Economy* 78: 35–59.

White, Erin. 2006. "The Best vs. the Rest: Companies Eschew across-the-Board Increases to Give Top Performers a Bigger Slice of the Raise Pie," *Wall Street Journal.* January 30.

Williamson, Jeffrey. 1997. "Globalization and Inequality, Past and Present," *World Bank Research Observer* 12: 117–35.

Williamson, John. 1990. "What Washington Means by Policy Reform," In *Latin American Adjustment: How Much Has Happened?* Edited by John Williamson. Washington, DC: Institute for International Economics.

———. 2000. "What Should the World Bank Think about the Washington Consensus?" *World Bank Research Observer* 15: 251–64.

Wolf, Martin. 2004. *Why Globalization Works.* New Haven, CT: Yale University Press.

Wood, Adrian. 1994. *North-South Trade, Employment and Inequality: Changing Fortunes in a Skill-Driven World.* Oxford: Clarendon Press.

———. 1995. "How Trade Hurt Unskilled Workers," *Journal of Economic Perspectives* 9: 57–80.

———. 1997. "Openness and Wage Inequality in Developing Countries: The Latin American Challenge to East Asian Conventional Wisdom," *World Bank Economic Review* 11:33–57.

Woodall, Pam. 1996. "The Hitchhiker's Guide to Cybernomics: A Survey of the World Economy," *The Economist.* September 28.

———. 2000. "Untangling E-conomics: A Survey of the New Economy," *The Economist.* September 23.

World Bank. 2001. *World Development Report 2002: Building Institutions for Markets.* Washington, DC: World Bank.

————. 2005. *World Development Report 2006: Equity and Development.* Washington, DC: World Bank.

————. 2006. *World Development Report 2007: Development and the Next Generation.* Washington, DC: World Bank.

————. 2007. *Global Economic Prospects: Managing the Next Wave of Globalization.* Washington, DC: World Bank.

Yeats, Alexander. 2001. "Just How Big Is Global Production Sharing?" In *Fragmentation: New Production Patterns in the World Economy.* Edited by Sven Arndt and Henryk Kierzkowski. New York: Oxford University Press.

Yergin, Daniel and Joseph Stanislaw. 1998. *The Commanding Heights: The Battle Between Government and the Marketplace that Is Remaking the Modern World.* New York: Simon & Schuster.

Index

Printed in the United States
128233LV00002B/9/P

9 780230 600898